DEVIZES AND CENTRAL WILTSHIRE

Devizes and Central Wiltshire

JOHN CHANDLER

illustrated by

MICHAEL CHARLTON

Wiltshire

A History of its Landscape and People 2

First published in the United Kingdom in 2003 by
The Hobnob Press, PO Box 1838, East Knoyle, Salisbury SP3 6FA

British Library Cataloguing in Publication Data
A catalogue record for this book is available from the British Library.

ISBN 0-946418-16-0

Typeset in 11/15 pt Souvenir Light
Typesetting and origination by John Chandler
Printed in Great Britain by Salisbury Printing Company Ltd., Salisbury

Contents

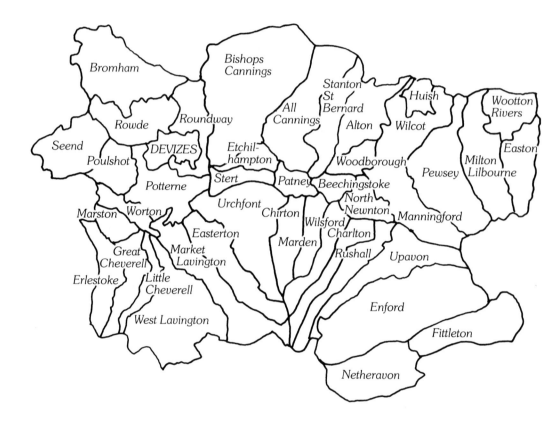

JOHN CHANDLER was born in 1951, and brought up in Winchester and Exmouth. He studied classics at Bristol University, and obtained his doctorate for research into the history of the later Roman empire. He qualified as a librarian, and worked for Wiltshire County Council until embarking on a freelance career, writing, lecturing and conducting historical research, in 1988. He has written or compiled some twenty books, including histories of Salisbury, Swindon, Pewsey Vale, Shaftesbury Abbey and Wiltshire churches, as well as editions of the works of the travellers John Leland and John Taylor. He is editor of the Wiltshire Record Society and joint editor of the *Wiltshire Archaeological and Natural History Magazine*. As Hobnob Press he typesets and publishes his own and other books of local interest. He has lived in Wiltshire since 1974.

Introduction

OUTSIDE LOCAL GOVERNMENT CIRCLES people do not naturally identify themselves with the modern administrative district in which they live, preferring to explain that they come from 'near Devizes', or 'near Marlborough', or more vaguely 'in the depths of Wiltshire'. And yet the post-1974 districts – in the present instance Kennet – are useful arrangements for the local and regional historian, because they enshrine much older economic and social allegiances of town and country, market, work and travel.

In 2001 I finished and published *Marlborough and Eastern Wiltshire*, first of a projected seven-volume series which will describe in historical terms everywhere in Wiltshire. With the publication of this book, *Devizes and Central Wiltshire*, I have achieved the more modest goal of completing my work on Kennet district. Anyone acquiring both volumes will find that they have a short history of every parish in Kennet, Wiltshire's largest district in area, but also its least populous.

I have been heartened to press on with this project by the favourable response *Marlborough and Eastern Wiltshire* received from reviewers, historians and local people; and I hope that many of that book's purchasers will want to have this one too. They will, I am sure, excuse me if, for the benefit of those who are only interested in the Devizes area, I repeat some of the information and explanations about the series given in the introduction to the earlier volume.

This project was conceived in 1984 and begun in 1985. I was then Wiltshire's local studies librarian, and during 1985/6 I was granted part-time leave of absence to work on it by my employer, Wiltshire County

Council. In 1988 I resigned my appointment, in part to continue and complete it, and I have worked on it intermittently ever since.

The initial idea was a single-volume landscape history, or topography, of Wiltshire, which would examine the county as a whole and each parish individually. My model was to be the classic *Devon* by the late William Hoskins (1954) – a book which I have admired since I was a teenager. I began writing short parish histories, and slowly – too slowly – colouring in the map of Wiltshire. The histories became wordier as I gained confidence, and took longer to write. My publisher, Tony Martin of Hobnob Press, and I despaired of ever seeing the book in print. Eventually, and with a certain reluctance, we agreed that the work had outgrown its single volume. So, *Wiltshire: a History of its Landscape and People* has been rethought and reworked to appear in seven parts, each devoted to a region of Wiltshire and its major town. An eighth, if health and strength permit, will distil the parish histories into a synthesis, a 'making of the Wiltshire landscape'. Work is well advanced on *Swindon and North-Eastern Wiltshire*, and *Salisbury and South-Eastern Wiltshire*, and I anticipate that the latter will appear as volume 3 in 2005.

The best way to learn a subject, someone must have said, is to write a book about it. And as I have been working on the history of Wiltshire, so it has been working on me. My book and I are maturing together. As we have progressed I have come to the conclusion that all local historians should have a twofold goal: to explain their surroundings, and to humanize the past. That is what the 260-odd vignette parish portraits which will eventually comprise the whole are aiming to achieve.

Friends to whom I have described my work have categorized it as, 'the poor man's VCH', or, 'the thinking man's Arthur Mee', and I am not unhappy to be either. The ubiquitous Arthur Mee wrote pleasant but anodyne county topographies during the 1930s; the Wiltshire *Victoria County History* (VCH), if it is able to continue (and its future is in jeopardy as I write) will eventually provide detailed, scholarly histories of everywhere in Wiltshire. My aim is to occupy the middle ground, by offering non-academic and (I hope) readable introductions to the history of towns and villages, a prelude perhaps to an afternoon's exploring, or a handy compendium on any Wiltshire bookshelf.

In evolving a 'house style' I am trying to produce books which are attractive to own and pleasing to use. Michael Charlton's illustrations have been specially commissioned to enhance the text, and I include also facsimiles of late nineteenth-century Ordnance Survey one-inch scale maps, which have not been reprinted before. I assume, incidentally, that readers will have access to modern Ordnance Survey sheets at 1:50,000 or (preferably) 1:25,000 scale. Without overloading the text with references, I have included a note on sources after each parish history; in addition the standard checklist of sources which I have used throughout is summarized in an appendix. I retain the copyright of my words, but have no objection (provided the source is acknowledged) to non-commercial organizations quoting passages in minor publications, such as church or village guides, without seeking my permission to do so.

The arrangement of this book is simple. It consists of forty-two historical essays, one devoted to each of the modern civil parishes in Kennet district which surround Devizes, from Bromham, Seend and Erlestoke in the west, and extending eastward to take in the Lavingtons, Pewsey and all the parishes of Pewsey Vale, as well as the upper Avon valley as far south as Netheravon. Very occasionally I have ignored recent changes to parish boundaries, and discuss topics in the context of the parish with which they are historically associated. The essays, which are alphabetically arranged like a gazetteer, vary in length according to the size, population or historical interest of the place in question. Devizes itself has the longest treatment, although much has already been written by others about this exquisite town, and I have given almost equal attention to some of the larger villages in the area, such as Milton Lilbourne, Bromham and Enford, as well as the small towns of Pewsey and Upavon, about which information is more scattered and elusive.

The essays are historical in the limited sense that they espouse the twin aims set out above, to explain one's surroundings and to humanize the past. They are therefore concerned with landscape and people, as the series title suggests. Far more meticulous parish histories are provided for every parish in this book by the Wiltshire *Victoria County History* (in volumes 7, 10, 11 and 16). And I have already published an overview of the landscape history of much of the area covered by the book (*The Vale of Pewsey*, 1991; 2nd edition, 2000, Ex Libris Press). The short bibliography appended to each essay will guide the reader to these and other sources of further information. The present book has been written sporadically over more than fifteen years, and there is inevitably some unevenness of treatment. I have revised and augmented each essay during 2003, but am sure to have overlooked some recent changes and developments – for which I apologize.

Acknowledgements

A BOOK SO LONG in gestation must accumulate many debts of gratitude, some for individual acts of kindness long forgotten by those who bestowed them, others for tasks perennially and so often repeated that they are in danger of being taken for granted. In respect of the former I must ask that my many friends in the Devizes area and in the local history community within Wiltshire generally will take the publication of this book after so long as recompense for their help in producing it. In respect of the latter I wish to pay tribute to the help given me by the agencies of Wiltshire history without which it would have been quite impossible to write it. They are the following: First, the Wiltshire & Swindon Record Office, at times my second home, and the staff who run it, in particular Steven Hobbs, for his friendship and constant interest in my work; and Ian Hicks, Jane Silcocks, their colleagues and predecessors, who have been responsible for finding, producing and then replacing thousands of documents for me over the years. Second, the staff of the Wiltshire Local Studies Library at Trowbridge, perhaps my third home (and once my responsibility), in particular Michael Marshman, Nicola Pitman, Linda Matthews, Daphne Perkins and Wendy Bate. Third, the Library of the Wiltshire Archaeological & Natural History Society at Devizes, especially its Sandell Librarian, Dr Lorna Haycock, as well as her predecessors and the many volunteers who have helped to maintain it.

Acknowledgements made in the first volume of this series are gratefully and warmly repeated here: to my late wife, Alison Borthwick, and my erstwhile publisher, Tony Martin, for the interest and support they gave me over many years; to Michael Charlton, who with his wife Annette has once again travelled around the region to capture its quintessence with his pen and brush; and to David Cousins, whose striking painting adorns the cover. In addition I have incurred specific debts to Roy Canham, County Archaeologist, and his staff for access to the Wiltshire Sites and Monuments Record and the Extensive Urban Survey documents; to David Landeryou, of Wiltshire County Council's Environmental Services Department, for supplying 2001 census data; and to Lorna Haycock, the doyenne of Devizes historians, who kindly read my essays on Devizes and Roundway. To Julie Horne and John Phillips of Salisbury Printing should go much of the credit for this and other Hobnob Press books appearing as intended and I owe a great deal to their cheerful advice and friendship. At a personal level my greatest debt is to my partner Ruth Smalley, who has shared with me the discipline, excitement and occasional drudgery of trying to complete a book such as this.

That this book contains mistakes and misunderstandings I have no doubt. They are mine alone and I take responsibility for them. But if you spot them please let me know (as gently as possible) and I shall correct them if another edition is ever forthcoming.

JOHN CHANDLER

East Knoyle, November 2003

All Cannings

C ANNINGS IS AN INTERESTING NAME, one of a small group (notably Hastings) which originally referred not to a place at all, but to a tribe – the followers of *Cana*. Such names are thought to have originated at an early stage (though not the very earliest) in the colonization of southern Britain by groups of Anglo-Saxon settlers in the sixth and seventh centuries. *Cana's* tribe settled around the marshy bowl which heads the western end of Pewsey Vale, and which came therefore to be known as Cannings Marsh. The territory which they carved out for themselves, or which already existed before they claimed it, seems to have comprised the later parishes of Bishops Cannings and All Cannings, including its tithing of Allington. These three at Domesday (1086), although by then lying in different hundreds, were assessed in total at precisely one hundred hides, and so – it may be assumed – constituted the original hundred of Cannings.

The boundaries of the original hypothetical Cannings, before Bishops Cannings was granted to the bishop and All Cannings was granted to St Mary's nunnery, Winchester, ignore Wansdyke, a defensive linear earthwork probably of the fifth or sixth century. But they use in part a Roman road, suggesting that the unit may have been originally laid out in the Roman period, several centuries before *Cana* and his tribe acquired it.

The headquarters of this supposed Roman estate have not been discovered, although a Roman well, discovered in 1913 west of All Cannings Cross Farm, lies close to an area known in the late-eighteenth century as Black Lands, a name often associated with settlement remains. About 500m north-east of Black Lands lay an early Iron-Age village (of

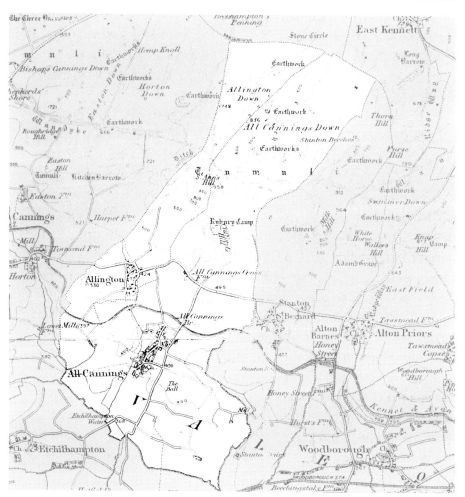

Ordnance Survey 1892 revision, 1 inch = 1 mile

around 650–400BC), excavated between 1911 and 1922, which has given its name – All Cannings Cross – to a type of early Iron-Age pottery discovered there in profusion. A further 500m north-east, on a spur of the chalk hills beyond, lies Rybury Camp, an Iron Age hillfort on the site of a much earlier earthwork, a Neolithic interrupted ditch enclosure or causewayed camp, of about 4,000–3,000BC.

Continuity in the landscape is a fashionable concept, and at All Cannings it can be made to sound quite convincing – a Neolithic site reused as a stronghold in the Iron Age by villagers from All Cannings

Cross, displaced by a Roman villa estate, its territory taken over in turn by Saxon settlers who made their base on the site of the modern village. But 6,000 years cannot be so easily bridged, and unless archaeological discoveries are made to strengthen each link, continuity at All Cannings, thus glibly stated, must remain conjectural.

Returning to surer ground, the ancient parish of All Cannings included Allington and Etchilhampton, although the latter was created a civil parish in 1866, and is described separately in this volume. It was probably not, in any case, an original portion of the Cannings territory, as it name appears to mean 'a farmstead added to an already existing larger settlement'. A small detached portion of the ancient parish, Fullaway, is now in Stert. Cannings is first documented in the Anglo-Saxon Chronicle, which records that in 1010 a Danish force penetrated Wessex as far as *Caneganmersc* or *Caningan maersc* before returning home. Cannings Marsh still existed as a field name immediately north of All Cannings village in the eighteenth century, but it probably originally referred to a larger area, as we have suggested. Allington was described as being in Cannings Marsh in 1394; and it is still found on a map of about 1775, strangely transformed to 'Vale of Candle Marsh'. Since the name *Aldekanning* ('Old Cannings') was in use by the thirteenth century to distinguish All Cannings village from Bishops Cannings, and since the latter has Norman and perhaps Saxon work in its church, it is reasonable to assume that there was a settlement on the site of All Cannings before the conquest.

The present village is closely built for about 1km, on lower chalk, along either side of its street, which runs between church, manor farm and green at the south, to an area known as Townsend, with a smaller triang- ular green (formerly containing a pond and the village pound), at the north. A certain regularity about the layout, particularly the survival of a common boundary and footpath behind the plots east of the street, seems to denote a planned village between the two greens, with Townsend a later addition. South of the church the street continues as a footpath through the farmyard to Etchilhampton Water, 1km further south, where a mill existed in the eighteenth century. Boundaries continuous with those in the village run parallel on either side, and building debris has been found in this area, so it is very likely that the village once continued south of the church along this footpath. On the ground, however, all trace has now disappeared.

In the fourteenth century All Cannings was one of the most populous parishes in Pewsey Vale, and probably in the seventeenth and certainly in the nineteenth century it had a larger population than today. Between 1851 and 1951 the combined population of All Cannings and Allington dropped by 47%, although it has since climbed.

A stroll along the village street offers many reminders of its substantial past. Good vernacular houses and cottages, of timber frame and thatch, and later of brick, survive in profusion, and they are interspersed with more modern houses, including some very early (1860s) examples of concrete construction. Two larger houses at the northern end of the street, The Grange and Bridge House, and one at the southern end, The Old Rectory, were the homes of village notables. Bridge House was built by the 4th Lord Ashburton, of the Baring banking dynasty, which owned the principal manor for most of the nineteenth century. The Grange belonged to the Hitchcock family, lords of a smaller manor in the parish, which had once belonged to the Ernles (commemorated by a spectacular monument in the church). The Old Rectory was rebuilt by a Cambridge academic, Robert Byng (who erected an inscription in Greek on his house), just before the Civil War – and his ejection from the living. A later incumbent was the philanthropic and evangelizing Thomas Methuen, rector from 1810 until his death in 1869. He built in 1833 a village school close to the church, which continued in use until its replacement, across the green, was completed in 1999. Shortly before he died, and under the supervision of his two clerical sons, the extravagant high Victorian chancel of the parish church was completed.

Allington, 1km north of All Cannings, and separated from it by the Kennet and Avon Canal, which wanders across the parish obeying the contour, is a good example of depopulation. The village lanes form an irregular letter D; on a map of 1773 houses clustered on either side of its curve, which widened, perhaps into a small green. Other houses lay in the centre of the D, along a road marked now only by a footpath. At the northern end a church had existed and was still remembered by old inhabitants in 1869; it, or its predecessor, is mentioned in a document of 1100. A Baptist chapel, the centre of an evangelizing campaign in Pewsey Vale by a seceded Anglican priest, Rev J C Philpot, was built in 1829 by a local farmer, Joseph Parry, and survives in use.

Baptist fervour in the nineteenth century posed one threat to the Church of England, represented in All Cannings by its large and impressive parish church of many architectural styles, from Norman to Victorian, and once dedicated to St Anne. Competition from another quarter was acted out on St Anne's day, 6 August, each year (until discontinued after 1932) at Tan Hill (a corruption of St Anne's Hill) on the downs above the village, which shares with Milk Hill the distinction of being the highest point (294m) in Wiltshire. To connect the name with pre-Christian fire ceremonies and Celtic deities, as some have done, is perhaps fanciful, but Tan Hill Fair certainly was held in the late middle ages; the earliest record is a grant of 1499. It became one of the most celebrated of all the downland sheep fairs, and played an important part in the agricultural and economic life of central Wiltshire, which in turn (although there were and are no proper roads to the hill) impacted on the pattern of tracks and paths leading to and across the parish. A remote and windy spot (the year the beer-tent blew down lingered long as a folk memory), Tan Hill with its fair was nevertheless a kind of metropolis for Marlborough Downs shepherds, who spent their working lives in view of it. A late-eighteenth century map marks 'a Building for the Receptacle of the Implements used at the Fair,' on the fairground site, alongside the 'Jockeys Stauls' and the 'Devills Church.' Other less than Christian activities continued in the village until the mid-nineteenth century, in the shape of back-swording, a maypole on the green, and mumming at Christmas.

NOTES (location: SU0762; area: 1,841ha; population (2001): 616)
General: *VCH* 10, 20-33; *WANHM* 11, 1-40, 194-203; Gough, B M, *All Cannings in the past*, 1956; Ozzard, R P, *One street in Wiltshire: a history of All Cannings*, rev. ed. 1997. *-ingas* names: *Medieval Archaeology* 10, 1966, 1-29; All Cannings Cross: Cunnington, M E, *The Early Iron Age inhabited site at All Cannings Cross Farm, Wiltshire*, 1923; Early map: WSRO 1553/75; Houses: Ozzard, R P, *A walk in the street: a tour of the houses of All Cannings* [ca. 2000]; Methuen: Young, S, *Memorials of a happy home*, 1995; Tan Hill Fair: Smith, C S ('Peter Gurney'), *Shepherd lore*, 1985, 18-20.

Alton

WITHIN ITS BOUNDARIES Alton encapsulates many of the themes which recur in the history of the Wiltshire landscape. It is an unprepossessing place, revealing its attractions only to those prepared to climb the breast-shaped hill to its nipple, Adam's Grave, or to examine the footings of the simple Saxon church.

Adam's Grave, which tops Walker's Hill, 1km north of the village, will be our starting point. 'Old Adam' (Little Eve was the name given colloquially to one of the two sarsens at its south-eastern end) commands a fine view across Pewsey Vale and beyond. A nineteenth-century rector, William Crowe, accustomed to find through his telescope three distant landmarks from this spot – Salisbury Cathedral spire, Alfred's Tower above Stourhead, and Fonthill Abbey – was surprised in 1825 that only two were visible; Fonthill had collapsed since his last visit. Today Westbury cement works chimney, more than 25km away, is clearly visible to the naked eye. Adam's Grave is a chambered long barrow of Neolithic date, and so is broadly contemporary with the earthworks of an interrupted ditch enclosure (or causewayed camp) on Knap Hill, across the coombe 1km to the east. Excavations at Knap Hill, while not determining the function of the monument, have suggested that open scrub predominated on the hillside in Neolithic times and that the area was used for cattle-rearing. Land hunger in the late Neolithic and Early Bronze Age periods seems to have resulted in the cultivation of some of this high marginal land, as cereal pollen has been found beneath a Bronze-Age barrow near Wansdyke 1.5km north of Adam's Grave. Iron-Age activity in the area is represented by an enclosed settlement site, known in the Saxon period as

Eorth byrig on the parish boundary with Stanton St Bernard. In Roman
times sheep farmers appear to have colonised part of Knap Hill, and a
Roman villa estate was probably established at Stanchester, a field near
West Stowell in the vale; marginal lands were again brought into cultivation in the extreme north of the parish, although these had reverted to
pasture by, or soon after, the end of the Roman period.

The combe which lies between Adam's Grave and Knap Hill,
although dramatically steep-sided, offers the gentlest incline in the vicinity,
and was used by the prehistoric Great Ridgeway as it descended into
Pewsey Vale. A second track, the Workway Drove, which climbs the slope
beneath Knap Hill to cross the Ridgeway north-east of Adam's Grave, was
probably in use in the Saxon period. It may have been partly in order to
block the access to the south which these two roads provided for hostile
invaders penetrating the Kennet valley from the east that Wansdyke was
constructed across the north of the parish in the fifth or sixth century. Red
Shore, the defensible gap in Wansdyke through which the Ridgeway
passes, was known as *read geat*, the 'red gate or gap', to the Saxons, and
it was probably in connection with defending this gap that two battles
known as *Wodnesbeorg* (identified with Adam's Grave) were fought, in
592 and 715.

The present road (turnpiked in 1840 but in use earlier), once it has
descended the hill, skirts the western edge of Alton, and housing has
developed along it since the nineteenth century, but the Ridgeway
continued due south, passing close by Alton Priors church. We shall follow
it into the village. Prehistoric and Roman activity in the Alton area was not
of course confined to the higher lands which we have so far considered; it
is for the most part only there, however, that the evidence survives. Only
from the Saxon period onwards, with standing buildings and documentary evidence, can we begin to interpret the valley. Although it perhaps
began as a single settlement, 'the farmstead by the source of the stream,'
Alton village had been divided into two before the end of the ninth
century and perhaps before 825.

The churches of Alton Barnes and Alton Priors which served the
two communities lie no more than 200m apart, separated by the stream
which divided their flocks. To walk between them, from Barnes to Priors,

along the narrow metalled path which crosses the puzzling but pronounced earthwork remains of the settlements for which they were built, is
always a moving experience. Arriving at Priors churchyard one pays one's
respects to the venerable yew tree – 1,700 years old according to the
certificate in the church. And then one reflects that, if this is true, since the
church cannot be so old, here is not a tree in a churchyard, but a church
in a 'treeyard'!

Throughout their history it is likely that Alton Priors was the larger community, and its church, though now redundant (and beautifully maintained by the Churches Conservation Trust), is the larger and grander building. It was not, however, autonomous; as a manor of St Swithun's Priory, Winchester, it was administered, along with West Stowell (a hamlet in the extreme east of Alton parish and now in Wilcot), as a tithing of the neighbouring Winchester manor of Overton. Alton Barnes, on the other hand, was a separate parish, but it remained small and poor, and consequently never replaced its Saxon church. 'If the pebble-dash could be removed and the fabric made good,' wrote an archaeologist who excavated part of the church in 1971-2, 'the nave of Alton Barnes could be seen as one of the most complete Saxon naves in England.' In the area between and around the two churches, especially north of Alton Priors church, village earthworks provide evidence of shrinkage.

The difficulty of deriving a living from thin chalk soils is illustrated by the failure of downland settlements in Alton and its neighbouring parishes, Huish and Overton. The medieval village of Shaw lay 1.5km north of Huish where the border between Alton and Overton now runs, immediately south of Wansdyke. By 1066 it was divided between two owners, and so it continued until its demise, which may have occurred in the fifteenth century. By 1377 It was the smallest economic unit in Wiltshire to be taxed, with only three payers; it is missing from a list of small settlements in 1428, and so had probably by then given up as a place to live. It remained an identifiable estate, however, which was mapped in about 1618 and 1766. Its fourteenth-century church was quarried for building material, and three of its windows seem to have found their way into Alton Barnes church; the site of the churchyard was nevertheless remembered as late as 1838, when it was marked on the tithe map, and an excavation to discover the foundations was carried out in 1929. Village earthworks are still visible ranged along a street which runs from south of Shaw Copse in a north-westerly direction towards Wansdyke.

The disappearance of the two estates at Shaw followed the desertion of the village; their lands were taken over by Overton and Alton Barnes (hence the present boundary drawn through the area of former settlement), and the farming pattern of the area was further disturbed in the late-sixteenth century by one William Button, who for a time occupied the principal farms of both Altons and both Shaws. His memorial brass, depicting him smugly entering the portals of heaven, may be seen in Alton Priors church.

A similar process of consolidating landholdings occurred again in the late-nineteenth and early twentieth centuries, when members of the Stratton family began to farm the majority of Alton, including Shaw. Arthur Stratton, who was killed in 1918 by a train at Woodborough Station, was a pioneer in the use of steam-ploughing tackle, and operated a successful hire company from Alton Farm. Recent Strattons, like William Button, have their memorials – delicate engraved glass quarrels in the windows of Alton Barnes church (and missed by the casual church visitor). They are the work of Laurence Whistler, who for many years was their neighbour at the former rectory.

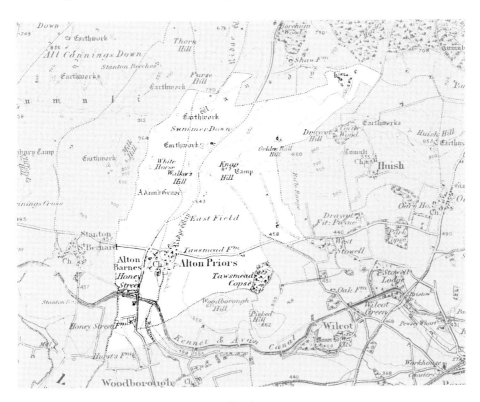

Ordnance Survey 1892 revision, 1 inch = 1 mile

Much more in evidence in Alton Barnes church are the several memorials to men of New College, Oxford. New College has owned Alton Barnes, including patronage of the rectory, since the college was founded in 1385. Consequently many distinguished Oxford men have held the living, including a poet, William Crowe (rector 1787-1829), and Augustus Hare (rector 1829-33). The latter's biography, *Memorials of a quiet life*, by his nephew, records in affectionate detail four years of happiness and benevolence at Alton, marred only by the agricultural riot of 1830 (which is recorded in contemporary letters and a diary) and by Hare's illness, which proved fatal in 1834. Towards the end Hare resorted to Italy for respite from his tuberculosis, and his duties were taken by a curate, Robert Kilvert (the father of the diarist Francis Kilvert). Crowe and Hare are remembered in adjacent monuments in the chancel.

The folly of one of Crowe's contemporaries, Robert Pile, a farmer, leads us back on to the hills above the village. The Alton Barnes white horse, although sired by the Cherhill horse, lacks its parent's equine grace. It was commissioned by Pile in about 1812, but John Thorne, his would-be leucippotomist (as cutters of white horses have grandiloquently been dubbed) proved dishonest, and absconded with the £20 fee before the work was completed. He was subsequently caught and hanged.

Marks of a different kind on the hillside were heralded by barking dogs during a July night in 1990. Next morning a strange line of circles ranged along an axis some 200m in length and with various enigmatic appendages was discovered in standing corn. It was by no means the first of the modern surge of crop circle phenomena, but this one, because of its complexity and oddity, became international news and an instant tourist attraction. Crop circles have appeared in Alton frequently since 1990. Most are of unexplained origin, but obvious hoaxes have included a stylized tree and a Japanese saloon car.

The white horse, Adam's Grave and much of Alton's downland form part of the Pewsey Downs national nature reserve, publicly accessible and a popular resort for walkers and lovers of chalkland landscape. An archaeologist at Adam's Grave in 1950 was told that if anyone ran round the barrow seven times the giant would come out, and although a test by the author failed to confirm this assertion, a visit to 'Old Adam' is always an exhilarating experience.

NOTES (location: SU1162; area: 1,019ha; population (2001): 229)
General: *VCH* 10, 8-13; *VCH* 11, 181-203 *passim*; Gee, T R, *Souvenir notes of a local history exhibition at Alton Barnes*, 1952 [typescript in T].
William Crowe: *WANHM* 67, 163-6; Knap Hill: *WANHM* 60, 1-23; Cereal pollen: *WANHM* 68, 120-2; Stanchester: *WANHM* 45, 504-5; 66, 71-5; Alton Barnes church: *WANHM* 68, 71-8; Shaw: *WANHM* 45, 156-65; Arthur Stratton: *WANHM* 40, 278-9; New College: WRS 13; Augustus Hare: Hare, A, *Memorials of a quiet life*, 1872-6; White horse: Marples, M, *White horses and other hill figures*, 1949, 92-5; Bergamar, K, *Discovering hill figures*, 4th ed. 1997, 60-1; Crop circles: Andrews, C, *Crop circles: signs of contact*, 2003; Silva, F, *Secrets in the fields*, 2002, 19-20; Devil: Grinsell, L V, *Folklore of prehistoric sites in Britain*, 1976, 113.

Beechingstoke

A PARISH OF MODEST PROPORTIONS defined by streams and ancient roads, Beechingstoke sits on the floor of Pewsey Vale, with no finger of land projecting up on to the downs. Instead it boasts in its centre a very modest hill, a chalk outlier rising no more than 15m above the streams, which is known as Stoke Elm from the tree which (alas no more) crowned its summit. The chalky soil made arable cultivation feasible, so that the three small settlements, which lay by the streams at the parish edges, shared a common field which covered and embraced their hill.

Until recent changes Beechingstoke retained the boundaries described in a charter of 941. These followed minor headwaters of the Avon, described as 'Ring-bourne' and 'Stoke-brook', which flowed in barely perceptible valleys, 'Rush-slade' and 'Mere- (or boundary) dene', and which 'ways' crossed at 'Stone-ford' and 'Weevil's-ford'. All these

14

places can be identified today, although the modern parish has lost land in the north to Woodborough (the new boundary follows the railway), and in the south-west to Marden. The latter change has removed from Beechingstoke its important archaeological sites, the enormous henge monument known as Marden Henge, and the destroyed Hatfield Barrow.

Three hamlets appear to have existed in the medieval period, occupying sites close to the east, south and north-west boundaries. Beechingstoke itself (like Erlestoke in this volume) was often simply known as Stoke. Colt Hoare spelled it Beauchamp Stoke, but the true derivation is less classy, the name probably one of reproach, meaning 'the bitches' enclosure'. It hugs the north-western boundary stream ('Stoke-brook'), and consists of no more than a small church and churchyard in a cul-de-sac dominated by a large rectory (which cost the enormous sum of £2,000 to build in 1830), and a few houses, including a thatched manor house, clustered around a road junction which may have been a small triangular green.

The eastern corner of the parish contained a settlement called Bottle, described as *botan waelle* ('Bota's spring') in 892, and commemorated now in the names Bottle Farm and Bottlesford. Precisely where this settlement lay is not clear. A Victorian rector of Beechingstoke knew a tradition that a church had existed in a field in the area, and a priest's dwelling is mentioned near present-day Broad Street in the charter

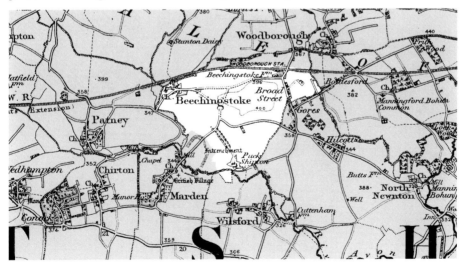

Ordnance Survey 1892 revision, 1 inch = 1 mile

of 941. Perhaps the linear village of Broad Street, first mentioned by name in the eighteenth century but probably much older, superseded the earlier 'Bottle'. It lies along part of the Great Ridgeway (hence its name) and shared in the economic revival of the area in the nineteenth century.

This began with the opening in 1810 of the Kennet and Avon Canal and its wharf at Honeystreet, and was continued by the Kennett and Amesbury turnpike of 1840, and the construction of the Devizes railway with a station (called Woodborough Station) in the parish in 1862. The turnpike trust improved not only the north–south route towards Upavon, but also the minor road which crosses the parish from south of the railway bridge at Beechingstoke Farm (known as Bottle Farm in the nineteenth century), through Marden Henge and across the stream (where a new bridge was constructed) to Marden itself. Woodborough Station closed in 1966, although the sidings and access roads remain and may be seen from the road bridge; the railway line remains open, and high speed trains thunder along the embankment past Beechingstoke village.

A third medieval settlement, with the enticing name of Puckshipton ('the goblin's cattle shed') lay in the south of the parish. Aerial photography suggests that a village site may lie east of the present Puckshipton House, and therefore close to *Wifelesford* ('weevils'-ford'), the point at which the Great Ridgeway crossed the River Avon. Any houses which remained in the village were probably swept away around 1700, when a large house was built by the tenant, Charles Raymond. Raymond may also have been responsible for alterations to the parish church in 1693, perhaps in order to obtain lead from the church roof to assist in building his mansion. He seems to have converted the droveway which led from Puckshipton to Beechingstoke into an avenue lined with a double row of elms. A map of 1726 shows a large house within formal gardens, from which tree-lined avenues radiate, with a smaller house at its shoulder. It is the smaller house, the old farm house which was later rebuilt, that survives – the mansion had gone by 1790.

NOTES (location: SU0859; area: 361ha; population (2001): 157)
General: *VCH* 10, 14-17; WANHS Library, notes by Richard Nicholson.
Turnpike: WSRO A1/370/195; 1726 map: WSRO X3/46H.

Bishops Cannings

W ILTSHIRE MEN AND WOMEN have a special regard for Bishops
Cannings, not only because of the quintessentially Wiltshire view of
it they catch from the main Devizes–Swindon road – a miniature Salisbury
Cathedral set against a backdrop of rolling Marlborough Downs – but
more especially because the village is the reputed home of the moonrakers,
the heroic symbols of Wiltshire patriotism who have given its residents
their sobriquet. The moonraker legend, which in its fully developed form
probably dates from the eighteenth century (it is recorded in 1791 and
cannot pre-date the introduction of excise duty in 1643), concerns a group
of Wiltshiremen smuggling brandy who, to avoid discovery by a passing
exciseman as they were fishing their contraband out of its hiding-place in
a pond, pretended that they were trying to recover what they took to be a
cheese, but which the exciseman correctly identified as the reflection of
the moon. Once he had gone, chuckling at their stupidity, the brandy was
safely recovered. Variants of the simple motif – raking for the moon
believing it to be cheese – are recorded for over forty places in Great
Britain, and Bishops Cannings is only one (albeit the most persistent) of
several Wiltshire places which claim to be the home of the moonrakers.
The legend's association with Wiltshire was strengthened by its adoption
by the Wiltshire Regiment in the late-nineteenth century, and the
'definitive' version was published in a poem by Edward Slow in 1881.

On the face of it Bishops Cannings, which has no village pond,
seems an unlikely venue for the story. But this difficulty can be easily
explained. Firstly, what would seem to be an ideal pond for moonraking –
the Crammer on Devizes Green – actually lay within Bishops Cannings

parish until 1835. Secondly the village has long had a reputation for idiocy, or feigned idiocy, which made it the butt of many folk tales recorded in the nineteenth and early twentieth centuries. The miniature steeple over the church tower staircase was ridiculed, and it was rumoured that the builders had manured it to make it grow; the village cooper was alleged to have employed his son to help mend a barrel by holding up one end from inside, but then had to knock out the other end to remove him; a large watch found on the downs by a shepherd was identified by the sexton as a 'dangerous ticktoad,' and smashed up before it could cause any damage; a farmer was greatly impressed by a gas fire which he saw in a Devizes ironmonger's, and bought it, but on taking it home could not make it work – Bishops Cannings had no gas supply.

Gentle teasing of this kind seems to have been affectionate rather than malicious (nor was it restricted to Bishops Cannings) and there is no need to find its origin in Saxon tribal differences, as an eminent historian suggested in 1944. The village's special qualities have been charmingly chronicled by Ida Gandy, who grew up in the vicarage in the late-nineteenth century, the daughter of a gentle bee-keeping vicar, the Rev Hony. Of the topography of the parish she wrote: 'All round the church was scattered the village. There was no concentration of houses in any particular place; they just gathered in little groups along the roads and by-lanes, like friendly neighbours met for a gossip. Some, of a less sociable nature, had set themselves right in the heart of the fields.'

Bishops Cannings is in fact a very large parish, the third largest in Wiltshire after Calne Without and Ramsbury (or fourth if Swindon be regarded as a parish), and nearly 50km in circumference. Before the Victorian and later expansion of Devizes it was larger still, embracing Roundway, Southbroom and adjoining hamlets right up to the town defences; as well as Chittoe, a more remote detached member of the parish beyond Bromham. Since 1934 it has consisted of five settlements: Coate and Horton on the lower-lying Upper Greensand at the head of Pewsey Vale, and Bourton, Easton and Bishops Cannings itself at the foot of the chalk slopes which mark the southern edge of the Marlborough Downs.

The bipartite terrain of chalk downland and Greensand vale has influenced the pattern of communications through the parish. Three

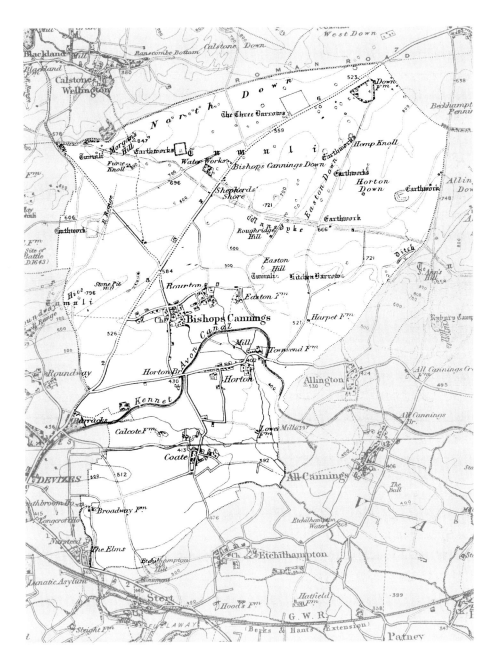

Ordnance Survey 1892 revision, 1 inch = 1 mile

generations of the Bath road cross the downland. The most northerly is a stretch of the Roman road from Mildenhall to Sandy Lane, which forms the parish boundary. Further south the road until about 1800 ran from Beckhampton along the present main road for about 3km, then branched slightly north of the present line to breach Wansdyke at a point known now as Old Shepherd's Shore, then beneath Morgan's Hill towards Heddington and Sandy Lane. At Old Shepherd's Shore a road branched south to rejoin the present main road at West End. This fell out of use when the present line was constructed around 1800 to become the main Bath–Devizes–London road, but its course is clearly discernible from the modern road. Descending the steep slopes from the chalk were (and are) several tracks linking the tithings' upland pastures to their respective arable and meadows.

A more interesting track, now largely vanished, ran from Morgan's Hill, along the hillside north of Bourton and Easton to Harepath Farm and All Cannings Cross, where it becomes the modern road towards Pewsey. As the farm name suggests it was a *herepath*, or Saxon military road. South from it branched a second ancient track, which passes beside Bishops Cannings Church, through Coate to Etchilhampton, on its way to form the Lydeway and the old Salisbury road across the plain. The valley bottom is shared by the Devizes–Pewsey road through Horton, and a stretch of the Kennet and Avon Canal, completed in 1805-6, and here meandering along its contour to remain level.

The downland territory is archaeologically rich, sharing with the neighbouring parish, Avebury, an abundance of prehistory. The land use of these downs, sheep runs and more lately training gallops for racehorses and a golf course, has until recent years been gentle on its archaeology, and barrows, field systems and parts of the Roman road are extant, or may be discerned from the air. In 1992 one of the largest hoards of late-Roman coins (over 7,000, including more than 1,500 silver coins) was found by metal detector on these downs. Wansdyke, the massive defensive work probably thrown up in the fifth or sixth century, and a recurring theme in the history of the northern Pewsey Vale parishes, is clearly seen from the main road, which meets and crosses it at right angles. Also visible, though only distantly from the Pewsey road, are massive strip lynchets or cultivation terraces rising in steps of 3m or more up the hillside north of Horton. These were sectioned archaeologically in 1957-8, and the results showed that, although they had interfered with prehistoric and Roman ploughsoil, they were formed later, presumably as a result of land hunger in the middle ages.

Some 600m north-west of the main road crossing along Wansdyke, at Old Shepherd's Shore (a *shord* was local dialect for a gap or opening), was the *Shepherd's Rest Inn*; a medieval enclosure on the hillside nearby may have served as a sheepfold. At Old Shepherd's Shore in June 1613 Anne of Denmark, queen of James I, was accosted by the villagers of Bishops Cannings, led by their vicar, George Ferebe, who sang her a song especially composed for the occasion, and invited her to listen to the church bells pealing in the distance in her honour. Thirty years later, in July 1643, the noise of battle echoed from the hills around Old Shepherd's Shore as Sir Ralph Hopton's Royalist army defeated Sir William Waller's Parliamentary forces at the battle of Roundway Down. The *Shepherd's Rest Inn* disappeared after the main road was diverted away from it; it was perhaps the 'strange old place, built of a kind of shingle, inlaid, as it were, with cross-beams, with gable-topped windows projecting completely over the pathway, and a low door with a dark porch,' described by the bagman in Dickens's *Pickwick Papers*, first published in 1836-7.

To the west of Old Shepherd's Shore, at the limit of the parish, is Morgan's Hill, part of which is managed as a nature reserve by the Wiltshire Wildlife Trust. The name is supposed to derive from one John Morgan, who in 1720, having robbed his uncle, murdered him to avoid detection, but was caught and hanged on the hill before a large crowd. The post hole of the gallows was still visible in 1894. A few years later the existing golf course was laid out nearby, and before 1914 masts (not the present landmarks) were erected for the first of a series of wireless stations.

The five settlements which make up Bishops Cannings parish all have a shrunken appearance. In view of the likely priority of All (or Old) Cannings as the headquarters of the territory of *Cana* and his followers (as described under All Cannings) they probably all began as subsidiary farmsteads or hamlets, but by 1086 the territory had split and Bishops Cannings had taken the lion's share. The village now called Bishops

Cannings may not have acquired its prefix until the thirteenth century, but it was probably the chief settlement in the bishop's parish long before, and may have possessed a church before the conquest (it was claimed that Saxon masonry was found during church restoration in 1880). The present church, largely of the twelfth and thirteenth centuries, owes its noble proportions to its episcopal connections, and it was joined in the fourteenth by a manor house belonging to the bishops of Salisbury, which stood south-east of the churchyard, near Court Farm. Ploughing in 1949 beside the extant mound uncovered foundations, pavements, paths and masonry, including an ornamental gablet.

The main axis of the village probably lay east of the church, along the Street, a north-south lane parallel with the modern road through the village. Here a cross-roads was formed, with routes eastward to Bourton and Easton, and westward into the churchyard. The Street itself broadened at this point and ran away south to form the track to Horton, as well as looping back on to the modern road, which leads to Coate. Thus all the settlements were connected with their church. An undated map of around 1770 shows many crofts deserted in Bishops Cannings village, although it is clear from another map (of 1773) that houses then still lined the roads leading west and south from the village. Shrinkage has continued, although in places modern housing has replaced the casualties.

Bourton and Easton (the 'fortified farmstead' and the 'eastern farmstead') have undergone similar deflation. Disturbed ground south of the road at Easton testifies to former occupation (two houses marked on a map of 1773 are absent from another of about 1790) while at Bourton a complicated and irregular former street plan suggests a community of some importance. Fishwater, a marshy hollow at Bourton, has the distinction of being the source of the western headwater of the Salisbury Avon. The infant river's effect on the Greensand of the vale is doubtless reflected in the name Horton ('muddy farmstead') through which it next passes.

The original nucleus of this settlement seems to have been south of the stream, where the road from Devizes makes its first bend. Later an area further north, characteristically known as Townsend, was added, and a planned addition along the road to the west, with regular crofts, a back lane, and narrow strips of land extending south to a stream. Coate similarly exhibits planned and apparently random elements, with many gaps and tell-tale disturbed plots. Apart from the present settlement along two parallel north-south lanes, other foci existed at Little Horton to the north, Calcote to the west, and east of Manor Farm. As at Worton and Marston on their Potterne estate, so at Horton, Coate and Bishops Cannings itself on their Cannings estate, the agency of the medieval bishops of Salisbury as village planners and colonizers may perhaps be seen.

The disappearance of houses has been paralleled by the disappearance of people. Between 1831 and 1931 the population halved, from 1,365 to 665, and only the recent new housing (especially on the fringe of expanding Devizes) has brought the total back to and above the 1831 figure. Bishops Cannings was unlucky to decline so markedly. In the seventeenth century, according to John Aubrey, it 'would have challenged all England for musique, foot-ball, and ringing;' the piety of its then inhabitants may still be witnessed in the church, in the shape of an extra-ordinary penitential seat, painted with a giant hand (the hand of God indeed) and texts to remind them of their misdemeanours. But it remains a parish of great charm and variety, and a desirable place to live. Cannings folk are wiser than their reputation.

NOTES (location: SU0464; area: 3,598ha; population (2001): 1,566)
General: *VCH* 7, 187-97; Gandy, I, *A Wiltshire childhood*, 1929; Gandy, I, *Round about the little steeple*, 1960; *WANHM* 6, 129-59.
Moonrakers: Briggs, K, *Dictionary of British folk-tales*, A2, 1970, 192-3; Stupidity: *WANHM* 50, 412-14, 481-2; Stern, J L, in *WF* 1(2), 1977, 5-8; Coin hoard: Guest, P, *et al*, in *Coin Hoards of Roman Britain*, vol. 10, 426-62; Strip lynchets: *WANHM* 57, 163-72, 322-38; Morgans Hill: *Devizes & Wilts Gazette*, 31.5.1894, p.5; Golf course: Lumley, J, *North Wilts Golf Club, 1890-1990*, 1990; Early maps: WSRO 248/143-4; 1553/79; Coate: Smith, S J, *In a Wiltshire hamlet*, 1993.

Bromham

I F WILTSHIRE WERE A GARDEN, then Bromham would be its vegetable
patch. That, at least, is the impression to be gained from the main
Devizes–Chippenham road (A342), which passes level fields of fine brown
tilth, cloches, and small busy tractors working between long lines of tender
plants. Bromham parish roughly coincides with the only significant
outcrop of Lower Greensand in the county, and this produces a fertile,
easily drained, iron-stained soil well suited to market gardening. It has also
encouraged broom, a plant still found on the escarpment nearby, but rare
elsewhere in north Wiltshire. From broom the community derives its
name.

The Lower Greensand predominates in Bromham, but the parish
boundary encompasses a slice of the larger geological layer-cake. West of
the village Clackers Brook, a tributary of the Bristol Avon, has downcut a
miniature ravine into the older Oxford Clay of the west Wiltshire vale. At
Westbrook and Spye Park spurs of Corallian limestone have encouraged
the growth of woodland. And in the east of the parish the terrain sweeps
upward beyond the Gault and Upper Greensand to the spectacular
rounded chalk hill known as Oliver's Castle. Bromham, therefore, like its
neighbours to north and south, provides a step or slope between
Wiltshire's chalk and cheese countries.

Across this 'tilted tract of sandy country', as an official report once
described it, the settlement pattern is complex, and somewhat layered.
The most recent of these layers, of smallholdings and market gardens
spread across the southern half of the parish, is superimposed on
dispersed scatters of domestic weavers' cottages. Hamlets such as

Netherstreet, Hawk Street and St Edith's Marsh, although their origins may be earlier, have the characteristic form of the rural clothmaking and pasturing communities on the edges of commons around the west Wiltshire towns, which became so widespread after enclosure on the claylands from the seventeenth century. The northern half of the modern parish, more broken and wooded, attracted country houses in parks and pleasure grounds – Westbrook, Nonsuch, Spye and Bromham House itself – from the Tudor period onwards. Underlying these layers is the medieval landscape of nucleated villages, with their open fields, common pasture and woods. Bromham itself remains a comparatively large village, its streets and paths converging on the parish church and its comfortable houses extending northward to take in the formerly distinct hamlet of Horsepool. Chittoe, a separate village to the north, is now very small, and a third medieval settlement and manorial centre to the south, Clench or Clinghill (if indeed it ever was a separate village) has all but disappeared.

These layers of settlement sit, in turn, upon a more ancient landscape. Across Spye Park, and still well preserved in places, runs the bank of the Roman road between London and Bath, which crosses Wiltshire from east to west. At Wans House, on the northern parish boundary next to Sandy Lane, the road's alignment changes, because here it entered and left a small town, generally known by its Latin name *Verlucio*. The size and extent of the Roman settlement are only vaguely known from limited excavation and fieldwork in 1986-7 and 1993, but it must have straddled the present boundaries of Bromham, Heddington and Calne Without. Like many Roman towns it seems to have begun as a military outpost soon after the conquest which attracted a civilian enclave outside. Later, probably in the third century, the town expanded and took over the site of the now obsolete fort, which has been identified between Bell Farm and Hayfield Copse on the parish boundary. Finds of slag suggest that the town's inhabitants were exploiting the local ironstone for metalworking, as well as marketing the farm produce of local villa-estates. They may also have maintained a *mansio*, or government posting-station for official travellers.

Such towns did not sit in isolation. The fortunes of *Verlucio* were linked not only to the traffic along the main road which it had sprung up

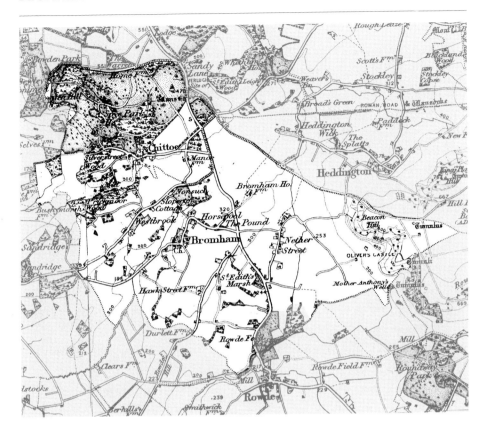

Ordnance Survey 1892 revision, 1 inch = 1 mile

to serve. It also controlled a territory – perhaps extending over many miles – within which were villa estates dependent on it. In Bromham parish a Roman villa with a fine mosaic pavement was known in West Park Field in the eighteenth century, and the site (which is cut by the main road north-east of the village) was investigated in 1810, 1840 and 1880. Other villas were reported on Chittoe Heath and at Silver Street, west of Chittoe; another, near Mother Anthony's Well beneath Oliver's Castle, was identified before 1908 by a cropmark of poppies growing in a cornfield with 'brilliancy and peculiar regularity', from which the buildings' outlines could be traced. Thus was Omar Khayyám's speculation almost literally confirmed: 'I sometimes think that never blows so red | The rose as where some buried Caesar bled.' A second Roman site was found nearby in 1963, possibly connected with working the local iron ore.

Another legacy of *Verlucio* is suggested by its position on boundaries. Chittoe, although since 1934 subsumed within Bromham, was anciently part of Bishops Cannings, and within Cannings hundred. Close to *Verlucio* no fewer than four of these Saxon and medieval territories, the hundreds of Chippenham, Melksham, Calne and Cannings, all kiss, and it has been suggested that they somehow reflect the break-up into four parts of the Roman administrative area once *Verlucio* had ceased to function at its centre.

Chittoe carries in its name a Celtic word for woodland, which could therefore have been heard on people's lips – when *Verlucio* was still flourishing – to describe this tract of secluded, broken, wooded country, carpeted in blue every spring and gold every autumn. Such woods must have been a valuable resource for faraway Cannings, where most of the land was treeless chalk. At Chittoe a medieval village developed, with its own mill and chapel of ease. The surviving mill complex, presumably on the site of its medieval predecessor, has not been used as such since about 1870. The site of the medieval chapel has been lost, but the knot of modern footpaths pointlessly criss-crossing the fields to the south of the present hamlet suggest where one might look. One such path, 'the burying road', struck east across the downs to Bishop's Cannings; since Chittoe chapel had no right to bury its own dead, corpses had to be carried to the mother church. But in 1845 a T H Wyatt church was built overlooking the winding village street, and this was the first of many innovations.

J W G Spicer, an army officer whose investment in a brewery had made his fortune, bought the Spye Park estate in 1863, and over the next twenty years reordered the lives of his tenantry. Six farms were rebuilt, cottages were demolished and their inhabitants moved to new roadside hamlets at Westbrook and Chittoe Heath, and at Sandridge (in Melksham Without). A school was built with teacher's house attached, a vicarage for the new church, and an enormous kitchen garden. Most dramatically of all, he demolished his seventeenth-century mansion, a curious pile described as, 'like a long barn . . . [with] not a single window on the prospect side,' and replaced it with something considered at the time to be far worse. Visible for miles perched on its hillside, the redbrick Spye Park

of 1864-8 was a sore thumb of a house, which provoked Spicer's
neighbour, Lord Methuen of Corsham Court, to complain about it in *The
Times*. Most of it was burnt down, and the rest demolished, in August
1974, on the day following the house-warming party for the fifth member
of the Spicer family to have taken up residence there. The park, privately
owned, retains many buildings associated with the successive mansions,
and with the kennels of the Avon Vale Hunt - the Spicers were enthusiastic
huntsmen. Back in the village, the school closed in 1906 and the church
was converted to a house in the 1980s. The churchyard remains
accessible, however, and here the Spicers have their memorials. Below
them in the idyllic valley, alongside the kitchen garden and partly
concealed by trees, sit those cottages that remain, quiet and trim now in
their new-found affluence.

The Spicers, whose domain from 1864 included the manor of
Bromham as well as Chittoe, were only the latest of a long line of
powerful manorial owners who controlled the parish. Medieval Bromham,
from about 1087 until the dissolution in 1538, belonged to Battle Abbey
in East Sussex, the house founded by William I as a thank-offering for his
victory. Its special status favoured it with privileges of autonomy and
jurisdiction over its lands which were not shared by many landowners. As
a result civil and criminal justice in its manors was dispensed by the abbey,
not the shire, and Bromham was termed a liberty. When Battle was
dissolved Bromham was acquired by the abbey's steward, Sir Edward
Bayntun (such 'management buy-outs' were quite widespread in the
1530s), and he set about building himself a mansion on his estate.

Bromham House stood away from and to the east of the village,
behind the present Bromham House Farm (a field here is called 'The
Moats' on the tithe map of 1847). Bayntun salvaged material for his
project from the ruins of Devizes Castle, a royal manor house at Corsham
and (possibly) Bradenstoke Priory. What he accomplished was said to
have been nearly as large as Whitehall, and a palace fit to entertain a king
– which it did, apparently, on at least three occasions. The magnificent
house lasted little more than a century before succumbing to the Royalist
army, who burnt it down in May 1645, so that only walls and chimneys
were left standing. The Edward Bayntun of the day, rather than rebuild his

ravaged house, removed to Spye Park where he had built by 1654 the
house (with by now third-hand materials salvaged from the gutted
mansion) which Spicer eventually demolished in 1864. One fragment
remains, however. The gatehouse to Spye Park's approach from the
Lacock–Sandy Lane road near Bowden Park is an authentic survivor from
the Tudor Bromham House.

The Bayntun family continued as owners of the former Battle
manor until 1864, and in the eighteenth century built a dower house
(Battle House) in the village, perhaps (since it contains medieval material)
on the site of the abbey stewards' house. A much later owner, between
about 1896 and 1912, was the *Punch* cartoonist Leonard Raven Hill, but
by about 1960 the house had been converted to flats. One other large
house in the parish deserves mention. This is Nonsuch, on the main road
at Westbrook, which was rebuilt about 1700 in Queen Anne style by
William Norris. The last of his family, James, was a recluse who died in
1835; he lived in such squalor that his solicitor when visiting always lit a
cigar to counteract the stench. Nearby, on the opposite side of the busy
main road, is Sloperton Cottage, the home from 1818 until his death in
1852 of the Irish poet and lyricist, Tom Moore. He was part of the circle of
talent attracted to and supported by the Lansdowne household at
Bowood, and is commemorated in Bromham churchyard by a large Celtic
cross, some 6m high.

Bromham church stands in the centre of the village, where three
roads meet. The churchyard wall incorporates an eighteenth-century lock-
up or blind house, unusually of timber construction. The church is very
fine. It is largely of the thirteenth and fourteenth centuries, with fragments
of a Norman predecessor, and a spire of 1510 surmounting its central
tower. The spire has needed frequent repair, having been damaged by the
rope of a 'steeple-flyer' or stuntman in 1735, and later struck by lightning.
The highlight of the church is its south chapel (very similar to one in
Devizes St John's) which was built to house a chantry established in 1492
by Sir Roger Tocotes for himself and his relations, including members of
the Beauchamp family. Tocotes was a politician and civil servant who
managed to steer his way unscathed through the tumultuous fifteenth
century and died in his bed at Bromham – he had married into the

Beauchamps in 1457, who owned a subsidiary manor in the village. Unscathed is not the word one would choose, however, to describe his alabaster effigy, which has attracted perhaps a finer assortment of graffiti, spanning several centuries and in every conceivable part of his ensemble, than is to be met with in any other Wiltshire church. The chapel contains in addition an interesting collection of Bayntun monuments, and is sometimes referred to as theirs.

Within a short stroll of the church are the principal buildings of the village. The Chantry (or Porch House) at the top of Church Hill (partly now the village shop) is contemporary with the chapel and was probably built (as its name suggests) for Tocotes's chantry priest. Below it is a Wesleyan chapel of 1799, rebuilt about 1860. The large house virtually opposite, Hillside, was built in 1811 alongside a brewery (demolished in 1895); and below it the old people's bungalows of 1964-5 replaced, despite concerted protest, a row of six almshouses which dated from 1612. In High Street beyond the lock-up is another medieval house (Church House) and the *Greyhound Inn*, with its fine collection of jugs.

The village car park adjacent to it was a community project, having been created in 1963 from the proceeds of the Bromham horse show. East of the church, in the area known as the Pound, is the village school of 1878, which began as a British or nonconformist school (since much extended and rebuilt); it stands next to the former Baptist chapel of 1873, replacing an earlier building of 1828. A much earlier nonconformist meeting, of Quakers, existed from the seventeenth century, and had a building on Bromham Common (west of the village, in the valley). The congregation had dwindled to one by 1814, and the meeting house was demolished in 1863, although the Quaker burial ground remained.

Beyond the village centre are reminders of Bromham's economic diversity. There are warehouses and industrial buildings associated with the vegetable-growing and market-gardening activities prevalent throughout the southern half of the parish. There is also a factory making furniture, and formerly a brush factory which also made butter churns and spinning tops. From the sixteenth to the nineteenth century, as noted above, Bromham like most west Wiltshire communities combined agriculture with domestic clothmaking. Bromham weavers are recorded in 1580; and in 1622, during a period of recession, there were said to be 44 looms out of use in the parish. Hand-loom weavers were still at work as late as the 1870s, supplying their work to one of the large Trowbridge businesses.

The careers of two Bromham worthies can serve to illustrate its inhabitants' versatility. William Gaby of Netherstreet, who kept a notebook covering the period 1656 to 1694, was a carrier or haulier, who supplemented his income by supplying draught oxen to help coaches and waggons up and down Bagdon Hill on the old Bath road across the downs. But his main business was as small-time clothier, the middleman who brought weavers their raw materials and delivered and sold the finished product in local towns or to London factors. Clearly he was a considerable figure in Bromham, who appears to have served as parish constable and overseer. Later generations continued to participate in local society, and Edward Gaby, a direct descendant, was responsible in the 1860s for building St Edith's House, beside the main road at the southern end of Netherstreet.

Henry Season (1693-1775) has a monument in the church porch. He was the son of a Bromham weaver, and was born, lived and died in the parish. He taught himself quack medicine and surgery, which he practised around local villages, and prepared various treatments such as ointment for the eyes and whitening toothpaste. But he was also an astrologer, who from 1733 produced an annual almanac, with calendar and prognostications. In these flimsy publications, which continued to be published long after his death, he gave vent to his personal opinion on all manner of subjects, such as that 'noxious venomous herb' (tobacco), 'a disgraceful evil' (stage plays), and life on the moon.

NOTES (location: ST9665; area: 1,913ha; population (2001): 1,807)
General: *VCH* 7, 179-86, 187-97 *passim*; Webb, W A, *Bromham: a history of a Wiltshire parish*, 1913 [typescript in WANHS Library]; Davis, H, *A history of Bromham*, 1965 [typescript in T].
Geology and soil: Ling, A W, *An agricultural and soil survey of the Bromham district of Wiltshire*, 1938; *Verlucio*: Chippenham College fieldwork report in SMR [T]; Spye Park: Spicer, S J L, *The Spicers of Spye Park*, 1981 [WANHS Library]; Liberty: WRS 12, 129-41; Bromham House: *WANHM* 15, 320-8; 38,432-4; WRS 43; Raven Hill: *Wilts Local History Forum Newsletter* 31, 4; Nonsuch: *WNQ* 2, 190-201; Church: Powney, D, *Bromham: the parish and its churches*, 1997; *WANHM* 1, 351-2; Chantry chapel: *WANHM* 49, 283-7; 95, 93-9; Gaby: *WANHM* 46, 50-7, 336-49; Season: *Wiltshire Life*, October 2003, 64.

Charlton

PLACES CALLED CHARLTON (and there are four in Wiltshire alone) are thought to be part of the residue of large estates which fragmented during the Saxon period, and represent an enclave of free peasants (*ceorls*) who lived apart from the demesne settlement, but performed labour services for it. In the case of Charlton St Peter, to give our parish the distinguishing name (from its church dedication) by which it has often been known, it probably began as a component of a royal estate based on Rushall and Upavon, and seems to have achieved separate parochial status by the thirteenth century. There are architectural indications that its modest church (which retains a chantry chapel and tower of about 1500, but was otherwise largely rebuilt in 1857/8) began life in the twelfth century. The lofty roof of the Victorian restoration obscured from the view of the village a painted sundial on the tower, which survived in 1890, but could only be seen from the high hill above. The manor of Charlton was given to endow a monastery in northern France in about 1187, and a reference in 1323 to a prior of Charlton suggests that for a time a small monastic cell or grange existed in the parish, but its position is unknown.

Like neighbouring Wilsford, Charlton village lies north of the present main road across its parish, which was turnpiked in 1761/2. Wisely, this chooses the chalk hillside in preference to the lower-lying village street, which clearly once formed part of an older road along the vale. Maps of the eighteenth and nineteenth centuries, made before serious depopulation set in, depict what appears to have been a planned medieval village with regular rear property boundaries parallel with the street on both sides. Many of these boundaries survive as low earthworks, and recent survey and analysis suggest that the regular planning of the settlement may have coincided with the period of monastic control, the twelfth to fourteenth centuries. Before this happened the village was perhaps focussed on a circular enclosure, traces of which can be detected as boundaries on the early maps in the area of Gatlow Lane, and this was perhaps the farm of the *ceorls* from which Charlton takes its name.

Several seventeenth-century thatched cottages remain, and a large manor house, dated 1625 but since remodelled, of brick and stone; alongside them are more modern brick houses, including pairs of old people's bungalows. The population of the parish seems to have remained fairly static, at around 150, from the middle ages until the Victorian period. By 1861 it had risen to 222, but thereafter it declined, and was down to one-third of that total in 1991. Cottages on wasteland at the west end of the village, some of seventeenth-century origin, are marked on the 1841 tithe map, but had gone by 1886. They lined White's Lane, which runs north from the *Charlton Cat* to the river. At its eastern end the village street bends to become a made-up footpath which leads to Rushall, a mere 500m away. At the bend, on the northern side, where a building is marked on maps of 1773 and 1817, but had gone by 1841, are substantial earthworks; the bend presumably signifies the limit of the medieval village. The remains of watermeadows may be seen beside the river west of the village, and mention in the tithe award of Mill Mead at this point suggests that nearby had been the village mill.

Charlton's proximity to Rushall has probably caused the failure of attempts to sustain both school (1844 to about 1871) and chapel (1893 to before 1925) in the village. Its pub survives, however, and is a focal point for surrounding, less fortunate, villages. It stands in a commanding position on the main road at its junction with Charlton Drove, and its present name, the *Charlton Cat*, is believed to be a corruption of its address, 'Charlton Cut', since there is a deep cutting at this point. The present building, rebuilt after a fire in 1821, was originally named the Poore's Arms, after the family who purchased the manor in 1784. Their arms incorporated a leopard as a supporter, which was represented on the signboard; hence 'cut' became 'cat'.

Between 1897 and 1899 Romano-British settlement remains were discovered and investigated on a remote area of Charlton Down, and meticulous fieldwork and survey a century later have revealed it to be a very large village, with more than 200 hut sites extending over 26ha into neighbouring parishes. The village had streets, a green area with a pond or reservoir (the settlers were excellent water managers), and – like modern villages – was extended in piecemeal fashion within the pattern of earlier fields that surrounded it. Its heyday seems to have been between the second and fourth centuries, and its purpose was agricultural. With the end of Roman rule intensive cultivation of the downland seems to have finished and the village went largely out of use. Its counterpart in the Roman period was a villa on the valley floor, north-west of the modern village on the parish boundary. It is suggested that here, as elsewhere around Salisbury Plain, the villa-owners controlled the activities of the downland farming communities, and their villas acted as collecting-points for the cereals they produced.

Different arrangements were in place by the late Saxon period. A narrow strip parish, like its eastern and western neighbours, medieval and later Charlton had its share of meadowland around the western headwater of the River Avon (including a few fields known in 1841 as Ruslet – 'rushy valley' – north of the river; arable fields extended southwards up the slope from the village and on Cleeve Hill; and rough sheep pasture lay beyond,

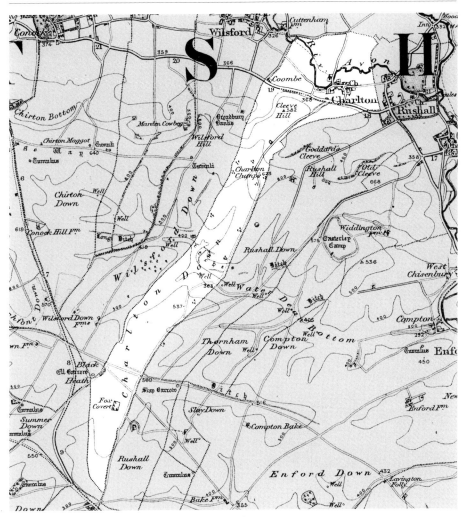

Ordnance Survey 1892 revision, 1 inch = 1 mile

stretching deep into the heart of Salisbury Plain. The parish was enclosed in 1780, and had been consolidated into three farms by 1841. The down-land was purchased by the War Department in 1898, and it has been estimated that eight million shells have landed on Charlton Down since then (rendering any alternative use in future impracticable). The remaining farmland, apart from Charlton Manor farm occupying the north-western corner of the parish, has from 1919 formed part of Rushall farm; since the 1970s it has been farmed organically by Barry Wookey, a leading proponent of organic farming.

Of the countless farm labourers who have cultivated Charlton since prehistory, one distinguished himself and is still periodically remembered. Stephen Duck, a poor thresher on a weekly wage of 4s. 6d. (£0.23), taught himself to read and began to write poetry. In 1729 he was discovered and, much to the chagrin of other, better, poets, became the protegé and favourite of Queen Caroline. His work was published in 1730, and includes 'The Thresher's Labour', a poem of rather more historical interest than literary merit, in which he describes the farming round experienced by a Charlton thresher. Duck enjoyed his success at court for more than twenty years, despite having to endure numerous parodies (usually involving his surname) from his rivals. His Charlton wife having died, he married the queen's housekeeper, Sarah Bigg, took holy orders, and was presented to a rich living in Surrey. But he became depressed, and eventually, on a journey back to Charlton in 1756, he drowned himself at Reading. It was, as a modern critic commented, 'the bad rhyme to end a life which did not scan'. His memory has been preserved, however, by an annual 'Duck Feast', which is still held each June at the *Charlton Cat*; it was originally meant for Charlton threshers and was financed by the profit from a small plot of land (Duck's Acre) purchased for this purpose by Lord Palmerston in 1734. The feast is presided over by the 'Chief Duck' (sometimes a member of the local Fowle family!), who wears a hat adorned with duck feathers. Toasts are drunk to Lord Palmerston and the Reverend Stephen Duck.

NOTES (location: SU1156; area: 702ha; population (2001): 73)
General: *VCH* 10, 33-40; Smith, N, in *Patterns of the Past* (ed. P. Pattison *et al*), 1999, 77-84.
Name: Finberg, H P R, *Lucerna*, 1964, 144-60; Cat: *WANHM* 51, 618; Roman village:
McOmish, D *et al*, *Field archaeology of SPTA*, 2002, 90-4; *WANHM* 90, 141-3; Organic
farm: Wookey, B, *Rushall: the story of an organic farm*, 1987; Duck: *WANHM* 34, 313-23;
Furnival, R G, in *Cambridge Journal* 6 (8), 1953, 486-96; *History Today* 27 (7), 1977,
467-72; Duck, S, *The Thresher's Labour*, 1989 (Merlin Press ed., with intro by E P
Thompson).

Chirton

DOMESDAY BOOK records both Chirton and Conock (the two tithings which make up Chirton parish) as ten-hide estates; in 1377 Chirton had slightly more adult taxpayers (73 to Conock's 59), and in 1851 Chirton's population was almost twice that of Conock. Recent house-building in Chirton has pushed this imbalance a great deal further. Both tithings are typical strip territories running north–south from the Cannings arm of the stripling River Avon (and a tributary, the Lul or Lulland brook), over rich, flat Greensand (The Sands), and up gently sloping lower chalk loam (The Clays) to the Salisbury Plain escarpment and wild downland beyond. The boundary between them, as it makes its way towards the scarp, is depicted on the 1845 tithe award as irregular, as if respecting the right-angled corners of early furlongs. By contrast the boundaries with the neighbouring parishes to east and west are mostly regular. They include a straight stretch between Chirton and Marden which is marked by a substan-tial bank; and the boundary with Urchfont follows an ancient downland road, a continuation of the Lydeway. The implication is perhaps that the tithing boundary is later, and that the territory defined by the medieval and modern parish is an early unit which was divided during the Saxon period (after the lower chalk had been divided into furlongs), rather than that two separate units (Conock and Chirton) combined to form the parish.

Conock, first recorded as *Cowic* (probably a misreading of *Connic*) in 1086, seems to derive from an obscure Celtic hill word *cunaco*, which is found, for example, in Consett (Durham) and Cannock. It is hardly appropriate here to the negligible rise on which Conock village sits, and so

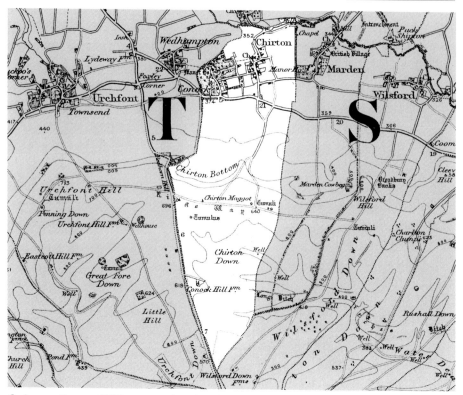

Ordnance Survey 1892 revision, 1 inch = 1 mile

presumably (like Crookwood in Urchfont) refers to the prominent chalk
escarpment. It may, therefore, have been used to describe the whole
territory, of which Chirton (*cirice-tun*, 'the church settlement') was a more
specialised part. However, as we have seen from the opening statistics, it
was Chirton (*Ceritone* in Domesday, and often spelt Cherrington and
variants up to the twentieth century), that gained the ascendancy over
Conock in the middle ages, and which has developed into a populous and
lively village. Conock meanwhile has subsided into a comfortable, shrunken cul-de-sac, complete with Victorian wall letter-box. Both tithings lost
their downland to the War Department's firing range in 1899, but both
retain working farms in their village streets – a hallmark of the chalkland
parishes to which enclosure came late (Chirton 1808, Conock 1816).

The first church, for it to have named the village by the eleventh
century, must undoubtedly have been Saxon and dating from a period

before churches were commonplace. The present building which adorns Chirton village is later, but it boasts fine transitional Norman features – a south doorway, ornamented roof timbers, north and south arcades ('terribly scraped', Pevsner observed), and a font depicting the twelve apostles – all of which are probably connected with the gift of the church in 1167 to Llanthony Priory, some thirty years after it was refounded in Gloucester. Various tell-tales suggest an early settlement around the church. There are awkward bends in the village street; a holloway running up the eastern side of the churchyard; possible earthwork features north-east of the church; a suggestive field name – Darkmead (on the tithe award) – north-west of the church; and the predominantly east–west orientation of footpaths and tracks in this area.

Yew Tree Cottage, east of the church by the second bend, is thought to be a former vicarage, which is referred to in glebe terriers from 1609; a 1783 terrier describes in great detail its oak frame, brick panes, thatched roof, elm-boarded rooms and wainscotting. Patney Road, which has carved itself a deep cutting as it runs northwards down the hill to the river, reminds us that the village is built on Greensand. From the foot of the slope, past Plummers Farm and squatter cottages on the right, and modern houses set behind trees on the left, there is a good view across Pewsey Vale to the Alton white horse. A lane leads eastwards to the former Church Mill, where converted buildings and a malthouse occupy a secluded spot in a hollow by the river where Chirton, Marden and Patney boundaries meet.

The church tower looks south down Chirton Street, which retains at its northern end something of the flavour of the linear green which it once was. A pond stood by the church corner in 1808, near another former vicarage, and several encroachments occurred to narrow the street between 1808 and 1845. The National school, of 1845 and still in use, stands where the street is widest and most green-like, and between the school and Manor Farm a number of Victorian and earlier brick cottages have survived. George Watts, a farmworker who was hanged for arson in 1835, was responsible for destroying a number of farm buildings along the street. Southwards from Manor Farm and along Small Street most houses are modern, and include small residential closes – The Orchard, Yew Tree

Close and Miller Close. The southern end of the Street connects Chirton
village with the main Devizes–Upavon road (A342), which was turnpiked
in 1762. This portion of the Street, as well as Small Street, were incorporated in the roads of the late (1840) Kennett and Amesbury turnpike
trust, which helped to open up Pewsey Vale to the outside world; by 1885
two inns, the *Three Horseshoes* (now a private house) and the *New Inn*
(now the *Wiltshire Yeoman*, but until quite recently displaying the old
name) were the sole buildings in this area.

Conock village shares with Chirton a number of characteristics. It
sits on the Greensand, is approached by a turning off the main road, and
lies along a north–south street which leads down to a river-crossing. But
there the similarity ends. Conock now has the appearance of an adjunct to
a gentleman's park, adorned by driveways and plantations, lodges and
cottages in various picturesque styles, and with few traces remaining of the
closely-built village depicted along its street on a map of 1773. There are
in fact two manor houses, Conock Manor, with its striking stable block
graced by a gleaming copper cupola, and Conock Old Manor, lower and
less dominant. They are of similar date, around 1700 with later alterations, and both were associated with the related Yerbury, Ernle or
Warriner families until the nineteenth century. From the 1960s until his
death in 1997 Conock Old Manor was the country home of Woodrow

Wyatt, a descendant of the architectural dynasty, remembered as an unpredictable socialite and controversial confidant of famous politicians. Across the lawn at Conock Manor, by contrast, lived Bonar Sykes, respected diplomat and steady champion of Wiltshire's heritage, who died in 1998. His father, Sir Frederick Sykes, one of the founders of the Royal Air Force, had bought the estate in 1945.

Slight earthworks north and north-west of the manor houses may indicate the site of the medieval village, which had a chapel-of-ease recorded between 1224 and 1410. The continuation of Conock Street towards Wedhampton, and the footpath which leads to Chirton church (and which has the appearance of a lychway) are presumably relics of early alignments. They seem to be portions of a valley road (superseded by the turnpike) which connected all the villages between Urchfont and Rushall, and which gave Wilsford and Charlton further east their village streets. A good view of Conock and Chirton is obtained from Redhorn Hill, on the Chirton–Urchfont boundary. Here the old Devizes–Salisbury downland road climbed the escarpment, and crossed the great ridgeway at the top, where now an army vedette sports its red flag.

NOTES (location: SU0757; area: 779ha; population (2001): 393)
General: *VCH* 10, 60-71.
Arsonist: church guide; WSRO 511/29; Wyatt: Wyatt, P, *Father, dear father*, 1999; Sykes: *WANHM* 92, 150-1; Ash, E, *Sir Frederick Sykes and the air revolution 1912–1918*, 1999.

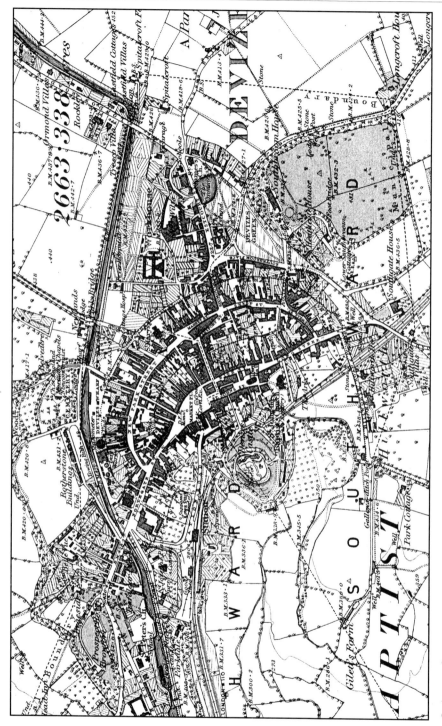

Ordnance Survey 1885 survey, 6 inch = 1 mile

Devizes

APTLY-NAMED, Devizes is a division in more ways than one. It straddles ancient manors, hence the name, but it also divides the two great Avon river systems of Wiltshire. Observant travellers approaching from the east, accustomed to rolling chalk hills on left and right, find as they pass through the town that a new vista lies before them, of a flat clayland vale and distant limestone hills. Devizes sits on one of several platforms of Greensand which line the western edge of the Wiltshire chalkland; the land falls sharply away to the west, and the Gault clay extends in two dry valleys almost up to the castle walls. Perched on this watershed the town has no river (although the Kennet and Avon Canal offers an artificial substitute); and until 1877 virtually all drinking water was obtained from wells which burrowed through the Greensand to the water-bearing Gault beneath.

The disability of having no running water – for industry, power and transport – should not be underestimated, and may have hampered the town's development. Consequently the arrival of the canal, in 1810, to satisfy the last of these needs, gave Devizes a boost, and one of its most tangible effects may be seen in the fabric of the town's buildings. In general – although there are many exceptions – architecture earlier than 1810, other than churches and large public buildings, is constructed of brick (locally made from the Gault clay), while after 1810 Bath stone becomes the favoured building material.

Devizes Castle, the hub around which the town developed, occupies a site of considerable strength when approached from the west, and there have been suggestions that it was built over earlier fortifications, presumably in the form of an Iron-Age hillfort. Only archaeological investigation will settle the question, and at present the evidence of prehistoric activity underlying the town and castle is not impressive. On its eastern side the castle site is less easily defended, especially if much of the mound on which the present Victorian building sits in fact consists of rubble and made-up ground from the medieval castle. There is a similar dearth of evidence about Devizes in the Roman and Saxon periods, and it is possible that the medieval town was built on a virgin site, lacking any previous settlement.

If so the area was probably farmed from the late Iron-Age period from a focus slightly to the east of the town (off Brickley Lane and Nursteed Road in Roundway parish) which has only recently been encroached upon for housing. Sites excavated here in 1999 revealed an Iron-Age farmstead and considerable settlement activity during the Roman period, including the possibility that a shrine or temple stood nearby. A Roman villa estate seems to have been centred on an area to the south of the town, in the Pans Lane – Wick Lane area, where remains including burials have been discovered at various dates since 1861. Some spectacular finds, perhaps related to the villa, were found much earlier, including a large coin hoard on Wick Green in 1699, and bronze statuettes of Roman household gods, including Pan (hence Pans Lane) on the Green in 1713. During the Saxon period important settlements emerged at Bishops Cannings to the east and Potterne to the south, and it is likely that what was to become Devizes belonged to their outlying farmsteads, in particular Wick and Southbroom.

As an unsullied example of a certain kind of medieval town planning, Devizes often appears in textbooks on urban history. It is therefore of some importance to try to discover who was responsible for the plan and when. A good start is to establish *termini*, dates before and after which the town's foundation must have taken place. An agreement struck in 1152 refers to an earlier arrangement between the borough of Devizes and Bishop Roger of Salisbury, who died in 1139. Thus Devizes existed as a town by 1139. On the other hand there is no mention of Devizes in Domesday Book (1086). This in itself does not prove that Devizes did not then exist – many eleventh-century communities are not named in Domesday – but it is unlikely that a place approaching urban status would be omitted or submerged in the entry for somewhere else. Furthermore, the need to invent a name, or rather an address, 'at the boundaries', for the castle, is an indication that (unlike Marlborough) no named settlement lay nearby when the castle was founded.

From its shape it is obvious that the present town plan cannot pre-date the castle bailey defences which circumscribe it. The castle was certainly operating in 1106, suffered a fire in 1113, but was in use again in 1121, and was being rebuilt on a lavish scale in 1138. An oblique reference in a document of 1157 to rights in respect of Devizes exercised in the time of Bishop Osmund, who died in 1099, has been used to suggest an eleventh- rather than a twelfth-century foundation date for the castle. This is strengthened by the fact that the diocese of Salisbury remained without a bishop from Osmund's death until Roger's consec-ration in 1107 (though he had been elected in 1102), by which time, as we have seen, the castle was in use.

So far, therefore, the consideration of dates points to one of two men, Osmund or Roger, as the founder of Devizes. The latter is often given the credit, the founding of the town being seen as part of his great work of reconstruction after the fire which ravaged the castle in 1113. The first borough charter, now dated to 1141 (and so too late to have been a foundation charter) has nevertheless also been used to point to a later, rather than an earlier, foundation date. But only if secure dating of the outer defences to Roger's rebuilding programme in the early-twelfth century is brought to light through archaeology can the matter be resolved in Roger's favour. Meanwhile arguments may be put to suggest that Osmund could have laid out Devizes.

If it be accepted that the original castle was built between 1086 and 1099 (after Domesday but before Osmund's death) then it might be expected that some kind of settlement would grow up or be deliberately created nearby. Examples elsewhere (in Wales, for instance) suggest that this usually occurred when a castle was built away from an existing settlement, and sometimes, as at Launceston and Windsor, a settlement was moved from another site to be adjacent to, or within, the castle defences. The first Devizes Castle, therefore, probably presided over some kind of civilian community before 1099. But there is no indication in the planted borough's plan of any irregularity which might have been caused by taking account of an earlier settlement, and this points to the possibility that the planted borough may be an original feature of the eleventh-century castle complex. That a town should be built within the confines of castle defences is in itself an indication of early date, and similar instances (Richmond, Launceston, Trematon, Skipsea, Richards Castle, Belvoir and Oswestry have been suggested) are mostly of the eleventh century. Finally the reference to the time of Osmund in a document of 1157, mentioned above, involves not only the castle, but also the two parks and the borough. If it may be used as evidence that a castle existed, the argument may be applied to the town with equal force.

Whoever began the castle, by the time of the twelfth-century anarchy period it had become an impressive sight, and was admired by contemporary writers such as Henry of Huntingdon, who called it the most splendid castle in Europe. As such it played a strategic role between 1139 and 1141, successively captured and recaptured, and it continued to be of military and political significance, as stronghold and prison, until about 1300. In the later middle ages, like other royal castles, it became important more as an administrative centre and for its adjacent hunting parks; by the fifteenth century the buildings were falling into ruin, and after 1526 materials were taken from it to build Bromham House. Substantial portions of towers and walls remained, however, to be fought over in the Civil Wars until 1645. Thereafter the site was cleared and robbed of its remaining stone, windmills were built on the former motte, and eventually the present Victorian Norman fantasy was built between about 1840 and 1880.

So much for the castle's vicissitudes – we must now turn to the community which emerged in its shadow. To whichever century it belongs, Devizes deserves its place as a textbook example of a planned medieval town within a substantial defensive ditch. Its axis is a semi-circular street line (New Park Street, Monday Market Street, Sheep Street, Bridewell Street) which lies between inner and outer defences, also semi-circular, like jam in a slice of swiss roll. Burgage tenements ran back from the street to the defences on either side, and about halfway along the line the street widened into a rectangular market place with a church (St Mary's) adjacent, and another street running off the market place through the inner defences towards the castle. This original market place has suffered encroachment by a block of shops and houses, notably the *White Bear* inn, which now forms an island surrounded by Monday Market Street and Maryport Street. The semi-circle appears to have terminated at each end with a gateway through the outer defences, near the present Northgate (Wadworth's brewery) and Southgate (the south end of Long Street).

An oval or semi-circular plan of this kind is not unique to Devizes, but it is unusual. Pleshey, Tutbury. Eye and Clare, as well as Richmond and Launceston mentioned above, all have plans affected by castle baileys. An example closer to home is Trowbridge, which bears many similarities to Devizes. But Devizes, not content with its original plan, had taken the opportunity by about 1300 to fill the vacuum created by the diminishing importance of the castle, and expand into the bailey. This released a kidney-bean shaped area in the shadow of the castle, containing at its southern end the garrison church (now the impressive Norman parish church of St John's), and through the centre a roadway (either slightly north of, or on the line of, the Brittox, which takes its name from a palisade – perhaps part of a barbican – created to defend this means of entry from the original market to the castle. A broad area, shaped like a spindle or a cigar, and more than twice the size of the present market place, was dedicated as an open space for marketing of various kinds (a vigorous Thursday market is still held), and burgage tenements ran back from both east and west sides wherever possible. Patchy market infill has occurred in blocks between the present market place and St John's Church, thus creating High Street, Wine Street and St John's Street. The old market place by St Mary's Church was not, however, abandoned, as a second market, on Mondays, was being held there by 1567, and probably much earlier.

This, in outline, appears to have been the evolution of the medieval town plan. It should give us pause for reflection, and a few questions. First, and easiest to understand, is the obvious fact that, plan apart, modern Devizes does not retain the appearance of a medieval town, although a number of timber-framed medieval houses survive, particularly in the areas of market infill, and both St Mary's and St John's churches display work of the twelfth and later centuries. But New Park Street, sporting filling stations and goods yards. and Sheep Street, with insensitive council flats, Victorian chapel and modern post office, come as a disappointment to the medieval topographer. The loss of much of early Devizes is of course a consequence of the town. It seems unlikely that the

castle bailey became available for urban development until shortly before 1300, by when the era of medieval town building and expansion was several decades past. Few towns after 1300 needed, or could afford, to

double their built-up area, which was in effect the opportunity offered to
Devizes – the town seems, in any case, to have been suffering a decline
during the early-fourteenth century. Rather than envisage a close-built
medieval town, eagerly moving in to cluster around the new market place,
evidence for which has been obscured and renewed, it is perhaps more
realistic to think (at least until the Tudor period) of sporadic and piecemeal
development, or re-use of former castle out-buildings, along a single wide
street or within a large area of open space.

Before the sixteenth century little is known of the town's economic
life, although an impression is gained of a community whose importance
as a marketing and administrative centre for its region outstripped its
relatively small population, and whose burgesses had succeeded in
installing a successful textile industry to replace the income derived from
serving the moribund castle. By the mid-sixteenth century, when the
population may have stood at about 1,500, the town was 'most occupied
by clothiers', according to John Leland. Over the next two centuries the
population doubled, and the town diversified its interests in several
directions. Fortunes were still to be made and lost by manufacturers and
entrepreneurs in the textile industry, but new cloths and new techniques
had replaced the famous Devizes blankets of the later middle ages. Crafts
involving metal and leather, traditionally associated with country towns,
flourished, and the manufacture of beer and tobacco (largely in the form
of snuff) was introduced. But alongside all the hard work came an air of
fashion and frippery, greatly deplored by a cynical physician in the town
writing about 1750: 'You have turn'd the grating of your woolcombs into
the scraping of fiddles; the screeking loom into the tinckling harpsicord,
and the thumping fulling mills into a glittering and contentious organ . . .
Your market house (a stranger to woolpacks) is metamorphiz'd into a
theatre for balls, and concertos, and oratorio's.'

Devizes owes the more pleasing elements of its present appearance
to a great rebuilding and improvement programme which began soon
after 1700 and was more-or-less complete by 1871, when the population
reached a peak of nearly 7,000, twice the 1801 figure and not exceeded
until the 1930s or 1940s. Prosperity and people arrived in the town as a
result not only of its industrial enterprises, but also because of its position

as a coaching town on one of the Bath roads (diverted in 1790 from its more northerly downland route), and, from 1810, on account of the flourishing waterway traffic along the Kennet and Avon Canal. It also developed a consciousness of its potential as an administrative and service centre, not only for the countryside in its immediate vicinity, but also for Wiltshire as a whole.

These trends and aspirations are everywhere seen in the architecture of Devizes, particularly in the grander private houses, and in the sequence of notable public buildings. These include the former 'New' Town Hall (Cheltenham & Gloucester Building Society) of 1750-2; the Town Hall of 1806-8; the Market Cross of 1814; the former Assize Court and Market House, both of 1835; and the Corn Exchange of 1857. Apart from the Assize Court (in Northgate Street) all these buildings lie within the market area formed out of the castle bailey, and before venturing out into suburban Devizes it is worth considering how the three elements in its history – planted medieval borough, industrial centre, and place of fashionable importance – coalesce in the modern town centre. A fourth, less satisfactory, element (not so far mentioned) has been a savage programme of 'slum' clearance between the 1930s and 1960s, which removed much of the town's minor domestic architecture, and has left some areas (Sheep Street, for example) devoid of their former character.

The visitor should first grasp the feel of the medieval plan by walking the semi-circle. It is best to start at the New Park Street end by the brewery (so saving the better bits until later), and take in St Mary's Church, the island of market infill, and a surviving fifteenth-century house, Great Porch (opposite the *White Bear Inn*). Along the way industrial Devizes may be seen in the Northgate Brewery and the former factory adjoining Snuff Street.

Wadworth's brewery, for which outside Wiltshire one suspects that Devizes is best known, owes its name to the activities of a farmer, Henry Wadworth, who purchased a combination of earlier brewers and maltsters in the town in 1875. The present imposing brick structure was built ten years later. The snuff factory (now apartments) has a more unusual history. Snuff was ground and sold in Devizes by a firm of grocers founded by Richard Anstie in 1698, and around 1740 the windmills on

the castle motte were being used as snuff mills. A grandson of the founder,
John Anstie, established a highly successful and lucrative business as a
clothier, making high quality but fine and versatile cloth known as
cassimeres. He was one of the first clothiers to bring his workforce into
one building, or manufactory, and the factory which he built in 1785
fronting on to New Park Street behind the family grocer's shop is one of
the earliest to survive. John Anstie's venture quickly failed, but the snuff
business continued in premises behind the factory along Snuff Street.
Eventually, by 1917, the factory itself had been taken over for snuff and
tobacco making, which ended in 1961.

Moving further along New Park Street, Brownston House (Wiltshire
Social Services) of about 1703 is an early example of 'polite' Devizes, and
the *Castle Inn* of 1768 is one of the town's coaching inns. There is nothing
medieval to be seen, except the curving street line, in Sheep Street and
Bridewell Street, the remainder of the arc; but Long Street, its southern
termination, preserves a feast of Georgian architecture, in many cases
concealing much earlier structures behind the pleasing façades. In fact,
after Marlborough High Street, it is probably the finest streetscape in
Wiltshire, eloquent of the successful clothiers and businessmen of a town
at the height (around 1800) of its prosperity. Many, perhaps most, of the
houses in Long Street have at one time or another been private schools,
and two, 40-41, have since 1874 been home to the museum and library
of the Wiltshire Archaeological and Natural History Society.

Beyond the museum, as one strolls back towards the town, the
visitor must imagine that he or she is entering the castle bailey close to the
castle chapel – now St John's parish church – and into a colony of
medieval houses encroaching on an originally open market place. Behind
the Town Hall, in St John's Street, looking towards the church, a medieval
enclave survives, dominated by the heavy Norman church tower. A second
group of early (sixteenth-century) houses hides nearby in St John's Alley
off St John's Street. The castle mound, surmounted by a largely-Victorian
sham-Norman mansion, is hard by on the left, and lanes lead up to
forbidding notices by the moat.

Everything on the right, as far as High Street and the Little Brittox, is
market infill; here, and along the Brittox (which leads out of the bailey and

back to the earlier market place at Maryport Street) are to be found the
principal shops of Devizes. Careful scrutiny of the frontages in the Brittox
reveals slight realignments (more noticeable in nineteenth-century photographs than today) where the street punctures the outer bailey defences;
hereabouts, presumably, was the site of the palisade or barbican which
gave the street its name.

Into the market place proper now, and here the medieval town is
forgotten. With a few unfortunate exceptions everything is redolent of the
Devizes revival of the eighteenth and nineteenth centuries. The south-west
side is dominated by the Corn Exchange and the town's principal inn, the
comfortable old *Bear Hotel*; and opposite there is a graceful sweep of
shops and banks and offices, concealing (for the most part) their narrow
burgage tenements behind. Passages such as the Ginnel enable odd
tenements to be explored, and the line of the bailey defences is marked by
a slight realignment in Snuff Street (by the entrance to the small shop car
park).

A detour south-west from the market place along Station Road
enables the visitor to gauge the defensive power of the castle, and
examine from a distance a large textile factory, of about 1813, which lies
behind Northgate Street. It is indicative of the spacious layout of Devizes
relative to its population that industrial buildings of such size (the complex
alongside Snuff Street is another example) could occupy prime sites
adjacent to the market place. Station Road, as its name suggests, led to
the railway station, and now leads to the car park which occupies its site.
Devizes was linked to the rail network by a branch line from Holt near
Melksham to the west in 1857, and then – such was the economic muscle
of the Victorian railway – a tunnel was excavated in 1862 beneath the
castle site (its portals may still be seen) to continue the line eastwards to
Pewsey and Hungerford. This meant that Devizes lay on a through route
to the west country, and enjoyed good rail communication right up until
the line was closed, in the teeth of great protest, in 1966. Station Road
emerges into Northgate Street near the Assize Court and the brewery, and
just beyond the outer defences of medieval Devizes.

The modern boundaries of Devizes encompass considerably more
than the medieval town, and have been several times extended to take

account of suburban growth, at the expense of neighbouring Bishops Cannings, Roundway, Rowde and Potterne. The suburbs of Devizes do not ring the town; they lie mostly to the east and south-east, with fingers extending along the town's western and north-eastern approaches. The principal constraint on development has been, not the topography, but the two large parks, which lie south-west and north of the town. Old Park is an oval, about 2km x 1km, occupying the slope running away from the castle to the south. It appears to be an original feature of the eleventh or twelfth century castle complex. Parts of the park pale survive, and an inaccessible moat marks the site of the keeper's house. The Bath Road on its north, an old lane past Hartmoor (formerly an important southern approach to Devizes) on its south, and the Potterne–Caen Hill road on the west, define its extent. The park bounds have been violated for nineteenth- and twentieth-century housing only in the Hillworth Road area (immediately south of the castle), and at Avon Road (south of the Bath Road). New Park, which also existed by the twelfth century, lay north of the town, and now forms part of Roundway Park. Together with the canal it has effectively blocked serious northward expansion; it lies largely in Roundway parish.

The earliest settlement in the modern parish away from the town centre probably lay at Wick. This and Southbroom (named after a broom-covered area which may have evolved as the Green) remained in the parish of Bishops Cannings until 1835. St James's Church, Southbroom, although rebuilt in 1831, has preserved its rich perpendicular tower, which might suggest a prosperous suburb in the fifteenth century; but although some medieval ribbon development along the present Estcourt Street probably had taken place, its main function seems to have been to serve as a chapel for the various agricultural settlements (Roundway, Nursteed, Wick and Bedborough) in Bishops Cannings parish around Devizes. The site chosen was probably that of a leper hospital (defunct after 1338) rather than that of a developing suburb.

The church overlooks one of the best-known and best-loved features of Devizes, the large swan-frequented pond known as the Crammer. This is often identified as the scene of Wiltshire's moonraking legend, which is also associated with Bishops Cannings. In fact there is no

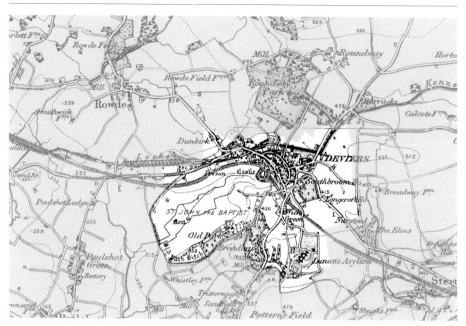

Ordnance Survey 1892 revision, 1 inch = 1 mile. Note that the present boundary is shown. Some land south of, and now within, Devizes is considered under Roundway.

inconsistency in accepting both versions since, as we have seen, Devizes Green (including the Crammer) lay in Bishops Cannings parish until 1835. Modern-day Southbroom is a product of the early-nineteenth century Devizes revival, described above, and its principal streets, Sidmouth Street and Estcourt Street (although already in existence) were remodelled and renamed after notable Devizes members of Parliament at the time – Henry Addington, Viscount Sidmouth; and T H S Sotheron Estcourt.

The canal, completed in 1810, had an immediate effect on the topography of Devizes in two ways. Its western approach to the town used (or ran very close to) the then line of the Bath road, thus requiring a new road to be laid out further north, between the Nursery and Prison Bridge. At the latter an awkward bend jerks the road back on to its old alignment before descending Caen Hill. Secondly an area north of New Park Street was dedicated for the development of a large wharf and associated buildings alongside the canal. This complex has been renovated, with theatre, shops, visitor centre and car park, to cater for the growing leisure use of the canal. Gasworks, a cottage hospital, the workhouse (later St

James's Hospital) and a foundry (the site now of a supermarket) all colonised the area between the town and the canal in the nineteenth century.

West of Devizes the canal's interference created a new road junction, where the Bath and Chippenham roads divide, in an area of Rowde parish (later known as Dunkirk and transferred to Devizes) which was already accommodating a few suburban villas. An elegant tollhouse erected around 1840 (and known as Shane's Castle) guards the fork, and opposite, set back from the road, is Trafalgar Place, a terrace of distinguished houses, of early-nineteenth century date. Meaner and later terraces lie further along the Bath Road, together with a Victorian church (St Peter's) and contemporary school. Almost opposite lay the county militia stores of 1856, which became the county police headquarters, and was used until 1962; and beyond the canal bridge (Prison Bridge) was the New Bridewell, or county gaol, an imposing circular building which opened in 1817 and was used until about 1920. Both symbols of authority have now disappeared.

The main thrust of twentieth-century suburbanisation was to the east and south of the town; it offers the usual range of housing style, size, age and quality seen in suburbs everywhere. One factor determining the topography of this area is the pattern of pre-existing roads and lanes – Brickley Lane (formerly the Devil's Jump – hence the Jump Farm estate), Pans Lane, Wick Lane, Drews Pond Lane and Hartmoor, as well as the present main roads. Other influences have been the engulfing of a former village settlement at Wick, the building-over of the grounds surrounding large houses, such as the Breach and Broadleas, the acquisition for development of farmland belonging to Wick Farm and Jump Farm, and the constraint imposed by unacquirable areas, such as Old Park and (until recently) the former Roundway Hospital and its grounds. Lesser growth points have occurred along the London Road (including the police headquarters), immediately north of the canal at Belle Vue and Rotherstone, and at the top of Caen Hill (Mayenne Place). At the turn of the millennium new housing development continues apace between the Swindon and Andover roads to the east and north-east of the existing suburbs, but almost all this recent growth has occurred in the neighbouring parish of Roundway.

In terms of total urban populations (based on wards, not parishes) Devizes is the eighth largest town in Wiltshire, and it is the natural centre of the county. As towns go it is not large, of course, nor is it Wiltshire's administrative centre. It lies on no really important highway and it is not an obvious magnet for tourists. But surely no-one interested in towns can fail to be stirred by their first sight of the magnificient market place, and dull indeed is the visitor who, faced with Monday Market Street and the Brittox, does not ask why.

NOTES (location: SU0061; area: 574ha; populaton (2001): 11,296)
General: *VCH* 10, 225-314 [reprinted as Pugh, R B, *A history of Devizes*, 2001]; Haycock, L, *Devizes: history and guide*, 1993; Bradby, *The book of Devizes*, 1985; Cunnington, B H, *Some annals of the borough of Devizes*, 2 vols, 1925-6; Waylen, J, *A history, military and municipal, of the ancient borough of the Devizes*, 1859; Wiltshire County Archaeology Service, *The archaeology of Wiltshire's towns, an extensive urban survey: Devizes assessment report*, 2003.
Iron-Age and Roman excavations: *WANHM* 95, 147-239; Castle: Stone, E H, *Devizes Castle*, 1920; 1750s physician: Davis, J, *Origines Divisianae. . .*, 1754; Anstie: Haycock, L, *John Anstie: an eighteenth-century Wiltshire clothier*, 1991; Railway: Priddle, R, and Hyde, D, *GWR to Devizes*, 1996.
Please note that there is an extensive literature on the history of Devizes, and that the foregoing bibliography is very selective. In many cases the general works cited include references to earlier published material. I am grateful to Roy Canham for allowing me access to the extensive urban survey report, and to Dr Lorna Haycock who has read and commented on a draft of this article.

Easterton

L YING AS IT DOES between Urchfont and Market Lavington, two
parishes of great topographical interest, Easterton comes as
something of a disappointment. Despite a surprising number of good
timber-framed houses the village lacks cohesion, and appears to consist of
little more than three concentrations of buildings: around Easterton Manor
and the *Royal Oak* (locally known simply as the *Oak*); near the church,
and at Eastcott strung along a secondary road (B3098) and interspersed
with modern housing. In part one's dissatisfaction stems (as for example at
West Kennet and Chicklade) from the loss of older houses as a result of
brutal road widening after World War Two and subsequently.

Easterton is not an ancient parish, and its present boundaries were
only established in 1934; it is made up of the tithing of Easterton
(comprising two manors), formerly part of Market Lavington, and the

tithing of Eastcott (pronounced 'Eskit' locally), which was formerly in
Urchfont. A map of 1773 suggests that there were then more buildings at
Eastcott and between Eastcott and Easterton than at present, and
therefore that the settlements have declined; the survival of timber-framed
houses in disjointed groups in an area where from the eighteenth century
brick buildings have predominated is consistent with such a decline. Both
names mean what they say: Easterton, 'the more easterly farm,' is self-
explanatory, since it lies east of its parent settlement, Market Lavington;
but Eastcott, 'the eastern cottage(s),' which lay at the extreme western
edge of Urchfont parish, cannot be so easily explained.

Easterton's territory is a carbon copy of Market Lavington, with
Gault and Greensand north-west of the road, and lower, middle and
upper chalk zones ascending the slope south-eastwards on to the high
plain. Across the parish run the same lines of communication, the
ridgeway along the scarp, the railway north of the Greensand ridge, and
the turnpike road in between. This forms the village street, where it is
bordered on the west side by a small brook. The brook, despite its
insignificance, is regarded reverentially by the villagers, who have bridges
across it to their cottages, and who have portrayed it on their village signs
as a major river. The street is in something of a hollow, so that gardens on
the east side rise very steeply and have been terraced up the slope. Paths
and lanes lead off the street to 'the Clays' on the east and 'the Sands' on
the west.

Market gardening and fruit growing by smallholders on the fertile
soils of the greensand became important as the traditional sheep and corn
husbandry on the chalk ('the Clays') declined following enclosure before
1800. Samuel Moore's jam factory was a legacy of the fruit fields. It began
in a small way in the early-twentieth century after an earlier venture had
closed, and became a major employer in the area, with 100 staff in 1972.
An extension was opened in 1985, but the whole enterprise closed during
the 1990s, and visitors to the village are no longer greeted by the all-
pervading aroma of warm strawberry jam.

The rich soils were doubtless exploited many centuries before the
surviving evidence of settlement, but Easterton, unusually among plain-
edge villages, can at least boast the presence of a Roman villa estate,

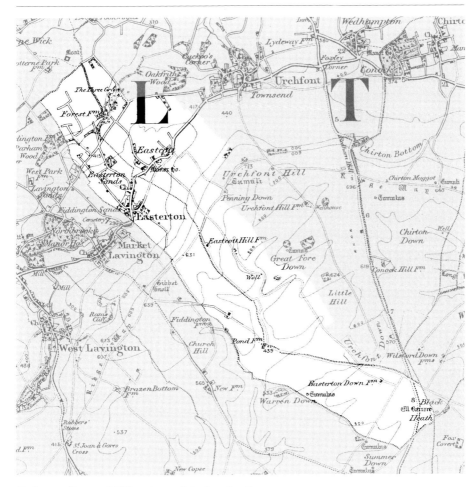

Ordnance Survey 1892 revision, 1 inch = 1 mile

known from stray archaeological finds in the area of Kestrels in Oak Lane, west of the village. This may be connected with a mid-fourth century coin hoard, discovered in an urn during the Victorian period and dispersed, although some coins passed to Devizes Museum. Another possible Roman site, deduced from place-name evidence, may lie at Wickham Green on the boundary with Urchfont (under which parish it is discussed) some 2km north of Kestrels.

Easterton was created an ecclesiastical parish in 1874, and its small brick-built church was opened shortly afterwards. Other Victorian arrivals in the village were a Methodist chapel, built in 1868 and converted to a private house in 1985; and a school – this was opened in 1867, replaced in 1875, closed in 1971 and demolished in 1973.

Apart from the attractive houses which remain, two vanished buildings are worth mentioning. Eastcott had a chapel-of-ease from before 1309 until dissolution in 1548; its exact site is unknown, but a field north of the road was known as Chapel Field in the nineteenth century. Wroughton's Folly was a mansion built near Crookwood, close to the Urchfont and Potterne boundaries, and was known variously as Folly House, Castle House and Maggot Castle (here, as elsewhere, the unflattering name is probably a corruption of 'Margaret'). It was built and enlarged by two members of the Wroughton family, Francis and Seymour, between about 1730 and 1780. After Seymour's high-speed accidental death in 1789 the house was left unoccupied and became a ruin. Its foundations, visible in the nineteenth century, have now entirely disappeared – only Seymour's ghost remains (according to local legend) recreating along his vanished driveway the furious carriage ride which proved his downfall.

NOTES (location: SU0255; area: 1,232ha; population (2001): 583)
General: *VCH* 10, 82-106, 173-90, *passim*; Judge, S M, *The history and development of Easterton village*, 1986.
Coin hoard: *WANHM* 78, 41-9.

Easton

MILTON AND EASTON are often pronounced in one breath, and Milton always comes first. Easton, as its historian points out, is therefore regarded as a Cinderella village to its larger neighbour, Milton Lilbourne. But Easton has the grander name, as it has been distinguished since the nineteenth century from other Wiltshire Eastons by the affix 'Royal'. Its connection with the king is not one of ownership, nor, as has sometimes been suggested, any link with the royal forest of Savernake (Easton lay outside its bounds after 1300); it results from the mistaken antiquarian belief that Henry VIII had made it a royal donative, a living wholly outside the jurisdiction of the bishop, and controlled by a royal appointee. The classy though erroneous affix has stuck, but remains unofficial. Easton church was indeed a donative from the thirteenth century, but the appointments were made until its dissolution in 1536 by and to members of a small monastic house, and by its manorial successors thereafter. Although generally known as Easton Priory, it was in fact a friary. A number of questions about this obscure monastery are still unresolved, but there is no doubt that it is the peg on which much of Easton's history has to be hung.

Although it has a Saxon name Easton, 'the eastern farm', is not recorded in Domesday Book. Like Fyfield and Milton, its neighbours to the west, it was probably then subsumed in one or other of the two large estates, based on Pewsey and Wootton Rivers, which controlled the western portion of Kinwardstone hundred. Easton is mentioned by name in the mid-twelfth century, when part of it was granted to Bradenstoke Priory, and it had a church by about 1200, since its ownership became a

63

matter of dispute shortly afterwards. Its first recorded incumbent
subsequently became Archdeacon of Wiltshire and was known as Stephen
of Tisbury, but his father was Sir Adam de Easton, a local landowner.

The role of this family was crucial because not only did Stephen, on
inheriting his father's house, use it to found the monastery; but also one of
Stephen's sisters married into the Esturmy family, hereditary wardens of
Savernake Forest, and thus forged a link between the village and the
successive Savernake owners – Esturmy, Seymour and Ailesbury – which
has continued up to the present century. The monastic order chosen was
the Trinitarian friars, founded in about 1197, who were devoted to ran-

soming captive Crusaders and offering travellers hospitality. Easton was
one of ten English friaries belonging to this order. It was a modest establishment, originally with three friars, and probably never more than six.

A friary serving travellers presupposes a thoroughfare, and this
Easton no longer has. However the Roman road, or Romanized trackway,
which ran between Mildenhall and Old Sarum must have ascended the

northern escarpment of Salisbury Plain close to Easton, and it has been suggested that the present village street is on its line. Perambulations of Savernake forest made in 1199 and 1244 used such a road as the forest boundary, with the result that Easton was split down its centre, half within and half without the forest. We should not, however, automatically assume that the thirteenth-century road ran along the modern street, as it is clear from the village's topography and from extant earthworks that there was a second, parallel road, some 100–150m to the east, which is now a footpath across fields and behind gardens. This, not the present street, seems to be the continuation of the track across the downs from Everleigh by way of Falstone Pond, which is the most likely contender as the line of the Roman and medieval road.

Whichever route the travellers took, it remained busy at least until the end of the fourteenth century, because in 1391/2 the friars attributed the house's poverty to, among other causes, the increasing cost of providing hospitality. But by the seventeenth century the main road, according to Ogilby's map of 1675, took a more easterly course through Burbage. The Easton route may have been abandoned because of emparking and therefore blocking its course further north, at Brimslade, or as a result of problems caused by marshy ground at the foot of the escarpment. This area, which is drained by one of the headwaters of the Salisbury Avon, was described as 'Floodgate Land' in a deed of 1324, which suggests that attempts were made to control the flow from an early date. Two large ponds here, which by 1773 had been divided by a road bridge, remained until 1955 when they were filled in.

Bound up with the question of roads through the village is that of the position of the friary. The medieval parish church and the friary church were distinct, and were said to lie some sixty yards apart. The former was demolished in 1369 with the parishioners' blessing, and material from it was used to enlarge the latter; but this was badly damaged by fire, along with the other monastic buildings, in 1493. Presumably, therefore, the friary and its church lay close together. Despite the fire both friary and church remained in use until 1536, and the church continued to serve the parish until it was demolished in 1590. The Esturmy and Seymour family tombs were removed at this time to Great Bedwyn. A replacement church

was built at Seymour expense in the following year and much of this,
despite drastic Victorian restoration in 1852-3 (by T H Wyatt, as usual in
this area), survives as a rare example of Elizabethan church architecture.

Meanwhile the friary buildings were converted to a Seymour
residence, which appears to have been altered in about 1680 and swept
away between 1735 and 1773. Village tradition, which identifies the site
of the friary with earthworks some 300–400m east of the present church in
a field known as Beech Meadow, is probably partly correct – correct, at
least, in remembering that the friary lay to the east of the village street and
not on the site of the Elizabethan church. But in 1953 floor tiles of about
1400 and other medieval masonry were discovered some sixty yards east
of the present church, in the field close to the Victorian cemetery (first
used in 1897). It is likely, therefore, that this was the site of the friary, and
that the Elizabethan church sits in the churchyard of its medieval predecessor. If the conventual buildings lay behind the friary church (viewed
from the street) and were reused by the Seymours for a mansion house,
the earthworks in Beech Meadow are probably the remains of garden
landscaping behind the house. Such a garden in this area would have
extinguished the parallel road as a thoroughfare and diverted all traffic
along the present village street. The name 'Beech Meadow' is itself
additional evidence, since it is believed to refer to a tree-lined avenue to
the former house.

Fortunately for Easton its street is no longer a through road, and
only village traffic now uses it. From a small former green area, where it is
crossed by the Pewsey–Burbage road (the Pewsey Herepath), it extends
southwards for about 1km to the foot of the great downland wall, sculpted
with lynchets and trackways, and surmounted since 1762 by Easton
Clump. Walking 'round the Clump' was at one time a regular feature of
village life, especially on warm summer evenings. In 1812 Sir Richard Colt
Hoare extolled from this 'delicious eminence . . . the beautiful and
extensive view which . . . so unexpectedly presents itself, over the rich and
highly cultivated vale'; this was long before the electricity pylons so
blatantly intruded themselves.

Along the village street the comfortable houses stand like old friends
enjoying each other's company. Apart from the grandest and the newest

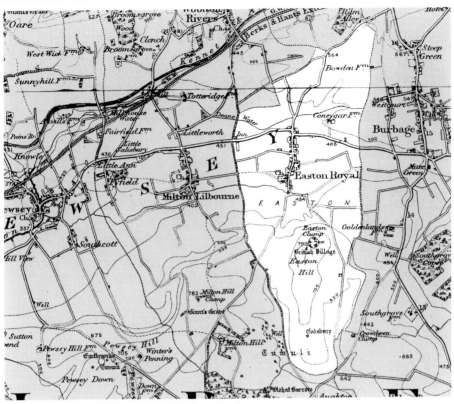

Ordnance Survey 1892 revision, 1 inch = 1 mile

they are mostly thatched, and many have the motif of a straw owl perched
over a gable. Three are late-medieval houses of cruck construction, and
several have seventeenth-century timber framing with brick infill. Others
are later brick and thatch cottages, or pairs of the showy estate houses
beloved by the Victorian Ailesburys. As commonly in parishes where
enclosure came late, most of the farms and farmhouses lie along the
village street, and they include a fine long thatched cartshed at Manor
Farm near the church, and a large farmhouse of 1783, now known as
Easton House. This was built, according to Easton's historian, Sir Henry
Bashford (who himself lived at the White House nearby) for Giles Herne,
and it is interesting to note that this surname (alongside the exquisite
Absalom Doggetail) occurs twice in a list of Easton taxpayers some 450
years earlier, in 1332. Such continuity of families and traditions is a strong
theme in Bashford's account of the village.

Apart from the church, farms and cottages, there are one or two specialized buildings typical of a village of Easton's size. The National School of 1873 replaced a charity school referred to in 1848; but schoolmasters are mentioned rather earlier, in 1805 and 1818. A plan in 1986 to close it was defeated by spirited parental opposition and it remains open. The Old Rectory, next to the church, was the childhood home of a hero of the American Civil War, one David Herbert Llewellyn, who as a young surgeon was drowned when a confederate steamship sank in 1864, and who is commemorated by a memorial in Easton church. The Old Forge, the Old Post Office and Chapel Cottage all recall former uses, and nearby is a cottage which was once an alehouse, the *Bleeding Horse*, and later the village post office. The only licensed premises within the parish now is the *Bruce Arms* on the Pewsey road. It is the successor to an inn known as the *Gammon of Bacon*, which stood almost opposite until it burned down in about 1848 and was replaced. The name may be a pun on John Gammon, a seventeenth-century inhabitant in the area. Later Victorian landlords of the *Bruce Arms*, Zebedee and Enos Price, operated the *Hope* coach between Lavington and Hungerford. One other tradesman worth recording is listed in directories from 1931–9; he was Albert Reynolds, castrator and rate-collector.

Easton's adult population total in 1377 was only 66, but this figure must reflect the depopulation, probably caused by plague, which was given as a pretext in 1369 for demolishing the parish church. Between the seventeenth and early twentieth centuries the total population of the parish was usually between 300 and 400. Apart from recent modern development along the Pewsey–Burbage road, there has been very little settlement away from the village street. The exceptions are Conygre Farm, a small portion of Ram Alley falling within the parish, and a few cottages which lay along Cock Lane until the nineteenth century, and which were known as Streches.

Farming in Easton was similar to that of its neighbours and reflected the local geology. Two large medieval open fields, East and West, ran southwards up on to the chalk hill, with sheep downland beyond and cattle pasture north of the village. The fields were sub-divided by the sixteenth century and some enclosure followed, but openfield farming remained in the south until 1773. In terms of its area much of the parish now consists of unpopulated downland beyond the escarpment. This has, however, yielded ample archaeological evidence of prehistoric and later activity. In addition to barrows and sherd scatters there are possible Bronze-Age habitation sites on Easton Hill and Crow Down, and extant earthworks of an Iron-Age and Romano-British settlement near Easton Clump. Saxon burials, too, have been discovered here and at the foot of the escarpment.

NOTES (location: SU2060; area: 897ha; population (2001): 283)
General: *VCH* 16, 140-9; Bashford, H H, *Easton Royal: a short history*, 1961; Bashford, H H, *Wiltshire harvest*, 1953.
Friary: *VCH* 3, 324-7; *WANHM* 51, 365-77; Llelwellyn: *WANHM* 68, 109-15;
Reminiscences: Pearce, J, *Accounts and recollections: tales of the Wiltshire village of Easton Royal*, 1996; Choules, A, *Village life: Easton Royal, Wiltshire, 1914–1929* [typescript in T].

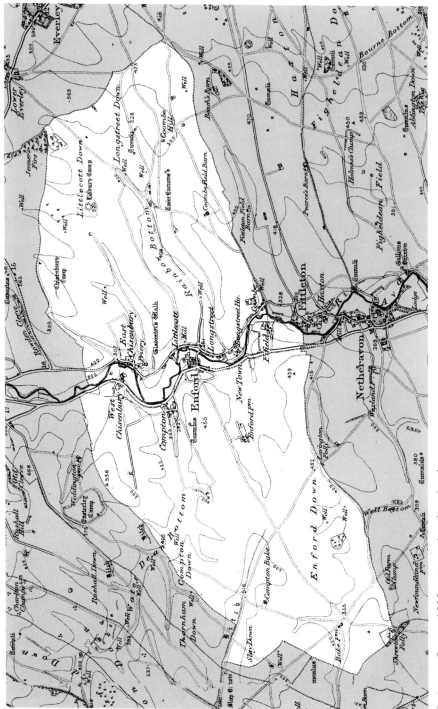

Ordnance Survey 1892 revision, 1 inch = 1 mile

Enford

A NYONE WHO HAS EXPLORED the chalk valleys of south Wiltshire will have noticed that close to each riverbank there is a village or hamlet every kilometre or two, and that each possesses a strip of land which runs from the river up the hillside and far away into the high downland. Enford, the first of the Avon valley parishes after the river's headwaters have united and left the Vale of Pewsey, consists of no fewer than eight of these small settlements, four on each bank. Together they preside over nearly 4km of meandering valley, and from its downland extremities the parish has a total wingspan (for on the map it resembles a large bird in flight) of about 11km. Each hamlet has its separate identity, and at first glance one might imagine that there has been little to bind Enford together as a community. This impression would be borne out by looking at its medieval history, where the descent of no fewer than eleven manors has been traced, and individual hamlets were often assessed for tax separately, or in conjunction with neighbouring parishes. But reading a volume of reminiscences published in 1986 by the former landlord of the *Swan Inn* one comes to appreciate the plethora of communal services, occasions and facilities which have existed to knit the Enford hamlets together.

Enford lay in the Bishop of Winchester's hundred of Elstub, a territory which at the time of Domesday appears to have been composed of the later parishes of Netheravon, Fittleton and Enford. During the middle ages other widely-dispersed properties of the bishop were added to the hundred. Elstub means 'elder-tree stump', and takes its name from a meadow in Enford parish between Fifield and New Town, which is now known colloquially as 'Nelstop'. Hundred courts were held in this meadow

71

during the middle ages and as late as the seventeenth century. Thus far the early history of Enford rests on fairly firm evidence; from here on the reconstruction is more speculative.

As well as being a secular unit of government it is likely that Elstub was also a Saxon ecclesiastical territory, with its minster church at Netheravon. When the minster system broke down in the later Saxon period and parishes began to emerge, the hamlets or tithings which had made up Elstub were regrouped into parishes. Fittleton and Haxton together formed one parish, and the former minster at Netheravon became a parish church, controlling Netheravon itself and West Chisenbury (which is now part of Enford). Part of Elstub – the tithings of Enford, Fifield, Littlecott, Longstreet and Coombe – had been granted by Athelstan to Winchester Cathedral as a single estate of thirty hides in 934, and became the major portion of the later parish of Enford.

It is possible that Enford tithing, which is roughly twice the size of the others, had been a ten-hide unit, and became the Bishop of Winchester's ten-hide demesne estate, which is recorded in Domesday Book. 'Fifield' means 'five hides', and the name was applied in the middle ages not only to Fifield itself, but also to Littlecott and Longstreet. This would suggest that each of them, and Coombe, had once been assessed at five hides apiece, thus accounting for the total of thirty hides. Two smaller estates, Compton and West Chisenbury, were separately assessed in Domesday Book, and they became part of the medieval parish of Enford. Finally, in 1885, West Chisenbury was transferred from Netheravon to Enford, and the present parish, with its eight constituent parts, emerged.

Continuing in a speculative vein we may assume that it was because the demesne farm was situated in Enford tithing that the decision was taken to build the church nearby. The later manor house stood in a bend of the river to the north of the church (the area is now called Manor Ground), and this probably marks the site of its Saxon and medieval predecessors. In 1826, according to Cobbett, only the stables remained standing. And Enford tithing, because it had contained both the principal house and the church, gave its rather lowly name to the whole parish – *ened*, the name's first element, means 'duck'.

The existence of Enford church is implied in Domesday Book, and the tall, narrow proportions of the present nave, with Norman arcades cut through its walls, suggest that it is of Saxon origin. The north wall of the chancel retains unusual medieval blind arcading, and a doorway leads into a strange octagonal vestry, which may have been built as a chapel. A second chapel was created in the fourteenth century by making a very large north aisle. The west tower until 1817 was surmounted by a spire, but in that year it was struck by lightning and fell, demolishing much of the western end of the church. Colt Hoare, writing before 1826, believed that the whole building was beyond repair. It presented a melancholy appearance, and he understood that there were plans to build a new church on the same site, reusing some of the fabric. In fact the damaged structure was repaired, rather inexpertly by a Devizes builder-turned-architect, and re-opened in 1831.

Three of Enford's hamlets, Compton, Coombe and West Chisenbury, had chapels-of-ease during the middle ages. All had ceased to function by the sixteenth century, but the site of Coombe Chapel, in Coombe Lane, is known, and the foundations are said still to be visible. Chisenbury chapel was dependent on Netheravon, and in 1405 it was reported that the chaplain kept his horse in it, tethered to the font. Three years later two parishioners claimed that it was totally ruinous. Part of a medieval cross, perhaps once a preaching cross from one of the outlying hamlets, now stands in Enford churchyard.

When Athelstan granted Enford to Winchester in 934, and so set in train many of these later developments, his gift was a tract of countryside already scarred and modified by millennia of settlement and cultivation. This is clear from the description of the estate boundaries accompanying his charter, which includes as landmarks features of varying antiquity, such as ditches and lynchets, walls, barrows and burial places, a prominent stone, pits and quarries, and roads of several kinds, including one which led to a Roman camp. Although most such landmarks have not been precisely identified, the archaeological fecundity of the downland on both sides of Enford's valley was recognized by Colt Hoare at the beginning of the nineteenth century, and our knowledge of it has been augmented by excavation, fieldwork and aerial photography.

Especially rich is East Chisenbury Down, which, besides barrows, linear earthworks and prehistoric field systems, includes two Early Iron Age enclosures, Lidbury Camp and Chisenbury Trendle, as well as one of the best preserved examples of a 'native' Romano-British village, Chisenbury Warren. To appreciate this site in its downland setting it is best to take the bridleway which runs south-west from Lower Everleigh. The earthworks of about eighty house platforms have been identified, ranged along a village street on the sunny south-facing slope of the wooded warren. At each end of the village, some 500m apart, the street divides to form triangular open spaces or greens, and all around are the low banks of the settlement's long, rectangular fields.

Even more remarkable is a site discovered in 1992 on the spur behind East Chisenbury village. This was a low mound of some 200m in diameter and nearly 4ha in extent, which proved on trial excavation to be an enormous midden or ritual feasting site, dating from about 800-600 BC. This was a period of transition from the Bronze to the Iron Age, and similar middens have been identified from Potterne and elsewhere in the region. Strange as it may seem to us, the creation of a rubbish heap of monumental proportions (a kind of inverted landfill site) and visible from afar, seems to have served as a status symbol, a boast to one's neighbours of conspicuous consumption.

Apart from Chisenbury Warren at least seven other probable late prehistoric or Roman settlement sites have been located on Enford's downland, including well-preserved earthworks on Coombe Down close to the Haxton–Everleigh road. In the valley archaeological evidence is more likely to have been masked or destroyed by later occupation, but debris associated with possible Roman villas has been recovered from two sites at Compton, as well as from East Chisenbury. Primitive Saxon pottery was also found at Compton, and a pagan Saxon cemetery was disturbed in 1928 during building work near the main road at West Chisenbury.

Enford's geology is uncomplicated, since almost the whole parish is upper chalk. The principal exception is the riverine gravel deposit which lines the floor of the valley, and extends up some of the dry coombes. The settlements are built on this gravel; indeed 'gravel' is the meaning of the first element of the name Chisenbury. Enford's agricultural history, like that of all its neighbours, is a consequence of its geology, and consisted until the later-nineteenth century of the normal sheep-and-corn husbandry. The arable fields of each tithing lay behind its hamlet, and stretched up the chalk loam of the hillside until the soil became too thin for agriculture, and gave way to rough downland pasture for sheep.

Between the settlements and the river the meadowland was 'floated', and the remains of hatches and artificial watercourses can still be seen, for example along the footpath between East and West Chisenbury.

At the East Chisenbury end this path is known locally as Milldrum or Milldrung, 'the drong (lane) which led to the mill'. Until 1960, when it was replaced by the present structure, the path crossed the river by a Victorian suspension bridge. The mill, referred to in 1923 but later burnt down, stood close to this path, and the mill tail and other evidence can still be seen. Mill buildings survive at Littlecott and Coombe, the latter with a large iron wheel, 3.5m in diameter, which is visible from the road. Compton also had a mill at the time of Domesday Book, but it is not mentioned later than the fourteenth century.

As a purely agricultural parish, remote from any major town and with poor communications, Enford's population has fluctuated in the wake of farming changes. In 1815, six years after much of the parish had been enclosed, it was claimed by Orator Hunt that half of Enford's labourers were paupers. Another social reformer, William Cobbett, who passed through Enford in 1826, commented on the abundance of food which the farms were producing, but the almost total absence of people who would be allowed to eat it. In fact the population fluctuated around 900–1,000 (considerably more than today) for the next fifty years, and then began to fall, as a consequence of poor harvests, the switch to dairying, and, after 1897-9, the acquisition of downland for military training.

Over time old cottages burn or fall down in most parishes, especially when thatch was the principal roofing material, but the casualty rate in Enford during the twentieth century seems to have been exceptional. In his 1986 book Fred Phillimore of the *Swan Inn* compiled from memory a list of vanished houses and their occupants, and allowing for a few uncertainties, his total was about 33 east and 40 west of the river. Most stood in the valley, but the field barns high on the downs also had their pairs of cottages for shepherds and farmworkers. The lonely hand-to-mouth existence of their inhabitants has been graphically described by another Enford autobiographer, Winifred Grace, a shepherd's daughter who spent her childhood before the first world war at Coombe Bake.

Two of Enford's medieval villages, Compton and West Chisenbury, retain substantial earthwork evidence of their depopulation. West Chisenbury, in particular, the site of which is crossed by the modern main road, is a particularly well preserved deserted village, and was surveyed in detail in 1991. Saxon or early-medieval settlement along two east–west streets included a manorial complex with barn and paddocks, a chapel and small dwellings. Probably around 1200 some expansion took place on to lower-lying ground within the meander, and this involved canalising the river into a new course. Shrinkage began during the Tudor period and after 1700 only a single farm remained with a few cottages

Notwithstanding these retrenchments and losses, both during the last hundred years and much earlier, sufficient remains to make a stroll through Enford's hamlets a rewarding experience. The fast, narrow and tortuous main road (A345), the former Kennett and Amesbury turnpike of 1840, which hugs the river's meanders on the western side of the valley, should be avoided as far as possible, and its eastern counterpart, the lane from Upavon to Fittleton, preferred. Early council flats in pleasant, garden-city style are the incongruous prelude to East Chisenbury; then, beyond the Primitive Methodist chapel of 1896, the village street turns next to a former beerhouse, the *Red Lion*. The diversion is caused by the grounds of Chisenbury Priory, a large eighteenth-century fronted house with formal Tudor garden and exquisite parkland, on the site of a medieval grange of the alien monastic house of Bec-Hellouin. The park is roughly circular, and is closed at its southern end by a tree-lined earthwork, probably the park pale but conceivably of prehistoric origin, which is known as Gladiator's Walk.

Littlecott, with a substantial modern housing estate hidden from the lane on the hillside behind, merges into the appropriately named Longstreet to form a linear settlement nearly 1km long, and it is here that most of the older village houses and cottages are to be found. The tithing boundary between Littlecott and Longstreet crosses the lane at the junction with the road to Enford, which until replaced in 1971 crossed the river by a Victorian cast-iron bridge. This road then continues past the driveway to the church, and climbs Enford Hill, where many cottages have been lost, to reach the main road. In Longstreet the most memorable

feature is the much-photographed signboard of the *Swan Inn*, which
extends across the village street. After the school and three notable houses
(The Grange, Baden Farm and Longstreet House) at the further end of
Longstreet, the lane continues to Coombe, which takes its name from the
dry valley at right angles to the road. Coombe Lane runs up this valley on
to the downs, and is built up with a straggle of twentieth-century housing
beyond the site of the medieval chapel. Opposite the turning a footpath
leads to a river bridge and to Fifield beyond, the most secluded of
Enford's shrunken hamlets, which is now a small cluster of thatched
houses and outbuildings, but which in 1831 recorded a population of 157.

It was on the bridge between Coombe and Fifield in 1913 that a
memorable crime occurred. Ernest Pike, the Enford policeman, whose
chance of promotion from constable to sergeant had been thwarted by a
disciplinary hearing earlier in the day, initiated by his superior at
Netheravon, reported here on his beat one evening. He took along a
shotgun and, when Sergeant Frank Crouch, the Netheravon policeman,
appeared, murdered him on the footpath. He then shot himself on the
bridge, and his body floated downstream.

Wrongdoing of a less heinous kind is recalled by one of the cottages
beside the main road at New Town, between Enford and the Fifield turn.
It has a large, low window, close to the road, and the occupant, who was
eventually deported, used it for abducting hapless sheep whenever a
drove was passing by.

NOTES (location: SU1451; area: 3,311ha; population (1991): 577)
General: *VCH* 11, 115-34; Phillimore, F, *Enford days,* 1986.
Chisenbury chapel: WRS 39; Lidbury Camp: *WANHM* 40, 6-36; Chisenbury Warren and
East Chisenbury midden: McOmish, D *et al, Field archaeology of SPTA,* 2002, 98-9, 73-4;
Antiquity 70, 1996, 68-76; Winifred Grace: Marlow, S, *Winifred: a Wiltshire working girl,*
1991; West Chisenbury: *WANHM* 89, 73-83; Chisenbury Priory: Sales, J, *West country
gardens,* 1981, 198-9; Police murder: Williamson, E, *Murder for the truth?* 2000.

Erlestoke

L IKE PEAS IN A POD – a former resident's description – the pretty
cottages of Erlestoke line their High Street, and hide beneath the
trees in their private little Greensand valley. Their refined quaintness was
largely the work of Joshua Smith, MP for Devizes, who from the 1780s
until his death in 1819 created this secluded arcadia for himself and his
tenants. He demolished the existing Elizabethan house and built a new
mansion higher up the hill east of the village, he landscaped the park with

cascades and lakes, he removed the cottages from one of the village
streets – Water Street, which ran south from near the present church
beside the stream for at least 400m – and on the vacated hillside and
valley slopes he planted trees. Along the High Street, part of the winding

Westbury–Lavington turnpike of 1757/8, he added picturesque estate cottages between the existing village houses, and incorporated pieces of sculpture and architectural fragments from the old mansion in niches and over lintels. These and the *trompe l'œil* windows on several cottages tease and amuse the visitor. Near the top of the High Street he provided a water house in 1786 to give the village a piped water supply.

When Smith died the house and estate were sold to a flamboyant and fabulously wealthy Jamaican plantation owner, George Watson Taylor. His fortune, derived from sugar but dependent on slave labour, enabled him to number among his close friends the king, William IV, and to throw extravagant entertainments. But when he failed in his campaign, waged as a Devizes MP, against the abolition of slavery this life-style became unsustainable, and after 1832 Taylor descended into virtual bankruptcy, dying in 1841. The house was let to another colourful figure, Byron's friend Cam Hobhouse, until around 1860, when the Watson Taylor family returned. Erlestoke became once more the centre of a large estate extending over many parishes until its sale and dispersal in 1919.

The Watson Taylor dynasty continued Smith's work of modifying the village. In the High Street the estate laundry of the early-nineteenth century had been converted by 1859 to be the village school, and is now a private house. The village cross and pound stood at the junction with Lower Road, near the present post office and opposite the seventeenth century *George and Dragon* inn. The church dates from 1880, and replaced a medieval building, said in 1859 to be, 'a very poor church, chiefly of debased inferior work, and moreover in a neglected condition.' Photographs of this building, near the end of its life, hang in the present church. Although it has gone its churchyard, railings and some tombstones remain in the park. A number of memorials and pieces of twelfth-century masonry were transferred to the present church.

Joshua Smith's vision of house, park and estate village has been several times dented. A fire destroyed thirteen houses in the village in 1865; after 1919 the mansion lay empty until occupied and run by an eccentric Spiritualist clergyman as a kind of retreat. It was purchased by the War Department before 1939 for use as an officers' training establishment, and a hutted wartime hospital for American servicemen was built in

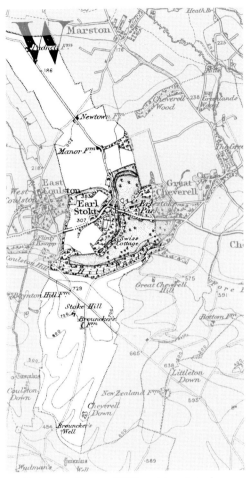

Ordnance Survey 1892 revision, 1 inch = 1 mile

the park. Much of the mansion was destroyed by fire in 1950, and after 1961 the surviving wings were incorporated into what was styled a detention or youth custody centre, and has become Erlestoke Prison. Modern buildings and barbed wire now occupy the eastern end of the former park, but the gatepiers, lodge, lakes and much of the woodland remain.

The parish of Erlestoke, like its neighbours, is a narrow strip of land, and extends some 7km from flat pasture lands on Kellaways Clay around Pudnell in the north, across Gault to Greensand, where the village sits, and south up the chalk escarpment on to Salisbury Plain. A possible Iron-Age hillfort, known in the seventeenth century as the Castle but since destroyed by quarrying, existed on the edge of the plain near the triangulation point beside the old Salisbury–Bath road. Areas of Romano-British and earlier settlement have been indicated nearby by stray finds and small-scale excavations on the golf course west of the village, around Brouncker's Court Farm, and within the prison enclave (where Roman burials and a midden were excavated in 1963).

Medieval Erlestoke lay in Melksham hundred and was an outlying estate of Melksham itself. The earl commemorated in its name may be Harold, pre-conquest owner of Melksham, although the prefix is not recorded until the thirteenth century, and the village (and more especially the park) was frequently known simply as Stoke until quite recently. The sequence of its medieval owners is complicated, and included a shadowy figure around 1200 known simply and incongruously as Terry the German. Ecclesiastically Erlestoke did not achieve parochial status until the old church (or more properly, chapel) was demolished in 1877; its remote position as a chapel-of-ease to Melksham, 12km away, may account for laxness and neglect. The chapel tower was allegedly used in the sixteenth century as a mew for hawks by the manorial owner, Sir William Brouncker, and a little later the vicarage house suffered a similar fate. Nonconformist groups of various denominations flourished before and after toleration in 1689; they seem principally to have been off-shoots of the vigorous Baptist cause in nearby Bratton. Services in the Anglican chapel-of-ease were said to be held irregularly in 1664, and in 1783 the curate responsible for the chapelry lived at Charlton, more than 16km away.

The plan and character of Erlestoke before the late-eighteenth century must remain largely a matter for conjecture, but there are some clues. The 73 households reported in 1309 were two more than in 1981, and there were 136 adult taxpayers in 1377. These figures suggest a fourteenth-century population of 250–350, much as it was in the 1980s, before the growth of the prison skewed the figures. Only 104 of the 2001 total – 522 – are women, reflecting the male prison population.

The orientation of the village before 1780 was probably north–south along the stream, rather than east–west along the High Street and B3098. Two mills lay along this stream, Manor Mill at the top of Water Street (now in Erlestoke Park Wood) and Marsh Mill near the north end of the present Park council estate. The former chapel and pre-1786 mansion were close together on the east bank of the stream, and a map of 1773 shows houses not only along Water Street, but also along Lower Road south of Park Farm. A continuation of Lower Road presumably ran northwards past Pudnell to Bulkington and so to the mother settlement at Melksham. High Street, according to the 1773 map, then had no buildings along its northern side – this cannot be completely accurate, as several cottages there now predate the map – but Smith certainly chose to develop High Street as the main centre of the remodelled village, away from his enlarged park. As for any village focus around the former chapel, that had already been obscured by the park and gardens attached to the earlier mansion.

The pattern of medieval farming can be plotted from an extent of 1309, and was of course dictated to a large extent by geology. Strip cultivation was practised on the lower and middle chalk south of the B3098, known as the Hill and the Clays, on the Greensand around the village (West Sands and Sharp Sands), and on the Gault (Lowfield). On the clay in the north of the parish was the demesne pasture (Pudnell) and common marsh; the high chalkland was sheep run; and the steepest slopes were wooded. In 1309 the land was divided equally between the lord and the tenants. The present position of farms in the parish, along Lower Road and on the downs, is largely a legacy of enclosure in 1782 and subsequent agricultural improvement.

The character of roads in the parish has also been affected by geology. On the clay the lane to Pudnell and New Road from Marston to Coulston (built in the late-nineteenth century) are flat, hedged and reasonably straight. (The main railway line from London to Exeter, built in 1900, also takes advantage of this flat terrain.) The B3098 road which connects Erlestoke with its neighbours beneath the escarpment follows the Greensand, and consequently has cut deep hollows in the soft rock like miniature ravines. That to the east of the village (greatly enlarged during the 1980s) cut through the park, and was until 1961 spanned by footbridges.

The contrast with the open, exposed, downland road from Bath to Salisbury, virtually disused by 1900, could not be greater. Known as the slow-coach road it climbed the escarpment at Tinhead and ran past Yarnbury to Serrington (part of Stapleford) in the Wylye valley. Milestones were erected along it in the eighteenth century (one on Coulston Hill bears the date 1753), and near Stokehill Farm survives the 'half-way' milestone, eighteen miles to each destination. Here on this lonely stretch of windswept road the traveller finally left behind his view of the claylands of north and west Wiltshire, with the Cotswolds and Mendips beyond, and caught his first glimpse of another country, as new and distant horizons began to emerge beyond the downland turf – Martinsell above Pewsey, Beacon Hill beyond Amesbury, and Grovely Great Ridge.

NOTES: (location: ST9653; area: 831ha; population (2001): 522)
General: *VCH* 7, 82-6; *WANHM* 33, 295-311; 33, 377-83; 34, 42-102.
Erlestoke Park: *WANHM* 93, 9-19; Britton, J, *Beauties of Wiltshire*, 1801, vol. 2, 199-205;
Romano-British finds: *WANHM* 85, 160; 92, 138; 95, 116-25.

Etchilhampton

A SMALL VILLAGE WITH A LONG NAME (sometimes shortened to
Ashlington) Etchilhampton has itself been shortened over the
centuries, and now presents a somewhat shrunken appearance. It is
aligned along a village street, now no more than a pathway in places,
which continues eastwards as a footpath towards Patney and Beechingstoke. Westwards, also as a footpath, it marks the parish boundary (and is
therefore probably medieval or earlier) running towards Tinkfield, an
outlying farm formerly within the parish, but since 1984 in Stert. The first
element of Tinkfield's name suggests that it was a place of assembly, and
so it may have been a meeting place for the Saxon hundred of Cannings
or Studfold.

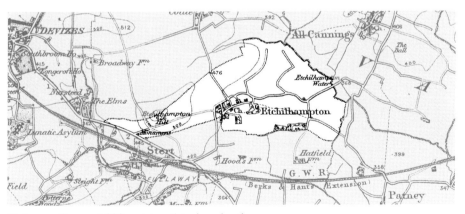

Ordnance Survey 1892 revision, 1 inch = 1 mile

Aerial photography has shown that village earthworks, in the form
of croft enclosures, extend at least 500m east of the present village, mostly

85

running south from the footpath in narrow strips to a common boundary line. West of the village, too, earthworks have been identified and were investigated in 1987. Nothing is known about the date of their creation or abandonment (though the latter had occurred by 1773), or indeed about their relationship to the present village. But it may be significant that through the village a second line (now a footpath) runs slightly south of the street and parallel to it, which defines the southern edge of the church-yard. The fourteenth-century church doorway and Victorian porch (replacing an earlier one) face south, suggesting that the main approach to the church was from this direction, and that the southern footpath marks the line of a former village street; although it must be said that the church also has a blocked north doorway.

The modern road pattern makes the problem worse; a road, which looks like a former back lane, runs in a semi-circle around the northern edge of the village and is met at right angles from the north by a road from Coate, which continues south into the village as a bridleway (appropriately called Dirty Lane) and then stops. It must, however, be the road from Old Shepherd's Shore (in Bishops Cannings) to Salisbury marked on a map of 1675, and so presumably once continued south of the village street, through Tichborne's Farm, to join the Lydeway. Whatever its plan before the eighteenth century Etchilhampton continued to lose houses and people, so that it has broken into two halves, with a 150m gap between the eastern (Manor house) and western (church) ends.

Etchilhampton parish is small, and is a former tithing of All Cannings, given separate civil parish status in 1866, although ecclesiastically remaining a dependent chapelry. Its name is difficult, but is thought to mean a piece of land added to an existing settlement, presumably Cannings or All Cannings. The parish lies mostly on Upper Greensand, but Etchilhampton Hill, which rises west of the village to give a panoramic view along Pewsey Vale and across Devizes to west Wiltshire, is an outlier of lower chalk offering good arable cultivation on its slopes. Much of the arable remained in open cultivation until the late-nineteenth century, when it was enclosed by agreement. The meadow lands of the eastern half of the parish, and pasture south of the hill at Tinkfield, had been enclosed much earlier, probably in the seventeenth century.

The village lies away from any important road, although both the A342 Devizes–Upavon road and the former Devizes branch railway (opened in 1862 and closed in 1966) cross the south-western corner of the parish beneath Etchilhampton Hill. The main road formerly took a steeper, more northerly, course across the hill, and part was turnpiked in 1707; the present, easier, realignment took place in 1768, and is commemorated by a monument to its creator, James Long, beside the road. The stone lion with an iron tail has become a landmark, and the section of road over which he presides is now usually known as Monument Hill.

Although at no great distance from the main road, and only a few minutes' drive away from Devizes, Etchilhampton retains a pleasantly remote ambience. It had no electricity, mains water or drainage until the 1950s; the telephone came much earlier – poles striding over Etchilhampton Hill from Devizes – but only because Wiltshire's chief constable in the early-twentieth century lived at Etchilhampton House. Another notable resident, at Tichborne's Farm, in the mid-nineteenth century was James Waylen, the historian of Devizes.

In common with many Wiltshire villages, which a century ago were almost wholly involved in agriculture, no Etchilhampton resident in 2000 was a farmworker, and all land in the parish was farmed from elsewhere. The Romany families which moved around the local farms before World War Two and who are buried in Etchilhampton churchyard – with names like Cinderella Bell and her daughter Britannia Black – have all long gone.

As for the village architecture there is a pleasing blend of old and new. There are surviving (but much altered) medieval houses in both halves of the village – Apple Tree and Littlewood Cottages in the east, and Church Holding in the west. The latter is believed to be the priest's house recorded in the early-seventeenth century as having been converted to a barn. The church itself retains its medieval nave, but the chancel and porch are Victorian; and it now boasts a splendid engraved millennium window by Simon Whistler. Other non-domestic buildings include the village hall, converted from the former school in 1971-3; the corrugated iron former Brethren mission hall, opened in 1890 and closed in 1958; and a motor-cycle garage, which began in 1946. Much of the village was sold by its owners, the Drax family, in 1928, and new housing has arrived in various places since then. Church View, a local authority development, begun in 1931, gradually expanded over four decades to seventeen dwellings; and the Mixon is a small private estate of the 1970s on the northern edge of the village. As commonly it was given the name of the field over which it was built, by someone presumably unaware of its meaning. The mixon was the village dung heap.

NOTES (location: SU0560; area: 354ha; population (2001): 152)
General: *VCH* 10, 71-7; Robertson, D, *Etchilhampton: a village portrait*, 2001.
Earthworks: *WANHM* 76, 17; 82, 177.

Fittleton

S KYLARKS AND HELICOPTERS provide the accompaniment to a walk
along the Old Marlborough Road, the Romanized trackway from Old
Sarum to Mildenhall which crosses Haxton Down and Weather Hill. Along
this road, which is now a metalled and well used army track, the walker
can see across most of Fittleton's extensive downland, and experience that
familiar feeling of looking out to sea – a petrified seascape of rolling chalk
breakers, incongruously dotted with trees, and extending beyond compre-
hension to a remote horizon in the west. Sidbury hillfort, in neighbouring
Tidworth parish, dominates the eastern skyline, and there are prehistoric
fields systems, linear earthworks, settlements and barrows in profusion.
Archaeological investigation in 1995 at Beach's Barn, high up on this
wilderness, suggested that a large Romano-British village, verging on a
small town, stood here in the first and second centuries. 'Antiquity,' it has
been noted, 'broods heavily over these downs.'

Fittleton is a typical chalkland 'strip' parish, extending some 7km eastward from the River Avon up on to the wild downland, which since its acquisition by the War Office in 1898 has been devoted to military training and aviation. The parish is divided lengthwise into two tithings, Fittleton and Haxton, and their settlements have coalesced in the valley. Neither is well known or much frequented, because the main road (the A345) runs up the western side of the valley, affording only a glimpse of Fittleton's steepled church beyond the meadows and fish lakes. Until 1840, when the present road was turnpiked, the more important valley route may have been up the eastern side through Fittleton. It was this, known as the Bourn road, which the Amesbury Trust turnpiked nearly eighty years earlier, in 1762. Neither, however, could rival the Old Marlborough Road for long-distance traffic; this was mapped by Ogilby in 1675 as part of the main road from Salisbury to the Cotswolds, was milestoned along its route in about 1740, and was considered in such good condition in 1761/2 as not to need the attentions of a turnpike trust.

Like Fittleworth in Sussex Fittleton is derived from a personal name, *Fitela*, although in Domesday Book the tendency of west country dialect to alter initial consonants (known as voicing) transforms the name to *Viteletone*. The owner in 1066 was in fact called Vitel, and we might imagine that he was responsible for the place-name, were it not for a reference in a Saxon charter of neighbouring Enford in 934 (some five generations earlier) to 'Fitela's slade'. A similar coincidence occurred later, when in 1665 William Beach purchased Fittleton, and so began its long connection with the Hicks Beach family. In fact Haxton in the fourteenth century had belonged to a family called de la Beche, or atte Beche, and it has been suggested that they, and not the later Beaches, may be connected with Beach's Barn on Fittleton Down.

Haxton is not recorded before the twelfth century, but also commemorates a person, *Hacun*, whose 'stone', rather than farm (*tun*), provides the second element of the name. For most of its history Haxton appears to have been more populous and wealthy than Fittleton; the 1332 tax list, for instance, enters a total for Haxton more than four times that for Fittleton. As late as 1817 the first Ordnance Survey map omits the name Fittleton altogether, and describes the whole settlement as Haxton. The parish church, however, lay just on the Fittleton side of the tithing boundary, and its name has prevailed for the civil parish too. Haxton in the middle ages had its own free chapel, with an endowment of land to support a chaplain. A Victorian tradition which located it in the Berry, the field south of the parish church, was probably mistaken. In 1718 the site was said then to be an orchard, and its glebe lay in the Berry. Most orchards in Haxton, according to the tithe map, lay along Lower Street or close to the Green.

Fittleton church is medieval, of several periods, and had various piecemeal restorations between 1841 and 1903. The soil of the churchyard has built up around the walls to a level in places a metre or more above the floor inside. The church is of flint, with a west tower, and the principal (now the only) entrance on the south faces away from the village across the Berry to Haxton. In fact the church is not at all obvious from Fittleton's present village street, which has clearly been diverted by awkward bends around the manor house. This alteration had taken place before a map of 1773, but the earlier course is probably represented by the paths which approach the church from north and south. An avenue of trees crossed the Berry from the church to Haxton Farm, and was known as Ghost Avenue because a spectral squire of Netheravon customarily drove his carriage along it.

In typical 'closed' village fashion, Fittleton's church has for near companions the two comfortable residences of the squire and the parson, the manor house and the former rectory (now Fittleton House). Both are of eighteenth-century character, with earlier and later work, and sit privately behind high walls. Beyond them to the north is a less predictable building, a substantial thatched house of brick with local flint and clunch, which was built in 1726 to accommodate a schoolmaster and ten poor schoolboys. The endowment, which was on the rector's initiative, followed two slightly earlier educational charities, in 1712 and 1717. The first master was appointed in 1718, and remained in post until 1773, when his son took over. Classrooms were added in 1843, 1872 and 1934, and in 1870 the building became a National school. From 1964 it was used as the junior school for both Netheravon and Fittleton, with accommodation for eighty children, but it has now closed.

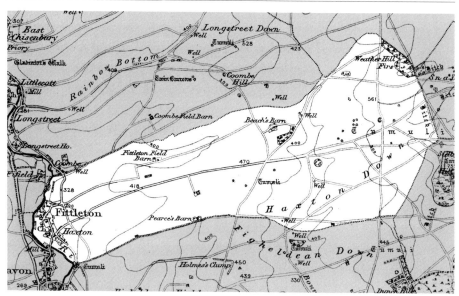

Ordnance Survey 1892 revision, 1 inch = 1 mile

The tithing boundary runs immediately south of Fittleton Manor, and so the cottages dotting the village street from here towards the small triangular green all belong to Haxton. The Green Vine has sixteenth-century work, and is a former pub, the *Green Dragon*. It retains inside an improving text as a wall painting, perhaps to discourage arguments between the clientele: "Disdain no man though he hath offended, The best of us will be amended'. Maps of 1773, 1817 and 1826 show buildings around the green, which was the site of the pound, but by 1889 most had gone, and now it is overlooked by old people's bungalows. Vacant garden plots along Lower Street, a regular linear continuation of the settlement south-eastward, mark the sites of other cottages lost during the nineteenth century. South from the green runs Fittleton and Haxton's main connection with the outside world, the lane to Netheravon across Haxton Bridge. The present structure dates from 1907, and replaced a Victorian suspension bridge.

Apart from gravel and alluvium in the Avon valley, and a finger of gravel extending up the dry coombe of the Nine Mile River near Beach's Barn, the whole parish lies on upper chalk, and the sheep-and-corn agriculture typical of Salisbury Plain parishes prevailed. Fittleton tithing was enclosed in 1796, but by then much arable land north and east of the

village was already held severally, and a downland farm of arable enclosures had been created around Beach's Barn. Haxton was not enclosed
until 1839. From William Beach's initial purchase of part of Fittleton
manor in 1655, the family (Hicks Beach from 1790) eventually acquired
the whole parish by purchases in 1734 and 1846. Fittleton and Haxton,
together with Netheravon, made up the Hicks Beach estate which was
compulsorily sold in 1898, under controversial circumstances (the vendor
was also Chancellor of the Exchequer at the time), to the War Office for
military training. The family, however, managed to buy back Fittleton
manor house and, after letting it to tenants, unmarried Hicks Beach sisters
lived in it between 1946 and 1965. East of the Avon military use was less
restrictive to farming than on the artillery ranges to the west. In consequence
rough grazing has continued on Fittleton's downland subject to limitations.

　　Except in one particular Fittleton escaped the suburbanization and
influx of population by which the military takeover has so affected most of
its neighbours to the south and east. The exception was Airfield Camp,
Netheravon, which despite its name straddled the parish boundary between
Fittleton and Figheldean, south-east of the village, and in 1991 accounted
for some 150 of Fittleton's total population of 370. The establishment
traced its history to 1912/13, when it was built as an airfield for the newly-
formed Royal Flying Corps, and it retains much of the original wooden
hutted accommodation. Its long flying career included training, testing and
operations, not only by the RFC and RAF but also, from the 1960s, the
Army Air Corps, and with helicopters and gliders as well as convention-al
aircraft. Since 1963 free fall parachuting has been one of its specialities,
and the drone of a light aircraft circling aloft as parachutes drift to earth
has become as much a part of the sights and sounds of Fittleton as the
swish of a fly fisherman's rod on the tranquil reaches of the Avon.

NOTES (location: SU1449; area: 1,300ha; population (2001): 234)
General: *VCH* 11, 142-51; Finch, R, *Netheravon with Fittleton: a short history* . . . rev. ed.,
1960; Anon, *Church of All Saints in the parish of Fittleton-cum-Haxton*, 1993.
Beach's Barn excavation: Wessex Archaeology, report 38814: Beach's Barn, 1995 [T];
Haxton chapel: Pearse, T, *Parochial history of Fittleton with Haxton*, 1867 [WANHS];
School: Pink, H R, *Fittleton school, 1772–1972*, 1972; Airfield camp: Ashworth, C, *Action
stations 5*, rev. ed., 1990, 134-8.

Great Cheverell

NATHANIEL SHUTE, who was rector of Great Cheverell, 1680–1711, wrote a short history and description of his parish – a very early example of the genre – and with evident pride was able to claim: 'Now as for the inhabitants they live friendly and neighbourly and are ready to assist each other upon occasion. They are generally industrious in their husbandry affairs and thrive by their industry.' His portrait of a well-rounded village is an important historical source, but much of it is also still applicable to Great Cheverell three centuries later. 'It is pleasantly situated on a sandy ground and enjoyeth an healthful air, it stands between the hill [Salisbury Plain] and vale [the west Wiltshire claylands and Pewsey Vale] being about three furlongs distant from the hills to the south, and yet it is seated upon an eminence above the vale to the north, so that it affords a most pleasant prospect for the space of 15 or 20 miles northward into the

vale country, where at one view you have a sight of diverse towns and
churches.'

Like its many neighbours along the northern escarpment of
Salisbury Plain Great Cheverell is a narrow strip parish, some 7km long
and never more than 2km wide, its feet in the stream (a tributary of
Semington Brook) which powered its mill, its head on Cheverell Down,
acquired by the War Department in 1933 and now part of the western
Salisbury Plain Training Area. Between the Portland beds and Gault clay
of the vale and the chalk downland of the plain a wide shelf of fertile
Greensand provides a platform for the village and, as Shute, pointed out,
an excellent panorama.

The village has a T-shaped plan, the result of three streets meeting at
a junction outside the *Bell Inn*, a large brick pub of about 1740 – in
Shute's time no alehouses were 'suffered' because of the 'ill consequence'.
Church Street, which runs west from the junction, leads not only to the
largely fifteenth-century church, heavily restored in 1868, but also to the
manor house of about 1690 and later – with contemporary former
manorial court house in the garden behind – and the former rectory. This
is a very grand affair of 1844 built in Fisherton brick (for a new rector who
came from Fisherton), and replaced an earlier rectory set nearer the road,
which was perhaps late medieval, and of which eighteenth-century gatepiers survive. The replacement was in turn replaced by a parsonage in
1937, but this too was later sold and there is now no resident incumbent.
Church Street turns into a track, and then a footpath leading to the former
common pasture grounds in the north of the parish, and to Common
Farm, built about 1700 when part of the common was enclosed. One
other building of note in Church Street, near the road junction, is Glebe
House, of about 1700, which is the former farmhouse of the rectory lands.

The other two village streets which meet at the junction are both
now called High Street, although formerly this name was restricted to the
road coming from the south, its counterpart from the north-east being
known (logically if unusually) as Low Street. A back lane, Green Lane,
serves the properties on the eastern and south-eastern sides of these
streets, and defines the former eastern extent of the village; council
housing built at Garston during the 1950s, however, extends beyond this

limit. High Street and Low Street present a good mixture of building styles, with a prevalence of local brick, derived from a brickyard which existed near the green from before 1700 until the 1880s. Most village amenities are in what was Low Street, and include at Hill Corner the Cheverell Stores, in a building of 1773, once the *General Wolfe* alehouse, on the site of Old House Farm; the village hall next door is a former Baptist chapel, Little Zoar, built in 1833 and converted to its present use after 1907 when a new chapel was built nearby. Across the road, on the site of the village pond, Kyte's garage, established in 1923, adjoins the picturesque National school of 1844/5, enlarged 1876/7, which is now privately run as the Old School Nursery. A school had been held in the south porch of the church between 1579 and 1680 (graffiti remain), and a charity school was endowed in 1730 and held in a cottage (demolished before 1920) near the *Bell Inn*. A new primary school has been built at Townsend south of the village.

High Street and Low Street each divide into two, at the southern and northern ends of the village respectively. The south end, Townsend, has 1970s council housing beside the school and playing field. The roads continue south to join the B3098 Westbury–Lavington road, which was turnpiked in 1757/8, and which links all the springline villages beneath the escarpment. An older road, from Bath to Salisbury, known as the slow-coach road, crosses Cheverell Down 2km further south, and Shute refers to this as, 'a most pleasant travelling over the green downes.' Low Street divides into Cheverell Road, which soon leaves the parish on its way to Potterne and Devizes, and the Green, which crosses the main London–Exeter railway line by a bridge built during the line's construction in 1902. Maps of 1802 and 1828 show that the Green was then lined with buildings near the site of the later railway, and it is known that a house, shop and cottages were burnt down by a fire during the construction of the bridge. The Green itself was a triangular area, now built over, north of the railway, and the road continues past it, over the insignificant Gang Bridge (mentioned in a document of 1513), and across the former common, on a line apparently laid out in the late-eighteenth century, to arrive at the parish boundary by the remains of Great Cheverell mill.

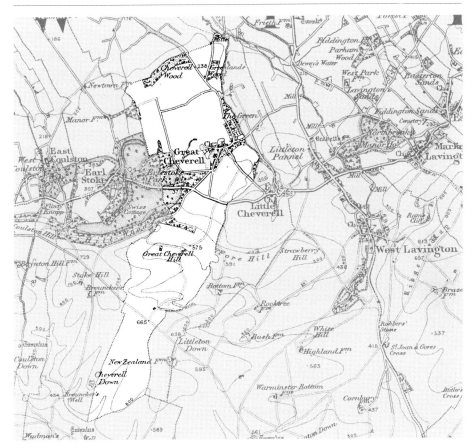

Ordnance Survey 1892 revision, 1 inch = 1 mile

The mill, recorded in 1324 as belonging to Henry and Walter Ennok, was referred to as Enock's mill until the seventeenth century, and then took the name of new owners, the Winsmore family, by which it is still sometimes known. Although in the middle ages it seems to have been a corn mill, it was being used for fulling in 1526, and continued under the Winsmores as a fulling mill until 1784. Between 1784 and 1843 new buildings were erected so that there were in effect two mills, one for corn, the other to provide power for an edge-tool manufacturer, James Potter. Potter later concentrated on making sheepbells from a workshop beside Hillview, the family house in the village, which bears a datestone 'E H Potter, 1757'. Millwrighting and the manufacture of iron water-wheels was carried on in Great Cheverell in the nineteenth century, probably using the

mill, and one of the leading exponents, Mark Sawyer, has also left a
datestone, 'MSS, 1843', on Laurel House, his High Street home and
workshop.

Cheverell is a name of uncertain meaning, possibly of Celtic
derivation, and the first mention comes in Domesday Book, when land
identified as lying in Great Cheverell was recorded as having formed part
of an exchange with the royal manor of Amesbury. An area of woodland
at Sutton Veny, near Warminster, was associated with the estate for much
of the middle ages, and may reflect a pre-Norman arrangement. To Norman
ears Cheverell sounded like *chevreuil*, French for a roe-buck, and the name
sometimes occurs in medieval documents as *Capreolus*, the Latin
equivalent. The Great Cheverell estate was divided in the thirteenth century,
and the two manors later became known as Cheverell Burnell (after an
owner who became bishop of Bath and Wells) and Cheverell Hales (after
Edward Hales, owner around 1400). In the early-fifteenth century both
manors, although retaining separate identities, passed into the ownership
of the Hungerford family, who used them to endow their almshouse or
hospital at Heytesbury. In consequence the Custos (warden) of Heytesbury Hospital was lord of the manors until 1863, when they were sold to
the Watson Taylors of neighbouring Erlestoke. This arrangement, besides
giving prominence in village affairs to the hospital's principal tenants,
members of the Merewether and Townsend families (the latter commemorated in extravagant fashion in the church), also benefited elderly male
paupers from the village, who might become residents of the hospital.

The early topography of the village, before it was lovingly described
in 1700, is conjectural, although it is likely that there were Romano-British
settlements on the clay in Greenland Wood and close to Erlestoke Prison
(but in Great Cheverell parish). In addition there are the earthworks
remains of a substantial Romano-British native village high on the Plain
on Cheverell Down, close to the boundary between the two Cheverell
parishes. A tradition that the village formerly lay higher in the fields (that
is, further south), because, 'severall foundations of houses have bin dug
up there,' was current in 1700, and may also point to a Roman settlement. Probable medieval earthworks and a holloway survive on the slope
north of the village, but small archaeological excavations here and on a

site to the east of the village in 1995-6 failed to reveal settlement features. The church, first recorded in the early-twelfth century, and the area around it, which includes the manor house and the manor farm (probably on the site of the demesne premises of the two manors), presumably represent the medieval focus of the village.

Always larger than Little Cheverell next door, Great Cheverell's fourteenth-century population of perhaps 125–150 is estimated to have risen to about 200 in 1539, and Shute's account of 1700 described the parish as then having about 300 inhabitants in 60 houses. The early-nineteenth century saw a rapid rise, from 457 in 1801 to 576 in 1831, but then a century of decline, to 270 in 1931. Council housing since 1928, as well as private dwellings, have arrested the decrease, and the local economy has been boosted in recent years by the development of Erlestoke detention centre and prison, which has included building a residential estate, Victoria Park, for prison officers' families, on the western edge of Great Cheverell parish.

The familiar pattern of agriculture, dictated by geology, supported the communities for centuries – common pasture occupied the northern claylands, the arable (with some gardening) lay around and south of the village on the Greensand and lower chalk, with extensive sheep runs on the chalk downland. The remains of terracing and field systems on downland slopes indicate cultivation on the high chalk, in prehistoric and medieval times, and manorial court records of 1776 suggest that attempts were then being made, illegally, to marl and plough up downland, several decades before Parliamentary enclosure in 1802.

But in addition to its agricultural concerns Great Cheverell has been involved in other rural activities – fulling, brickmaking, millwrighting, tool- and sheepbell-making have already been mentioned – which have given it an ecomonic diversity not shared by its smaller neighbours. Domestic weaving seems to have been important in the eighteenth century; three weavers and a clothier occur in parish register entries between 1701 and 1705, and there is a record (in the life of David Saunders, 'the shepherd of Salisbury Plain') of wool being taken from Littleton Pannell to Great Cheverell to be made up by weavers, probably towards the end of the eighteenth century.

NOTES (location: ST9854; area 747ha; population (2001): 588)
General: *VCH* 10, 41-53; Waley, M H, *Great Cheverell: a retrospect*, undated [1980s]
[typescript in T]
Shute: Waley, M H (ed), *A description and historical account of Great Cheverell in
Wiltshire in 1700*, 1976; Townsend (location): *WANHM* 77, 93-101; Mills: *WANHM* 64,
78, 93; Merewether and Townsend families: *WANHM* 60, 109-19; Tradesmen: WRS 55,
217-21.

Huish

THE SMALLEST PARISH in Pewsey Vale, in terms of both area and
population, Huish nevertheless has the distinction of being the only
place in Wiltshire to have more than doubled its population (from 30 to
64) between 1971 and 1981, and then halved it again by 2001 (to 28).
Fluctuation within modest bounds has indeed been a feature of Huish's
evolution, and is the main theme developed here. The parish, like its
western neighbours, sits on the south-facing edge of the Marlborough
Downs, here called Huish Hill, with the characteristic geological
progression from Greensand south of the village, through lower and

middle chalk on the hillside to upper chalk capped by clay-with-flints
beyond the ridge. The church and Huish Farm lie some 300m north of the
present village, along a lane which continues as a muddy track up the
hillside towards the now deserted village of Shaw 1.5km further north (see

Alton in this volume), and through the woods to Marlborough. Huish is
served now by a minor road running west from Oare, which replaced an
earlier, more southerly approach between 1773 and 1817. The road
meanders on past the village, following 'too faithfully the angles of old
fields,' (as Huish's historian put it) until at Draycot Fitzpayne it leaves the
parish and returns to Wilcot.

In the Romano-British period the area may have been farmed
from a settlement at Great Mead in the extreme south of the parish
adjoining Draycot Farm; the area had yielded Roman pottery before
1814, evidence of a villa was discovered in about 1882 (probably nearby)
and ten years later a tradition was reported that a great city once stood
there. Sir Richard Colt Hoare, visiting Huish in 1814, was told that
'British' (Iron Age) and Roman pottery had also been found north-east of
the church, but excavations in 1967 and 1968 on village earthworks in the
area uncovered nothing earlier than the twelfth century. However, the
medieval church contained shaped sarsen blocks, which may have been
robbed from an earlier, possibly Roman, building nearby.

The root meaning of the name Huish, which is common in
Somerset (where there are 21 examples) but rare outside south-west
England, seems to be 'household' or 'family farm'. It has been suggested
that Huishes are survivals of an older, perhaps pre-Saxon, farmstead-
based settlement pattern, which was largely replaced in the English
lowlands by planned open-field villages in the later Saxon period. This
description would fit this Wiltshire Huish, with its Romano-British
antecedent, its modest size, and its position hemmed between the villages
of Wilcot and Oare.

Where the household lived is not known, but between the twelfth
and fifteenth centuries, under the ownership of the Doygnel family and
their successors, buildings were laid out and successively renewed in an
area north and north-east of the church, later used as a conigre (or rabbit-
warren) and now very overgrown. The church, probably built originally in
the late-thirteenth century, lay within the village, which seems to have
been defined by a rectangular ditch embracing the area of the conigre, the
church and the present Huish Farm and farm buildings. Ponds 100m
south of the farm perhaps represent the southern limit of the ditch, which

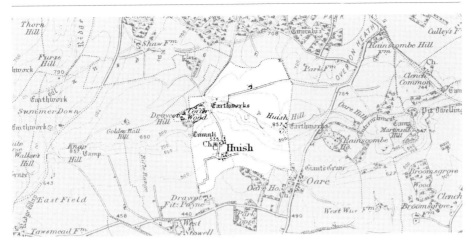

Ordnance Survey 1892 revision, 1 inch = 1 mile

is extant (although overgrown) to west and north. A second settlement existed in the parish in the thirteenth century, but its precise location is unknown; its name, *Hulwerk*, 'the earthwork on the hill', suggests that it probably lay above the main village, in or near Gopher Wood.

The village around the church had been deserted by 1500, perhaps because of its vulnerability to flooding, and the present site was in use (possibly after an interval of neglect and depopulation) by the seventeenth century, since several of the cottages contain work of this period. At about the same time parts of the downland in the north of the parish were enclosed, and eventually cultivated.

This expansion of the arable into an area not easily accessible from the village was probably the reason for the emergence of a secondary settlement, known as Huish Hill or Upper Huish. Today the area of this upland hamlet, which straddles the Huish–Wilcot boundary, is marked by a double-bend in the track, a stagnant pond close to over-grown building rubble, and one smart modern house masked by trees. It existed in 1773 and only fell into decline after 1920, as motor transport and agricultural changes rendered it unnecessary. The last house to survive was the bakery, which had enjoyed a reputation for lardy cake and fine bread baked partly from potato flour. It has been demolished since 1962. An earlier casualty was the Methodist chapel, erected in 1863 at a cost, it was said, to each inhabitant of ten shillings. One impecunious shepherd raised his contribution by selling his smock. A few years later, down in the valley, Huish parish church was rebuilt at a cost of £1,000.

NOTES (location: SU1463; area: 298ha; population (2001): 28)
General: *VCH* 10, 77-82; Ibberson, D, *Two Wiltshire villages*, 1963, 70-95.
Excavations: *WANHM* 62, 51-66; 67, 117-31; name: *Anglo-Saxon Studies in Archaeology and History*, 5, 1992, 65-84.

Little Cheverell

T HE SMALLEST of the sixteen parishes which climb the northern scarp
of Salisbury Plain from Bratton to Upavon, Little Cheverell is a
narrow, gently curving, strip of land, no more than 500m wide in places,
but over 6km from its northern tip at the confluence of streams on the
pasture lands of Kimmeridge clay to its southernmost point near New
Zealand Farm Camp, high on the upper chalk of Salisbury Plain. The
usual geological sequence – Portland beds, Gault, Greensand, lower and
middle chalk – crosses the parish in bands, and has affected the land use
(better documented than most of its neighbours) and influenced the
village shape and appearance.

A stream rises at Hawkswell, south of the village, and flows north
through the parish; near the church it is crossed by the B3098 Westbury–
Lavington road (turnpiked in 1757/8), notorious for the tortuous course it
has gouged along the Greensand. It here excels itself by plunging into a
narrow double bend in a deep hollow in its effort to climb out of the
parish and away to Littleton Pannell. At the crossing, now culverted, stand
the former school (closed in 1922) and schoolhouse, a cottage with a
Victorian letter box, and a converted malthouse (Bridge House), overlooking the junction with a minor lane.

This is Low Road, which leads northwards in the valley formed by
the stream, and beside it has grown up a ribbon of bungalows and older
houses and cottages. The first were probably built near the lane's northern
end, where, according to a map of 1722, it opened out into a funnel-
shaped green or common. Already by this date there were buildings along
the lane, and a hamlet, described as Fuzzy's Hill, had developed by 1773.

More houses were built in the mid-nineteenth century (notice datestones 1845 and 1854 on existing cottages) concomitant with a steep rise in population. One nineteenth century house in Low Road near its southern end became the *Owl* public house in 1939.

The earlier focus of settlement was probably in the vicinity of the church, Glebe Farm and Manor Farm, where more buildings than survive are marked on eighteenth- and nineteenth-century maps, including several between the church and the road, which probably took a narrower, slightly more northerly course. The church itself, perched on a bank above the road, was rebuilt in 1850, but retains a plain fourteenth-century tower. A chantry chapel was founded by the Cheverell family, eponymous lords of the manor, in 1298, but did not survive the middle ages. Their demesne house and premises may have been sited south of

the church, where fields named Court Closes are marked on the 1722 map, and an area of disturbed ground is still to be seen.

The Cheverell family are recorded as owners from the twelfth to the fourteenth century, and subsequent lords have included Hungerfords and Radnors. A twentieth-century owner, Col R W Awdry, 1881-1949 (a chairman of Wiltshire County Council and much else), built for himself between 1914 and 1920 Hawkswell House, in Arts-and-Crafts movement style; in 1941 it was commandeered by the War Office, who since 1934 had owned the manor, and was retained until 1979, when the Ministry of Defence sold it for conversion to flats. It lies, secluded from the road, beside woodland and lakes, south of the church.

Another notable resident of the village was Sir James Stonhouse, rector from 1764 until his death in 1795, who rebuilt Little Cheverell House in 1782-3, the former rectory. He was a distinguished physician who had founded Northampton Infirmary in 1743, and became an eminent member of Bristol society, where in later years he spent the winter months, away from his cold and bleak Wiltshire living. As Mr Johnston he is portrayed in a good light by his friend Hannah More, whose *The Shepherd of Salisbury Plain* tells the moral tale of David Saunders of neighbouring Littleton Pannell.

Population and farming records suggest that this small parish supported about 15–25 families through the middle ages and as late as the seventeenth century, when 58 adult inhabitants are recorded. However by 1785 there were 44 households and a total population of 195, probably as a result of development along Low Road; and the population reached a high point of 295 in 1841, declining thereafter. By comparison with farming in similar parishes the proportions of medieval and later demesne and glebe land were large, whilst tenantry land accounted for relatively little. As usual arable farming in strips was concentrated on the more fertile soils of the lower and middle chalk and Greensand to the south and around the village, with sheep runs on the high downland and pasture on the heavier clays in the north. The rector's glebe land, scattered throughout the fields, is described in meticulous detail, furlong by furlong, in a terrier made around 1600.

Since at least the fifteenth century there was a mill in the parish, probably on the site of Cheverell Mill near Great Cheverell Green. Enclosure began on the clayland in the sixteenth century, but much strip cultivation remained in 1722 around the village and along the eastern and western edges of the parish, although wholesale enclosure and reorganisation of holdings took place in 1767 and 1802. Bricks were made on the Gault north of Furze Hill in the nineteenth and twentieth centuries, close to the railway line which was built across the parish in 1900 on its way between London and Exeter. A downland farm, named

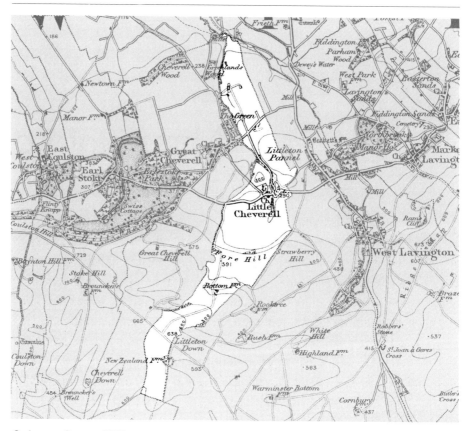

Ordnance Survey 1892 revision, 1 inch = 1 mile

New Zealand on account of its remote position, was built in the later-nineteenth century close to the 'slow-coach road' from Bath to Salisbury. In 1940 this distant corner of the parish began a new career as a military airfield for training pilots in night flying, and its now abandoned runways were expanded during the 1950s. When Imber was evacuated in 1943 the War Department took over the farm, and it remains active as a small training camp for soldiers exercising on Salisbury Plain.

NOTES: (location: ST9953; area: 415ha; population (2001): 139)
General: *VCH* 10, 53-60.
1722 map: WSRO 490/765A; Awdry and Hawkswell: *WANHM* 53, 127-30; *CL* 14.6.1979; Stonhouse: Waley, M H, *Great cheverell: a retrospect*, undated [198-], 110-14 [typescript in T]; 1785 Population: WSRO 1725/14; New Zealand: James, N D G, *Plain soldiering*, 1987, 176, 211.

Manningford

I**T WAS THE POET** Edward Thomas who aptly summed up Manningford, or rather (as he pointed out) the three Manningfords – Abbots, Bohun, and Bruce. 'All had their churches, graveyards, farms and byres, Lurking to one side up the paths and lanes, Seldom well seen except by aeroplanes.' Since his day, in 1934 in fact, the three communities have been united as a single parish, although the scattered pockets of settlement within this administrative unit remain aloof from one another, and there is nowhere in the modern parish which one might regard as its centre. Before 1934 Manningford Abbots and Manningford Bruce were autonomous ancient parishes, but Manningford Bohun had been a tithing of Wilsford (from which, geographically, it was detached) until it became a civil and ecclesiastical parish during the nineteenth century. The territories of the three adjacent Manningfords were similar. Each possessed a thin slice of Pewsey Vale and its southern escarpment, some six or seven kilometres from north-west to south-east, but nowhere much more than a kilometre wide. In typical Wiltshire chalkland fashion, therefore, each had its share of Greensand in the valley, alluvium by the stream, chalk loam on the hillslope, and rough pasture on the downland. The oldest and largest houses lie south of the stream, between the meadows and the main road, and include several timber-framed farmhouses and cottages, as well as substantial brick-built former parsonage houses and farms.

The name that the three Manningfords share is derived from a ford which carried the early road known as Hare Street across the eastern headwater of the River Avon. Hare Street appears to have been an important north–south route in Saxon and perhaps earlier times, linking

downland routes and ridgeways on the Marlborough Downs and Salisbury
Plain. It functioned in the same way, therefore, as the line of the Great
Ridgeway (through Honeystreet, Broad Street and Wilsford) and the
Lydeway, which both cross Pewsey Vale further west. The first element of
Manningford includes a personal name, *Mana*, followed *by -inga*, which is
usually translated 'the people of'. Names which include *-inga* (Cannings is
another local example) are usually thought to refer to places which were
colonized by a Saxon population at an early date, from some nearby
settlement which had already been established. In the case of Manningford
that earlier settlement may have been associated with the important
pagan Saxon cemetery discovered at Black Patch, south of Pewsey.

How and when 'the people of Mana' came to divide themselves
into three parts is largely a matter of speculation, but sufficient clues exist
to put forward a hypothesis. The three Manningfords share common
south-eastern and northern boundaries, the latter along another early
road which was probably in use in the Saxon period. This suggests that

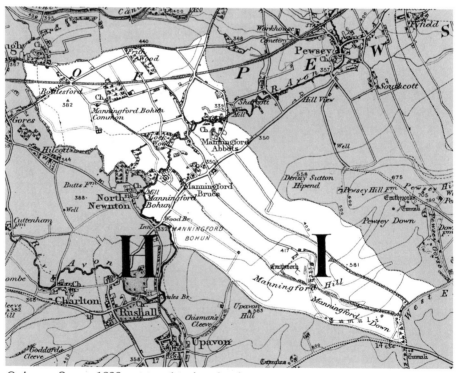

Ordnance Survey 1892 revision, 1 inch = 1 mile

we are looking at one territory divided into three, rather than three territories amalgamated into one. In 1985 a substantial Roman villa, probably
of courtyard design and with an elaborate mosaic pavement and the
remains of a bath-suite, was discovered adjoining the east side of Manningford Bruce churchyard. It was partially excavated between 1985 and
1987, and evidence of third- and fourth-century occupation was found. It
is possible that Manningford's boundary reflects the estate dependent on
this villa, which was then taken over by *Mana* and his followers.

We know that by 987 the territory of Manningford had been
divided, because in that year King Ethelred granted the part later known
as Manningford Abbots to a man named Aethelwold. Subsequently
Aethelwold bequeathed it to New Minster (the later Hyde Abbey) at
Winchester, which retained it until the dissolution, and from which it
derived its affix 'Abbots'. It is likely that the first division of Manningford
was into two, rather than three, parts. At the time of Domesday book
Abbots was reckoned at 10 hides, Bruce at 6½ hides and Bohun at 3½
hides. Abbots had its own mill, but Bruce and Bohun shared a mill, in the
proportions two-thirds to one-third. Clearly, therefore, Bruce and Bohun
together had once been a ten-hide estate with a mill, just as Abbots by
itself was a ten-hide estate. If indeed Manningford was initially divided into
two parts it may be significant that the boundary drawn between them ran
close, not only to the ford after which they were both named, but also to
Swanborough Tump. This is a probable Bronze-Age round barrow which
became the hundred meeting-place, conveniently placed for the purpose
beside the Saxon highway, and which lent its name to the large hundred
of Swanborough. The name's first element refers not to swans but to
swains – the 'common people' who assembled there.

Manningford Abbots had probably acquired a church by 987, as a
'church way' is mentioned in the charter as one of the landmarks. The
present church at Abbots is a Victorian reconstruction (1861–4) of a
medieval building. Manningford Bruce, however, has preserved one of the
purest and most charming of small Norman churches in Wiltshire, complete
with herringbone flintwork, simple nave and apsidal chancel. Moreover its
restoration in 1882, by J L Pearson, was carried out with sympathy, and
the new features which he introduced, such as the smart parquet ceiling in

the apse, tend to enhance rather than detract from the spirit of the original building. Presumably because the community which it served remained small and was never especially prosperous Bruce church fossilized at a stage in its development (the eleventh or twelfth century) beyond which most other parish churches evolved to become larger and more complicated buildings.

But it did at least achieve separate parochial status in the middle ages, unlike its neighbour Bohun. If we are right in assuming that Bruce and Bohun were once a single territory, it is possible that Bruce church originally served Bohun as well, and that a twelfth-century mention of a chapel-of-ease at Bohun in fact refers to the building which by 1291 had become Bruce parish church. This is purely speculation, but it is certain that for most of its subsequent history Bohun was dependent on Wilsford parish church, 3km away. Only in 1859 did it acquire a church of its own, and this was built at a remote site on Manningford Bohun Common, roughly equidistant between its two main groups of parishioners, at Bottlesford and Bohun itself. It was still in use in 1971, but redundant by 1973, and is now a private house. Partly, no doubt, because of the unsatisfactory nature of Anglican provision in Manningford Bohun it was there, rather than in Abbots or Bruce, that dissent flourished and chapels opened. A Strict Baptist chapel was built at Townsend in 1869, probably on the site of an earlier cottage used for worship since 1840. A Methodist meeting was being held in Bohun in 1819, and another Baptist congregation met at Bottlesford, in the tithing's north-western corner, from 1838 onwards.

The long fingers of land which extend south-east from the villages up on to Salisbury Plain conform to the normal pattern of chalkland agriculture. The common fields lay on the hillslope, and from an estate map of 1722 for Manningford Bruce it is clear that, although some furlongs had by then been enclosed, much strip cultivation remained. The last of the open fields in the Manningfords disappeared in 1812. In the vale the pattern was more complicated. The intractable Greensand was common pasture during the middle ages, and was then enclosed during the sixteenth and seventeenth centuries, so that only small commons remained. An outlying dairy farm, or 'wick', had perhaps existed on the edge of Bohun Common in Saxon or medieval times; the name Wyke occurs in 1330, and Wick Lane and Wick Close appear in the 1839 tithe apportionment close

to the site of the later Manningford Bohun church. There was also an area
of woodland, the Frith, near Swanborough Tump, which seems to have
extended into the territory of both Abbots and Bruce. In addition Bruce
had an arable field on the Greensand. During the twentieth century market
gardening has been practised at Bohun, in the area known as Free Trade.

Through the Greensand vale meander not only the eastern River
Avon from the Pewsey direction, but also a tributary rising near Alton,
which is followed by part of the western parish boundary. The two streams
meet in the meadows opposite North Newton church, and John Leland

reported in the 1540s that the course of the river had recently been altered
to alleviate flooding. The boundary continues to follow the former course,
and on the Bohun tithe map of 1839 this was marked as 'The Old River'.
Because of the marshy conditions created by these streams one imagines
that reliable fords were important, and therefore affected both communications and settlement. Thus in addition to Manningford itself, there is a
reference in the 987 charter to *mearc* or 'boundary' ford, which carried the
lane through Abbots across the Avon, and in a document of 1348 to
'Botwell's' ford (Bottlesford), which crosses the Alton stream. Woodbridge,
which takes the Devizes–Pewsey road across the combined streams south of
Bohun, is also a medieval crossing-place, recorded in a document of 1434.

Taxation records suggest that in the later middle ages each of the
Manningfords had fewer than 100 inhabitants; indeed Abbots in 1428 was
included on a list of very small parishes with under ten households.

Abbots and Bruce each had about 100–120 inhabitants in 1676, and Abbots remained small, with only 22 dwelling-houses in 1783, and a highest recorded population (in 1831) of 165. Bruce and Bohun, by contrast, seem to have been growing significantly during the eighteenth and nineteenth centuries, and each was approaching a total of 300 around 1850, declining thereafter. This period of growth is reflected in the settlement pattern. Cottages and more substantial houses, including in the 1840s a thatched school, appeared along the lane leading northwards to the site of the original Manningford, with further ribbon development from there towards the former common land in the north of Bruce parish. This gained the characteristic name 'Townsend', and the same name was also applied to an extension of the settlement at Bohun along the main Devizes–Pewsey road. Cottages extended along the lane leading eastward from Bottlesford, and at a remote crossroads (after 1862 also a railway bridge) a settlement sprang up. Its founders, reflecting presumably their liberal and anti-protectionist sympathies, christened it 'Free Trade'. Cottages were also built on the waste at Manningford Bohun and Manningford Abbots Commons. The former played host to the new Victorian church, already mentioned, and the latter to Manningford railway halt, which opened in 1932 and closed in 1966.

Because it belonged to Hyde Abbey throughout the middle ages Manningford Abbots tended to be associated with its neighbour to the east, Pewsey, which was also a Hyde Abbey possession. They remained under the same ownership until the eighteenth century. Bruce (de Breuse) and Bohun both owe their affixes to medieval manorial owners. Later owners of Bruce were members of the Nicholas family. Mary Nicholas, a sister of Jane Lane, is commemorated in Bruce church by a memorial, which describes her part in the rescue of Charles II after the Battle of Worcester. As 'Alice Lee' her role in this adventure (which occurred before she married into the Nicholas family and came to Wiltshire) was immortalized by Sir Walter Scott in the novel *Woodstock*.

NOTES (location: SU1458; area: 1,251ha; population (2001): 385)
General: *VCH* 10, 106-19, 204-14.
Roman villa: *WANHM* 82, 84-91; Swanborough Tump: *WANHM* 94, 239-43; Bruce church: *WANHM* 20, 122-37; Mary Nicholas: *WANHM* 26, 1-38.

Marden

UNLESS YOU KNOW THEM WELL, it is easy to confuse the placid villages of Pewsey Vale; but Marden sticks in the memory on account of its particularly fine church tower, set in a churchyard which seems to have been jostled away from the village street by a row of thatched cottages and a former vicarage, so that only a narrow stone-flagged path connects the church to the outside world. The fifteenth-century tower was condemned as unsafe in about 1850 – it had previously been lowered to counteract the weight of the bells on its foundations. But to his enduring credit it was rescued by a sympathetic restorer (C E Ponting) in 1885, who dismantled it completely and rebuilt it stone-by-stone and joint-by-joint to what he considered had been its original form. The underlying cause of its distress, as the admirable Ponting explained to a party of antiquarians when showing them round in 1890, was inadequate church foundations in the soft and shifting Greensand; he clearly understood and sympathized with his medieval predecessors, who had tried in vain to solve their problem by sinking large boulders into the sand as a foundation. The danger of building on sand is graphically illustrated by the otherwise splendid Norman chancel arch, now far from semi-circular, and known technically as 'depressed'. But any depression felt by the church visitor is quickly dispelled by the joyful gaudiness of Saints Peter and Paul (1958) and the evocative Wiltshire landcapes (1979), as depicted by J and M Kettlewell in modern stained glass.

The eighteenth-century cottages around the churchyard, which stand like gossips at a font, probably include former parish houses, and were joined in 1844, through the enthusiasm of the then curate, by a

delicate brick National school (closed in 1925) which is scarcely larger
than a domestic garage, though epochs removed, with ornamental bell-
cote and windows. Nearby, according to a sketch map of 1776, lay the
alehouse of Mary Dennis, probably trading as the *Swan Inn*. Its function
has been replaced by the *New Inn* nearer the river, which is marked,
though not named, on a map of 1886.

Marden probably means 'boundary valley', and Saxon charters of
neighbouring settlements locate the name to the meandering stretch of the
insignificant River Avon – later constrained by mill leats and water
meadows – around and downstream from Marden Mill. This (until very
recently) formed the parish boundary with Marden's neighbour Beechingstoke, but it was also the boundary between medieval rural deaneries,
which are believed sometimes to follow more ancient divisions; so the
boundary which existed when Marden's name was coined may have been
of more than local significance. There is another Marden (near Chippenham), of similar derivation, which was a medieval forest boundary, and
gave its name to the river which flows through Calne. A tradition survived
until the present century that our Marden had been the scene of a battle
between red-haired and black-haired men (a similar folk-memory existed
at Tilshead), and it was probably a version of this legend that led the
Elizabethan topographer, William Camden, to identify Marden with the
battle of *Meretune* recorded in the Anglo-Saxon Chronicle against the
year 871.

This identification is not now generally accepted, but it may have
been fostered by the proximity of an earthwork once assumed to be a
castle. On what used to be the Beechingstoke side of the river crossing
(but now by a recent boundary alteration reclaimed by the parish from
which it takes its name) lies Marden henge, a massive Neolithic henge
monument or earthwork enclosure even larger than Durrington Walls near
Stonehenge. As at Durrington parts of the bank and ditch may be seen
from the road, which bisects the roughly oval enclosure; but they are not
sufficiently striking to be noticed by the casual passer-by, and are partially
obscured by a small housing estate built within the monument.

In the eighteenth century there would have been no ignoring
Hatfield Barrow, a miniature Silbury Hill or Marlborough Mount some

15m high, which lay within this enclosure. William Cunnington conducted a disappointing excavation into this 'super-barrow' in 1807, when it was still some 7m high, but when Colt Hoare visited the site again in 1818 all trace of it had disappeared. The site had been levelled by one Perry – probably Leonard Perry, a small farmer who was living in Beechingstoke at the time of the tithe award in 1839. In the wake of exciting discoveries at other henge monuments in the 1960s, a limited excavation was carried out at Marden Henge in 1969, which discovered that it was contemporary with Durrington Walls and had contained at least one circular timber structure. Evidence was also found of earlier occupation from the same period as the interrupted ditch enclosures on the hills above Pewsey Vale, and a little indication that the occupants were involved in forest clearance.

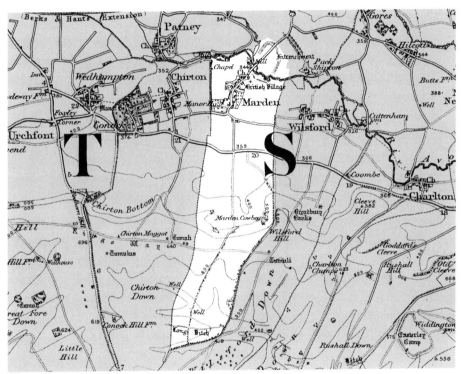

Ordnance Survey 1892 revision, 1 inch = 1 mile

Marden is one of about twenty strip parishes which climb the northern escarpment of Salisbury Plain to share in the chalky loam of the slope and the rough sheep pastures on the downland; like many of them it also enjoys the lush meadows and fertile Greensand of Pewsey vale. Its traditional sheep and corn husbandry was affected (though not extinguished) by enclosure in 1812, but in 1898 it lost its downland and rough grazing to the War Department's firing range. Marden village, like neighbouring Chirton, lies along a north–south street which until the nineteenth century was a broad green, similar to that surviving at Poulshot. It is depicted on a sketch map of 1776. By 1845, although still named on the tithe award, encroachments had limited this green to a small area north of the present Manor Farm stables. Between then and 1912 it was claimed that fifteen cottages had been destroyed, and some had been replaced by the red-brick estate houses which are now dotted along the street. Only Marden House Farmhouse, set well back from the road, respects the edge of the former green, but its limits may still be followed in the rear property boundaries on either side of the street. Part of the green was incorporated into the grounds of Marden Manor, a rendered brick house of the early nineteenth century, which was said to have replaced cottages on the same site.

This wholesale reorganisation of Marden was connected (probably cause and effect in equal measure) with fluctuations in the village population. In 1676 there were at least 175 adult residents, which may perhaps be translated into a total population of around 300, and the sketch map of exactly a century later suggests that about forty dwellings then lined the street. Through the nineteenth century the population climbed from 162 in 1801 to 247 in 1871, but had dropped to 152 by 1901. By 1981 it had fallen to 86, but then by 1991 had climbed again above its 1901 total by the acquisition from Beechingstoke of the housing estate within the henge (it has fallen back again since).

The western edge of Marden's former green represents also the western limit of river gravel deposits overlying the upper greensand. Also on the gravel, but closer to the river, lay an Iron-Age and Romano-British settlement, identified by Colt Hoare in 1814, and represented now by substantial earthworks behind the *New Inn*. Nearby, and perhaps confused with the prehistoric remains, are medieval village earthworks, suggesting that here, as at Chirton, the modern village has migrated to its green from an earlier focus further north. The tithe award of 1845 describes fields in this area as 'Isterton' ('Isetown' in a survey of 1702), presumably a corruption of Easterton or Easton, which would accurately denote a settlement here, due east of the church. The 1812 enclosure map shows a track branching from the present road to serve this area, and an arrangement of closes which appear to represent 'ghost' crofts of a former settlement. By the time of the 1845 map this ghost had been exorcised.

The present road alignment north-east of the *New Inn*, which crosses the faintly-visible water meadows on a causeway and the two streams by small bridges with iron railings, is not shown on a map of 1821, but had arrived by 1845, replacing a turning close to the mill. This alteration may perhaps be attributed to the Kennett and Amesbury turnpike trust, which turnpiked the road from Woodborough through Marden to Chirton in 1840. An earlier turnpike, of 1762, now the A342 Devizes–Upavon road, which it joins near Chirton, crosses Marden parish 1km south of the village.

All the inhabited buildings in Marden parish lie within the village or the henge, except for the *New Inn*, the nearby millhouse and associated cottages of Marden Mill, and a converted malthouse on the parish boundary near Chirton's former Church Mill. Marden Mill, probably on the site of its Domesday predecessor, suffered a fire during the nineteenth century, which presumably led to the rebuilding commemorated by a datestone, 1842; it was still a working corn mill in 1923, but the wheel was removed in 1932, and the buildings were later used by a pig breeder and an animal feedstuffs producer. Near the former malthouse on the Chirton boundary, which is dated 1844, a Baptist chapel is marked on a map of 1886; it was succeeded from 1899 until about 1951 by a chapel built on the west side of Marden's street.

NOTES (location: SU0857; area: 551ha; population (2001): 124)
General: *VCH* 10, 119-25; *WNQ* 7-8 *passim*.
Church: *WANHM* 25, 261-4; church guide; 1776 map: WSRO 510/11 (reproduced in Chandler, J, *Vale of Pewsey*, 2000 ed., 50); Battle: *WANHM* 54, 36-8; Henge: *WANHM* 56, 4-11, 251-2; *Antiq Jnl* 51, 177-239; Hatfield Barrow: Hoare, *Ancient Wilts*, 2, 4-7.

Market Lavington

I N THE ABSENCE of any more precise word for this type of settlement, Market Lavington may be described as a large village or a small town. A century ago, when its population was hovering around 1,000, one would have inclined to the former, but now as it continues to rise above 2,000 (and with a more than 40% increase over the past two decades), the latter definition is becoming more realistic. It is one of several minor trading centres – other examples are Westbury, Heytesbury, Amesbury and Pewsey – which developed in the medieval period around the edge of Salisbury Plain.

One consequence of the burgeoning housing estates which have caused the population increase has been that archaeological investigation in advance of development (between 1986 and 1995) has revealed a great deal more than was previously known about the settlement's early history. A Roman villa of some affluence (judging by the quality of the finds) existed somewhere close to the present settlement, probably 300m or more to the west of the parish church. It has not been excavated, but work on the Grove Farm estate (on the high ground immediately to the west and north of the church) discovered remains peripheral to this villa, and much more importantly the evidence of sunken buildings and a cemetery belonging to a very early-Saxon settlement, which functioned from the fifth to the seventh century.

This excavation is important and unusual for three reasons. In the first place it is rare to be able to investigate together the evidence of both life (the dwellings) and death (the burials) of a community of this date. Secondly it seems to have been established many miles west of other equivalent Wiltshire sites of this period, in an area where there is little other evidence of Saxon penetration at so early a date. And third, it suggests that at Lavington there may have been continuity of settlement from the first-century Roman villa onwards, the waning Roman presence being replaced by the early Saxon village, to be replaced in turn by successive late Saxon and medieval renewals, right up to the present. Particularly interesting in this respect is the site of the medieval parish church adjacent to and perhaps overlying the pagan Saxon village, a possible instance of the Christianizing of something older.

The name perhaps means 'the farmstead of *Lafa*' and is of course shared with its neighbour, West Lavington. Market Lavington has sometimes been distinguished from its neighbour with other affixes, including East Lavington and Steeple Lavington; and West Lavington was often known as Bishops Lavington. The two Lavingtons together with Potterne and their respective satellite villages had in the later Saxon period constituted most of a land unit known as Rowborough (which was subsequently divided and then disappeared). Potterne was probably the ecclesiastical centre of this territory, but the Roman villa at Lavington may have created its original boundaries. When Rowborough was fragmented its constituent parts were grouped by owner rather than location, so that the ancient parish of Market Lavington included Easterton and Gore, while West Lavington included Fiddington and Littleton Pannell. Changes in the nineteenth century have left the present geographically more sensible arrangement of three civil parishes, West Lavington (with Gore and Littleton Pannell), Market Lavington (with Fiddington), and Easterton.

The town (to give it the benefit of the doubt) is compact, centred on a cross-roads which has only lost its significance in the present century, with the closure of the Salisbury–Devizes roads across the military lands of Salisbury Plain. Most through traffic in the narrow streets is now travelling east–west along the Westbury–Pewsey road (B3098), which links all the northern plain-edge villages. Market Lavington has not simply developed around a cross-roads, however; it is possible to identify three elements in its plan, to all of which the cross-roads is incidental. The primary focus in the late-Saxon and early-medieval periods seems to have been in the area of the church, which sits on a high ridge between east–west flowing streams. The Grove Farm excavators found pits and evidence of small-scale structures of the twelfth century associated with this phase. The present parish church itself retains fragments of twelfth-century work, and the oldest secular building in the town (The Old House, Parsonage Lane), of early fourteenth-century date, is also on this ridge, north-east of the church. It is an impressive structure, the only fully aisled medieval house surviving in Wiltshire, and it was probably built as the demesne house for one of Lavington's two manors, that of the Rochelle family.

M C

A second focus lies further south, along White Street, at the area known as Broad Well. Here a strong spring (the main water supply until 1936) issues into a stream which runs alongside a track towards the church, endearingly and now officially named 'The Muddle'. This track, and White Street, which meet at an acute angle south of Broad Well, appear to have formed two sides of a triangular village green, suggesting that the medieval village spread southwards from the church to surround its water supply.

The third element in the plan may be dated with some confidence to the mid-thirteenth century, for in 1254 Richard Rochelle, owner of one of the two manors in Market Lavington, was granted a market charter. He was doubtless responsible for laying out tenements along the present High

Street, running north-east from the cross-roads, and for creating a market place abutting the High Street on its northern side. The back lane and most of the tenement boundaries south of the High Street still exist, but on the north their line has been lost, and – in a most regrettable piece of planning vandalism – most of the buildings surrounding the market place including the market hall, were demolished between about 1958 and 1961, thus extinguishing all the atmosphere of a market from what is now a rather meagre car park. To add insult to this injury, the local authorities then tried to charge the successors to the manorial owner, Dauntsey's School, for the cost of resurfacing their market place!

The parish of Market Lavington is a long narrow strip, some 9km long by between 1km and 2km wide. Its geology and consequent agriculture follow the pattern set by many similar parishes along the northern edge of Salisbury Plain, with Greensand and Gault pasture land (largely enclosed by the seventeenth century) north of the village, arable fields (open until enclosure in 1782) on the loamy lower and middle chalk slopes south of the village, and sheep pasture on the high downland beyond. Before Fiddington (a strip less than 400m wide in places) was added to its eastern side the town's territory was narrower still.

Along the full length of the parish, from north-west to south-east, runs the former Salisbury–Devizes road (turnpiked in 1757/8), now a mere track south of Gibbet Knowl, and this acted as the spine road and division for the open fields. These extended beyond the escarpment and much further south across the plain (nearly 4km, almost to Candown Copse) than the fields of most Pewsey Vale communities, and they remained under open arable cultivation until enclosed in 1781. Along the edge of the scarp, and hence across the short axis of the parish, runs a ridgeway (so-called in the middle ages) seen as a continuation of the Great Ridgeway of the Marlborough Downs. The Westbury–Pewsey main railway line, built in 1900, crosses the north of the parish, elevated on an embankment, with a station called Lavington (closed in 1966) north of Littleton Pannell.

Settlement away from the town has taken place largely along minor roads on the upper Greensand, known as Lavington Sands and Fidding-ton Sands. Housing here is scattered, and mostly of the twentieth century, but earlier foci may be at Northbrook and Townsend. Fiddington, first recorded in 1270 as *Fifede* ('five hides') is no longer a village. Its position was perhaps marked by Fiddington House (towards which Market Lavington High Street is aligned), but this was demolished after its long career housing a private lunatic asylum came to an end in 1962. The asylum had been established in 1816 in the High Street, but moved to Fiddington in 1834, and in 1844 was licensed to take 180 patients. Modern houses (Fiddington Clays) now occupy the grounds.

Tollgates stood across the main road at Dewey's Water (in the extreme north of the parish) and at Gibbet Knowl. Their removal, along with nine others in 1825, was achieved through the agency of a local miller, who encouraged villagers to buy out the lessees of the tolls. This was cause for great celebration. The gates were paraded through the streets and then turned into a bonfire on the plain. West Park and The Lodge, at Lavington Sands, imply an area of parkland at the northern end of the parish, perhaps adjoining the bishop's park in Potterne. Freith Farm, recorded in 1268, is derived from a word which often means 'scrubland on the edge of a wooded area;' the clay and Portland beds in this north-western corner of the parish may, therefore, have been tree-covered in the middle ages.

Although organised as two separate manors until the eighteenth century at least, Market Lavington shows little sign of having served two masters. Most landlords were absentees (in the later middle ages Edington Priory was the principal owner), and so, apart from Clyffe Hall of 1737, which was not part of a landed estate but became a country seat of the Radnor family, the parish boasts no great houses earlier than the Manor House of 1863-7. This was a mock-Elizabethan extravagance for a Radnor younger son, which lies west of the town and is now part of Dauntsey's School. The most influential action of a manorial lord was probably that of establishing a market in the thirteenth century, and so promoting Market Lavington to urban status. This affected not only the topography but also the economic life of the community. The market's success was modest – the proximity of Devizes must always have had a stifling effect (and Steeple Ashton too was seen as a threat in the early days) – but it continued until the mid-nineteenth century. Corn and malt were the chief commodities, according to a guide book of 1673, and still in a directory of

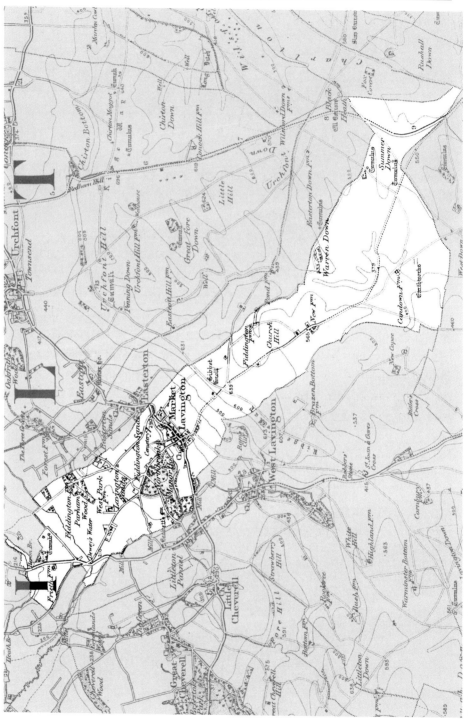

Ordnance Survey 1892 revision, 1 inch = 1 mile

1848. Malting and its concomitant, brewing, were supplemented by other trades more appropriate to a town than a village, including since the nineteenth century an agricultural engineering concern. Two trading families of local celebrity were the Elishas, tailors who have given their name to a playing field (Mr Elisha ran the football team); and the Potters, carriers and horse-bus proprietors, who from 1872 built up a flourishing transport business. As Lavington and Devizes Motor Services it ran 37 vehicles in its heyday, with regular bus services to Bath and Salisbury. As at Rowde and elsewhere the Gault clay north of the sands was suitable for brickmaking, and a large brickyard (subsequently a chemical manu-facturer) lies alongside the railway line.

Despite its urban pretensions, Market Lavington has remained pleasantly small, with an attractive variety of architecture and landscape. As the focus for several neighbouring parishes it has a range of services – comprehensive school, library, estate agent – unusual for a community of its modest size. Besides its impressive parish church it has a United Reformed chapel, heir to a long nonconformist tradition of Quakers, Independents and Methodists; the former Quaker meeting house of 1716 (now a studio) lies almost opposite the chapel in the High Street. Next to the parish church the former school (which was superseded in 1971) has been turned into a most interesting museum of local history and folk life.

NOTES (location: SU0154; area: 1,536ha; population (2001): 2,257)
General: *VCH* 10, 82-106; McGill, B, *Village under the plain: the story of Market Lavington*, 1995; McMahon, P, *The archaeology of Wiltshire's towns, an extensive urban survey: Market Lavington*, 2001 [WCC, unpublished].
Excavations: *WANHM* 85, 160; Williams, P, and Newman, R, *Excavations at Grove Farm, Market Lavington, Wiltshire* [unpublished Wessex Archaeology report]; Wessex Archaeology, *Grove Farm, Market Lavington, archaeological evaluation 1995* [unpublished report]; Eagles, B, in Ellis, P (ed.), *Roman Wiltshire and after*, 2001, 210-19; Asylum: Parry-Jones, W L, *The trade in lunacy*, 1972; Manor house: *HR* 3 (25), 246-60.

Marston

L IKE ITS LARGER NEIGHBOUR Worton, Marston was until 1866 part of
the parish of Potterne, and so its medieval lands and settlements lay
on the great estate of the bishops of Salisbury. The modern parish is low-
lying and reasonably flat. The scarp edge of Salisbury Plain, like a distant
wall, forms the southern horizon, its springs and streams draining on to the
heavy clay of Marston and its neighbours. One of these, Bulkington Brook,
flowing westward to the Bristol Avon, forms Marston's northern parish
boundary with Worton. The name, meaning 'marsh farm,' and that of its
outlying hamlet, Norney ('north of the marsh'), evoke the wet conditions
encountered by its medieval farmers; it is still subject to periodic flooding.

128

Like Worton the village perhaps began as a deliberate creation on a new site by the bishop of Salisbury; in Marston's case the name suggests that this was to harvest the resources of this marshland corner of his Potterne estate.

Away from any important road, and largely hidden along a cul-de-sac, the village is not well known, although it possesses a number of picturesque black-and-white thatched houses. It has retained a large and ragged green, which conveys the idea (historically correct) of a workaday area of communal rough grazing land. Broad driftways, for driving cattle to and from their pasture grounds, funnel into the green from south-east and south-west, the former retaining something of its medieval appearance. A map of 1657 suggests that the green was originally larger, and approximately square, but by then houses had begun to encroach upon its northern side. The original focus was perhaps slightly north and north-east of the green.

Marston green seems to have marked the crossing-point of roads which are no longer important. A track running north-west from the Cheverells becomes the modern road between Marston and Norney, and then reverts to a green lane until it meets the Worton–Seend road. A second route, which perhaps connected Edington and Potterne, carries the modern road from the south-west as far as Marston, but then degenerates to a path, crossing the stream by a footbridge. The other lanes and footpaths of the parish were probably access roads to the common fields, which lay east, south and west of the village, meeting at the green. By 1657 much of the south of the parish had been enclosed, and further enclosure took place under an act of 1824. North of the green, as far as the stream which marks the parish boundary, lay Ham Field. Substantial traces of medieval ridge and furrow remain in the northern part of this field, but the furlongs near the village were closes by the seventeenth century, their boundaries and a built-up lane apparently preserving the line of the former strip cultivation. Pronounced ridges may still be seen in one of these closes.

Marston seems never to have been a populous place. It is not mentioned in Domesday book (presumably it was submerged within Potterne) and the name first occurs in 1198. It was never a separate manor, merely a community of the bishop's Potterne estate. In 1377 the

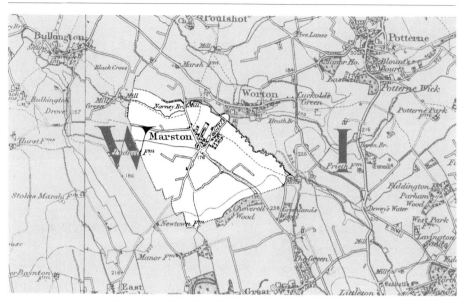

Ordnance Survey 1892 revision, 1 inch = 1 mile

adult population was recorded as 88, slightly more than Worton, to which
it has often been subordinate. The map of 1657 records over 60 buildings,
suggesting a population of 200 or more. In 1931 only 96 people lived in
Marston, half the number a century earlier, but infilling with smart new
houses in recent years has resulted in a modest increase. The village has
never had a church, and prior to 1843, when Worton church was built
close to the parish boundary to serve both communities, Marston
worshippers had to walk to Potterne, where a part of the parish church
was set apart for them. A Primitive Methodist chapel was built on one
corner of the green in 1835 and is still used, with six regular worshippers
in 2000. There is neither shop nor school nor public house; fewer working
farms remain than in the recent past, and a haulage contractor's yard is
tucked out of sight. For social life and village services Marston seems
increasingly to be allying itself with Worton, and an organization was
formed in 1998 to bring the two communities together – its first venture
was the practical one of restoring the footpath that links them.

NOTES (location: ST9757; area: 367ha; population (2001): 145)
General: *VCH* 7, 207-17 *passim*; *Worton and Marston Domesday book 2000,* 2001.
1657 map: WSRO 1553/110. See also sources for Worton.

Milton Lilbourne

ONDAY, 28 AUGUST 1826 was, in William Cobbett's estimation, as
pleasant a day as he ever spent in his life. Before breakfast he rode
from Everleigh across the downs and past Milton Hill Farm to a vantage
point on the steep escarpment above Milton Lilbourne, and from here he
spent half an hour sitting on his horse admiring the view: 'I never before
saw any thing to please me like this valley of the Avon.' Next, the way
down being too steep for his horse, he was helped by a boy driving pigs,
who led his horse and directed him through Milton to the farmhouse of an
old friend, nearby at Fyfield. 'I do not know, that I ever in the whole
course of my life, saw people so much surprised and pleased as this
farmer and his family were at seeing me.' He must have spent the day
discussing the local farming situation and collecting statistics, because in
his book he demonstrates that the parish of Milton produced food enough
to feed at least five times its population, and yet its labourers subsisted in
poverty and its two mansion houses were falling into ruin. Such was his
welcome that he postponed until the next day his famous ride down the
Avon valley to Salisbury, and stayed the night at Fyfield.

Were he to return today Cobbett would still find the view
invigorating – he would mourn the lost elms, no doubt, and be intrigued
by the electricity pylons – and he would look down on a parish with
virtually unaltered boundaries and roughly the same number of
inhabitants. The mansion houses (there are really four in the parish –
Milton Manor, Havering House, King Hall and Fyfield Manor) are now
rebuilt or restored and in good order, and the present-day 'labourers', not
so poor now, are well-housed and work, for the most part, outside the

131

parish, in places such as Marlborough, Swindon and even London. He would certainly be welcomed – as I have been – and would be amused and perhaps flattered to see a striking modern house (on the site of the old village hall) named 'Cobbett's Way'.

Milton Lilbourne is quite a large parish, and may be conveniently divided into three. North of the Pewsey–Burbage B3087 road (a former Saxon military road, the Pewsey Herepath, but never turnpiked) there is now a dispersed pattern of settlements on undulating Greensand, and with the domed hill of Martinsell as a backcloth. Until the nineteenth century much of this area formed the tithing of Clench which, with Little Clench, is the name given to a farm and hamlet in the north of the parish close to Wootton Rivers. Clench Common, now largely shared between other parishes, lies on the high chalkland behind Martinsell. First recorded in the thirteenth century, Clench means a lumpy or massive hill, and must surely be a reference to Martinsell. A document of about 1300 in the Cirencester Abbey cartulary describes *Wykclench* as one of Milton's three hamlets; *Wyk-* perhaps refers to a now vanished part of the settlement due west of the present East Wick Farm, which may be glimpsed as extant earthworks when looking down from the small car park at the top of the hill. Clench probably extended further south as well, as far as the complex of small closes near Broomsgrove Lodge; this area, with more buildings and boundaries than survive now, is marked as 'Clench' on the 1843 tithe map.

The second of Milton's hamlets also lay within our northern division of the parish, but within Fyfield tithing. In about 1300 it was known as *Mulecote*, 'the cottages by the mill', and the name occurs also as a local surname in the thirteenth and fourteenth centuries. The first reference to the name comes in 1236, and it is still called Milcot in 1632, but later it had been corrupted to Milkhouse, and since at least 1817 the nearby ponds have been known as Milkhouse Water. These ponds, presumably constructed as reservoirs for the mill, or in connection with the water meadow system downstream, were later used as watercress beds and are now a trout farm. The river here is a headwater of the Salisbury Avon, and a second mill, probably supplanting Milkhouse, was operating about 1km upstream by 1773. A hamlet known as New Mill developed around the substantial mill complex (which, augmented by steam power, still worked in the 1930s), and the *New Inn* (sometimes called the *Lydiard Arms*, after a Victorian landlady's surname) was functioning here by 1822

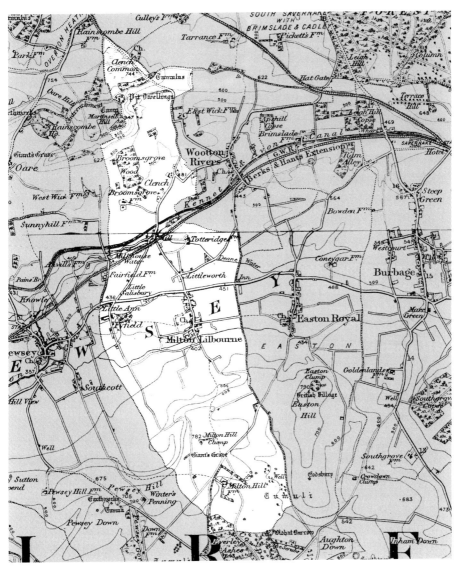

Ordnance Survey 1892 revision, 1 inch = 1 mile

and closed during the 1980s. The river here can never have been a particularly reliable or substantial source of power, and, especially after the thirsty Kennet and Avon Canal was completed along its valley in 1809, milling must have been a precarious business. Probably in consequence of this we find references in the early-nineteenth century to two windmills nearby, one near Totteridge, and the other south-west of New Mill. A small wharf was built on the canal at New Mill, and in 1862 an embankment took the Berks and Hants Extension Railway close to both New Mill and Milkhouse as the railway engineers pursued a course parallel to the canal between Hungerford and Devizes.

In addition to these hamlets there are two other significant farmsteads in the northern part of Milton parish. Totteridge takes its name from the projecting ridge formed by the confluence of the Avon with a minor tributary, Deane Water, close to which the farm stands. The first reference to the place has been claimed as 1199, but this and some other early instances may in fact refer to places elsewhere in Wiltshire with similar names, such as Timbridge and Tytherington. Broomsgrove sits on a slight rise in front of Martinsell, and is well seen from the Fyfield–New Mill lane. Near the farm in 1893–4 were discovered and excavated the remains of a Romano-British potters' settlement, one of the sources of the domestic pottery industry known as Savernake Ware, whose products appear to have been produced for the market at *Cunetio* (Mildenhall), and which are widely found on Roman sites in east and central Wiltshire.

Two squatter-type settlements had emerged along the Pewsey–Burbage road by the later-eighteenth century. Little Ann (a corruption of Little Land) straddles the Pewsey–Milton boundary near Fyfield, and has never been as substantial as Little Salisbury (alternatively known in 1773 as New Town), which boasted a beerhouse in 1880 (now the *Three Horse Shoes Inn*), and since the last war has been graced also by the rather obtrusive yard of a scrap car dealer. A third settlement, at Littleworth, seems to have comprised no more than one or two buildings before the mid-nineteenth century. A Wesleyan chapel for fifty worshippers was built here in about 1854 (successor to two earlier Methodist groups in Milton – Independent in 1825, and Primitive in 1843). Another Methodist chapel, now a private house, was built nearer Milton crossroads in 1932. And since the last war a group of eight bungalows and several other houses have appeared at Littleworth.

South of the main road lie the other two parts into which we may divide the parish; these are the hamlet and tithing of Fyfield, and the village of Milton Lilbourne itself, with extensive lands on the downs to the south. Fyfield is typical of the narrow strip tithings which are found right along the northern escarpment of Salisbury Plain. It extends from the Greensand of Milkhouse Water on the valley floor, across the main road at Little Ann, and past the now shrunken settlement. The community's arable fields (enclosed in 1822/3) lay south of the hamlet on the broad band of flat chalk marl at the scarp foot, and beyond them the chalk downland of Fyfield Hill, which is supervised by a well-preserved Neolithic long barrow, Giant's Grave, some 100m long, and excavated by Thurnam in 1865. The lane which leads from the main road to Fyfield (it can hardly now be called the village street) continues southwards as a kind of spinal track. This served the open fields, and leads to a derelict windpump and field barn in a muddy enclosure, before sweeping up the hill in a deeply-rutted chalk cutting to reveal a hidden dry valley behind. Extensive remains of a prehistoric and later field system and lynchets are carved into the sides and head of this secret coombe, and evidence of a possible Roman building has been found nearby.

Fyfield's regular western boundary had been defined by the tenth century, and its name (like other Fifields) suggests that it existed in the Saxon period as a separate five-hide estate. It does not, however, occur in Domesday Book, and was probably then subsumed within the entry for Wootton Rivers. The name is first recorded in 1230, and by about 1300 it was certainly regarded as one of the hamlets that formed part of Milton Lilbourne parish. In 1377 it had an adult taxpaying population of forty (probably including Milcot) compared with Milton's sixty-seven. The hamlet of Fyfield has probably never been very populous, and its shape (especially as seen on the 1822 enclosure map) suggests a small linear medieval settlement, with a planned arrangement of rectangular closes on the western side extending back to the tithing boundary. The eastern side of the hamlet is dominated by the house and grounds of Fyfield Manor (including a large wooded area known as the Wilderness, and formerly as the Vineyard). The present building, it has been said, is the house of a small squire of about 1700, although it conceals within it the foundations and roof of a typical fifteenth-century manor house. The Waryn or Warren family owned Fyfield from about 1200 until 1613, but the 'small squire' who rebuilt the house was probably a Hungerford, most likely Edmund Hungerford, who died in 1713 and is buried in Milton church. The estate passed by marriage via the Wyndhams to the Penruddock family in 1768,

and stayed in their hands until it was divided in 1919. A distinguished more recent owner was Lord Avon, the former Sir Anthony Eden, who lived in the house during the early 1960s, before moving to Alvediston in south Wiltshire.

Like Fyfield, Milton is absent from Domesday Book, although it is assumed that one of the two churches listed under Wootton Rivers in fact refers to Milton, and that, therefore, Wootton's apparently excessive totals include both Milton and Fyfield. However Milton, in the form Middelton ('the middle farm') makes its first appearance by name in 1195, and the affix Lilbourne is tagged to it soon afterwards to distinguish it from other Middletons. Logic dictates that the 'middle' refers to its position between Easton ('the east farm') and either Fyfield or Pewsey. Lilbourne is the family name of manorial owners from the twelfth to the fifteenth century. It was often written in the Latin form *de Insula Bona* ('of the good island'), and in fact refers to the family's place of origin, Lillebonne in Normandy, still a small town between Le Havre and Rouen.

Whatever Saxon Milton's relationship with Wootton Rivers, the first certain reference to its church, in 1195, tells us that it had by then been appropriated by Cirencester Abbey. The significance of this is that Cirencester had earlier acquired Pewsey church, so Milton may in the twelfth century have been a chapelry dependent on Pewsey. The architecture of the present church is mostly of the thirteenth century and later, but the imposts of the chancel arch are believed to be Norman. Cirencester retained the patronage until the reformation, and medieval features in the church include the Early English arcade and font, the Decorated chancel, and Perpendicular tower and some windows. Fragments of a wall-painting of the virgin and child are discernible near the pulpit, a few quarries of medieval glass remain in a chancel window, and there is the recessed arch of a tomb with encaustic floor tile fragments in the north aisle wall.

The church had become very dilapidated by the nineteenth century, to the extent that the pews were patched with wood from packing cases – one still bore the instruction, 'Wine With Care, This Side Up'. Church restoration took place in 1864 and 1875 and then, according to an inscription, 'the bones of unknown persons found within the walls of this church' were reburied under the nave floor. Galleries were removed at this time, but painted panels from the west gallery are preserved in the church, and one of the instruments formerly played by the village musicians there, an iron cello, is now in Devizes Museum. The well loved vicar at this period, who was patron of his own living, was John Henry Gale, who as Parson Gale achieved a reputation as a maverick magistrate and eccentric sportsman. The tombstone in the churchyard of a like-minded contemporary, George Carter, is a full two metres high, and lists his many hunting achievements.

The topography of Milton village is less straightforward than that of its neighbour Easton, with which at first glance it appears to share the same kind of north–south orientation. Easton, like Burbage, lay on a main north–south route, and has an essentially linear form; but the north–south village street of Milton seems to have had no more than local significance, and indeed was probably less important than a parallel track, known as the Packway, which forms the parish boundary between Milton and Easton, and leads to Wootton Rivers. Milton's street serves rather to connect two areas of settlement, an older nucleus of which the church, vicarage, King Hall and a small triangular green formed by the junction of three roads, are the key elements, and a later northward extension along the street to the Pewsey–Burbage road. The date of this expansion and its cause are not entirely clear – no buildings earlier than the seventeenth century have been identified in this area – but it may probably be linked to an unusual rise in population which occurred between the fourteenth and the seventeenth centuries. In 1377 the adult taxpaying population was recorded, as we have seen, as 67 in Milton and 40 in Fyfield; in 1676 the adult population of the whole parish was recorded as 362. There seems to be no evidence of expansion elsewhere in the parish (contraction is more likely, in fact), which suggests that Milton village witnessed a four- or five-fold increase in population (to roughly its present-day level) during the intervening three centuries. That the northward expansion occurred well before 1700 is also suggested by the presence of what appear to be the tofts of former buildings immediately opposite the main vista of the present Milton Manor, which was built between about 1710 and 1730. These buildings were presumably demolished at this period to improve the view.

Whenever it took place a degree of planning may perhaps be seen in the straight rear footpath running behind properties on the western side of the street, and by the narrow ginnel (opposite the village hall) which is known as the Drunge. This northern part of the street is lined with a mixture of eighteenth- and nineteenth-century cottages and several larger houses, including a Victorian farmhouse (Lawn Farm); and at the crossroads are twentieth-century council and private housing (including a former police house), and a large motor garage. A recreation ground on the eastern side of the street was given to the village by George Ferris, a well-known local land agent who owned Milton Manor from before 1870 until his death in 1929. Previous owners of this large brick Georgian manor house were members of the Richmond Webb and Somerset families.

Returning to the village nucleus we should examine its components in a little more detail. The church occupies an elevated position, which is exaggerated by the natural down-cutting of the street into the Greensand. From the churchyard may be seen the early-nineteenth century vicarage built on to a more modest, older house, and with an outbuilding against the street built of stone blocks. These are perhaps reused from an earlier building, as brick is the normal building material in Milton; indeed the tithe map of 1843 located brickmaking sites at Totteridge and Little Salisbury. A parsonage house and yard at Milton are recorded in a Cirencester document of about 1300, and these may well have occupied the same site. King Hall lies opposite. The present house is Victorian and was built by the owner of the rectory (or former monastic) manor, but its gates and some outbuildings are older, and there is a strong local tradition that it occupies the site of an important medieval house. In view of its position in the village, this may well be true; and if so it was possibly the manor house of the Lilbournes, which is mentioned in an inquisition of 1282 as possessing a courtyard, dovecote and garden, and in which the Lilbournes were permitted to build an oratory or private chapel in about 1300.

The Lilbournes were not, however, the only manorial lords in Milton. Two other manors, Milton Abbots and Milton Havering, existed in the middle ages, and were still referred to as late as 1781 in the enclosure award. 'Abbots' refers to Cirencester Abbey's rectorial holding, memory of which is perpetuated in the present Abbey Farm; and the de Havering family, who are recorded from the early fourteenth century, have given their name to Havering Lane and the seventeenth-century Havering House, which is perhaps on the site of their earlier manor house. Havering Lane meets the village street at what appears to have been a small triangular green, and here now are the village shop and the former school and schoolteacher's house. The school opened in 1878 and closed in 1985. Unusually in Pewsey Vale it was a board school, and replaced an earlier National school (recorded in a directory of 1859) on the same site. Instruction given in the National school was said to have been of an elementary kind, owing to the early age at which children were removed.

Like Fyfield, Milton conformed to the usual agricultural regime which prevailed around the edge of Salisbury Plain, and which Cobbett was able to record at first hand. The community's open fields lay around the village and extended southwards to the escarpment, with considerable arable also on Milton Hill. From an inquisition taken in 1628 we learn that the open fields were called East and West Sands, East and West Clay, and East and West Down. The latter, on Milton Hill, were still largely under strip cultivation until enclosure in 1781/2. Small enclosed meadows also existed in the seventeenth century, and closes adjacent to the village on its western side are remembered in the name 'Severals' (land held separately or apart) given to an area of predominantly twentieth-century housing, including council houses and a wooden bungalow, 'Dunmilken'. By the later eighteenth century a hill farm had been established in a lonely position on Milton Hill, and this now farms much of the downland in the southern part of the parish. A group of five Bronze-Age round barrows close to the farm complex was first noticed by Colt Hoare before 1810, and was the subject of a detailed excavation in 1958. The lower-lying farmland between the Pewsey–Burbage road and the foot of the downs was until recently controlled from Lawn Farm, but its farm buildings were sold for housing development, and farming operations are centred on Abbey Farm.

NOTES (location: SU1860; area: 1,411ha; population (2001): 512)

General: *VCH* 16, 165-81; Ferris, G, *A few notes on the history of Milton Lilbourne*, 1929 [typescript]

Roman pottery: *WANHM* 69, 67-84; Fyfield Manor: *Country Life* 30.8.1930, 260-5; Church: Tomlin, A, *Milton Lilbourne church*, 1994; Parson Gale: *Globe*, 31.5.1899 [copy in WANHS]; Ferris: *WANHM* 45, 104-5; Barrows on Milton Hill: *WANHM* 80, 23-96.

This account has benefited from discussions in 1991 with Betty Andrews and Frances Price.

Netheravon

EXPLORATION OF NETHERAVON should begin at the church. That is a sound rule for most villages, but at Netheravon the church makes an especially good starting point. No need to go inside, even (it is usually kept locked anyway) – most of what is important can be seen from the churchyard.

Netheravon church stands in parkland, and is approached along a fenced carriage drive, which is clearly a southward extension of the village street. A map of 1773 depicts this drive as a through route which looped around the church to cross the river by a bridge, and then doubled back to Choulston on the opposite bank. By 1790 it had been truncated to serve only the church and adjacent Netheravon House, in whose park it sits. And by 1817 a new road is shown skirting the northern edge of the park to a river crossing upstream from its predecessor. This is the line of the modern road to Airfield Camp, and it offers the best view of the church in its setting. Apart from Netheravon House, with its stables and appurtenances, there are no buildings within 200 metres of the church – an observation to which we shall return.

In 1907 part of a Roman villa, including evidence of a bath house, was discovered and excavated a short distance to the south of Netheravon House. Further evidence of a mosaic pavement was accidentally revealed nearby in 1936, and walls and Roman pottery were found in 1996 during a televised excavation. A second Roman villa, situated within an Iron-Age enclosure, was encountered in 1991, prior to laying a gas pipeline, about 1km south of the Netheravon House site, straddling the boundary with Figheldean. The juxtaposition of a Roman villa and a Christian church is

141

by no means unusual, in Wiltshire or elsewhere, and may in some instances suggest a continuity of a central place within a territory from the Roman to the Saxon period. Three pieces of evidence suggest that Netheravon was important as a Saxon estate centre.

First, in common with many early central places, it takes its name directly from its river. Northward up the valley the next high status settlement was probably also called 'Avon', and by the middle ages they were distinguished as 'Upper' (Upavon) and 'Lower' (Netheravon). Second, Netheravon's church is listed in Domesday as having possessed three estates, including the large holding of Stratton St Margaret near Swindon. Churches with substantial landholdings prior to the Norman conquest had usually functioned as Saxon minsters, or headquarters of missionary priests, and as such were generally established at important centres of population or local government. In the case of Netheravon the jurisdiction (known as its *parochia*) of the minster church probably coincided with the secular territory and hundred known as Elstub, which included the later parishes of Enford and Fittleton, as well as Netheravon itself. One tithing of Elstub, West Chisenbury, remained subordinate to Netheravon and its church until 1885. Third, as if to corroborate the documentary record, Netheravon church retains impressive late-Saxon features.

Several problems surround the church tower which cannot be entirely resolved. The narrow-arched openings to north and south are Saxon in character, and appear to have led into small chambers, known as porticus. If it was always a west tower, then the more elaborate arch, with carved capitals, on the western face may have emerged into a vestibule or narthex, perhaps housing the font. But it may have been originally a central tower, in which case this arch divided nave from crossing, and the porticus were rudimentary transepts. Whether or not the upper stages of the tower are contemporary with its base is uncertain. Indeed the dating of the earliest work is controversial. If it is Saxon, then stylistically it is very late, and perhaps just post-conquest. But Domesday Book in 1086 describes the church as ruined, unroofed, and on the point of collapse. All that can be said with any confidence is that its poor state in 1086 suggests that by then its period of high status as a minster church had passed, and that the Domesday description either did not apply to the tower, or that it was rebuilt in old-fashioned Saxon style very soon after 1086.

Whether still in ruins or newly rebuilt, Netheravon church quickly passed by royal grant to the chapter of the new cathedral at Old Sarum, where the income from it (somewhat depleted since the conquest) was used to create a prebend. The prebendaries and the dean of Salisbury, therefore, exercised jurisdiction over the church as a peculiar, including the appointment of vicars, throughout the middle ages and until peculiars were abolished in 1846. The present church retains medieval work of various periods, but it was substantially restored after 1839. Until then it had two porches, one of which at least existed in 1405 (the vicar at that time was reprimanded by the dean for using it as a stable and keeping his horse in the churchyard). The porches were removed during the Victorian restoration, which was executed with great zeal by a colourful vicar, Francis Jackson Blandy. He is said to have embarrassed himself by forgetting to invite the dean to the rededication service. Blandy died in 1866 when the village blacksmith performed an unsuccessful operation to remove a chicken bone from his throat.

Domesday Book describes Netheravon as a twenty-hide estate, and records an unusually large population of more than seventy families, as well as fifty-four staff on the demesne farm. This might represent a total population of 400–500, the same as in 1900. Ownership fragmented during the middle ages into at least five manors, as well as other estates, which were gradually reunited during the eighteenth and nineteenth centuries by the dukes of Beaufort, and later the Hicks Beach family. Netheravon House, the church's companion, is believed to stand on the site of one of the manor houses. It was begun in 1734 as a large villa or hunting box by the Beauforts, whose interest in Netheravon lay less in its potential as a typical sheep-and-corn chalkland parish than as a sporting estate for coursing and hawking on the downs. Stables were built at the same time, and the grounds had been laid out by 1755. But the Beauforts were not here for very long; by 1780 the house and principal manor had been acquired by William Beach, and it descended in his family for more than a century.

No map is known to exist before the creation of Netheravon House and park, so it is not possible to reconstruct the village topography and setting of the church prior to the eighteenth-century changes. However, the extent of new building elsewhere in the village during this century suggests that the park may have displaced earlier settlement around the church, thus leaving it in isolation. That isolation was accentuated in the nineteenth century. Maps of 1773 and 1790 show a built-up road, Netheravon Green Road, running across the park parallel to Kennel Row, as well as buildings along the lower end of what is now the drive to the church, and around an area of village green, with a pond, which is now crossed by the main road near the *Dog and Gun Inn*. Village earthworks west of the main road as it begins to climb the hill suggest earlier settlement in this area too. In fact we have the eye-witness testimony of William Cobbett, riding down the valley in 1826, that Netheravon had altered a good deal, and for the worse, since his previous visit eighteen years earlier. Buildings were in decay, the population was declining, the sites of large houses had become orchards, and even the roof of the dog kennel was falling in. Clearly the early-nineteenth century was a time of upheaval, partly no doubt as a result of the enclosure of the arable land and meadows in 1790, and one effect was to move the village focus northwards, creating the present linear settlement along High Street and Mill Road.

But that is not the end of the Netheravon House story. In 1898 the
Hicks Beach estate was compulsorily purchased by the government as
part of the War Office acquisitions of land for military training on
Salisbury Plain. The purchase was controversial at the time, and created a
storm in a political teacup, because to his opponents it appeared that Sir
Michael Hicks Beach (who happened to be Chancellor of the Exchequer)
had received a very favourable price for his land, by comparison with
other Wiltshire landowners and the depressed state of agricultural land
generally.

The army's interest in Netheravon, of course, was less in the house
than in the extensive chalk downland, which became part of the artillery
ranges. But the house, geared as it had been to sporting pursuits, was
well suited to a new career as the Cavalry School, which it became in
1904. Additional stabling and other accommodation was built in the
grounds, and it was this work which uncovered the Roman villa in 1907.
During the first world war the house was put to other uses, including
temporary quarters for a flying squadron, but the cavalry returned
between 1919 and 1922. From 1922, under various names, it was used
as a gunnery school, and was from 1948 until its closure in the mid-

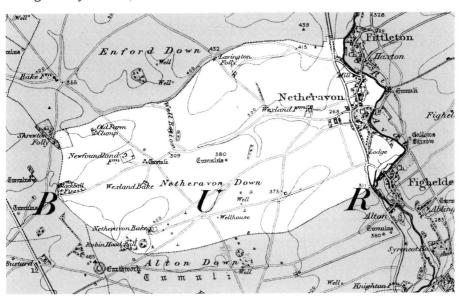

Ordnance Survey 1892 revision, 1 inch = 1 mile

1990s as the Support Weapons Wing of the School of Infantry. In the grounds, encircled by barbed wire, were houses, barracks and other buildings, and the house itself was used as the officers' mess. It is still in closely guarded military use, and is currently designated Avon Camp East and West.

Before we leave Netheravon church one other feature of its setting needs to be mentioned. That is the River Avon, which winds around the eastern edge of the park. The right to fish on 'Netheravon Water' has been controlled from the sixteenth century, and since this right was acquired by the army in 1898 the river ecology has been carefully stewarded and nurtured. Frank Sawyer, river keeper from 1928, became a legend among fishermen, not only for his innovative approach to keepering, but also for evolving the 'Netheravon' style of nymph fishing, which he expounded in his 1958 book, *Nymphs and the Trout*. He developed a method of cleansing the river using powdered chalk, and invented a humane vermin trap; he was also responsible for the construction of the lakes for rearing trout and grayling at Corfe End, opposite Haxton. It was said of him: 'The Avon was his river. He knew it as no other human being has ever done, or ever will!' And it was here, on the river at Choulston Shallows by Netheravon church, that he died in 1980.

Travelling northward on the A345 one does not receive a particularly favourable impression of Netheravon. After the barbed wire and armed checkpoints guarding the army camp at Netheravon House the road descends to cross the area of the former green, with barely a glimpse of the church. It then skirts the village, behind twentieth-century military, council and private housing, to leave the parish above Corfe End Lakes. The present alignment of the road, by-passing the village, is not shown on maps of 1817 and 1826, so may be attributed to the Kennett and Amesbury Turnpike Trust. This body (one of the latest in England) turnpiked the road in 1840, and this determined its future as the principal route up the Avon valley. It became more important after the military acquisitions, as downland routes of high antiquity were closed to traffic. Two of these led from Netheravon to Warminster and Devizes, and a third, the Wiltway, crossed the parish obliquely from Breaking Cross (the Mill Road junction) past Wexland Farm to Wilton, via Stonehenge.

The population of Netheravon rose significantly before World War One (from 440 in 1901 to 741 in 1911), and again between 1931 and 1951, when for the first time it exceeded 1,000. It is thus one of those Salisbury Plain villages which has become suburbanized by the army. New housing has sprung up in the area defined by High Street, Mill Road and the A345, and the older cottages along the High Street have been infilled by modern houses and a variety of commercial premises. Survivors from pre-1898 village days include the *Fox and Hounds* pub, with former malthouse and brewery behind; the old post office, which displays a clock on the wall outside; and the village school of 1846, now closed and replaced by a modern building nearby. It was by no means the first attempt to establish a school in the village. A quick-witted young clergyman who was later to make his name in literary society, one Sydney Smith, was curate of Netheravon from 1794-7, and persuaded the squire to subsidize a Sunday school where village children could learn to read and write. The project seems to have helped alleviate the tedium he experienced here. 'Nothing,' he wrote, 'can equal the profound, the unmeasurable, the awful dulness of this place, in the which I lye dead and buried.'

At the north end of the High Street the Primitive Methodist chapel of 1847 is hidden up an alleyway beside the village fish and chip shop (a sure sign of suburbanization), which also leads to a Baptist graveyard. The Particular Baptist chapel of 1820, which formerly stood there, was destroyed by fire in 1946. Beyond the Haxton turning, in Mill Road, the striking premises of a small independent brewer, Stonehenge Ales (formerly Bunce's), began life as a generator house to provide direct current electricity to the military camp at Netheravon House. It was built in 1914 on a former mill site, and operated until about 1925 employing water power from the river to drive a large turbine.

NOTES (location: SU1448; area: 1,429ha; population (2001): 1,064)
General: *VCH* 11, 165-81; Finch, R, *Netheravon with Fittleton: a short historical survey. . .* rev. ed. 1960.
Roman villa: *WANHM* 94, 148-53; Church: Taylor, H M and J, *Anglo-Saxon architecture*, 1, 1965, 456-9; Sawyer: Vines, F, *Frank Sawyer, man of the riverside*, 1984.

North Newton

T HE VILLAGE WHICH GAVE its name to the parish consists now of little
more than its medieval church sitting on a roughly circular, slightly
raised, churchyard, beyond a few cottages and a farm. Its name ('North'
merely distinguishes it from South Newton near Wilton, and Long
Newton near Tetbury) suggests that it was not the original settlement in
the parish, although it is mentioned in a charter of 892; if it was a satellite
from an earlier village, perhaps near Woodbridge (where pagan Saxon
burials were discovered in 1935) or Cats Brain (where aerial photographs
and fieldwalking suggest a Romano-British site), then the choice of site
was far from ideal.

It is here that the eastern headwater of the Avon is augmented by a
stream flowing south from Alton. Although normally placid and insignifi-

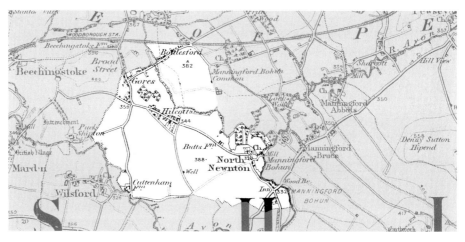

Ordnance Survey 1892 revision, 1 inch = 1 mile

148

cant this was not always so. John Leland, who visited the village in about 1545, explained the problem and its solution: 'there comythe a litle broke into Avon from northe west at the est ende of Newton churche. The course of it is latly changyd to the great commoditie of the village lyinge lowe,and afore sore troubled with water in wynter.' The parish boundary is faithful to the former course of the stream, which near the church is further disrupted by a mill leat. All the parish boundaries follow streams or ancient tracks; the western boundary is formed by the probable line of the Great Ridgeway, marked now by an overgrown double hedgerow.

North Newnton, like some of its small neighbours further west, is one of those Pewsey Vale parishes which does not enjoy a long strip of farmland extending up the escarpment on to the chalk downs. Perhaps as compensation it had as a detached portion of its parish an upland territory at Rainscombe north of Oare. But in the medieval period this was largely wooded, and seems not to have been exploited for the benefit of North Newnton. It was transferred to Wilcot parish in 1885. Despite their low-lying position, however, North Newnton and its tithing Hilcott had access to an outcrop of chalk, suitable for arable cultivation, in the shape of a low domed hill named Cats Brain (after the pebbly consistency of its soil).

John Leland's visit on his way between Marlborough and Devizes was probably not by chance. Since 934 the manors of North Newnton and Hilcott had belonged to Wilton Abbey, and a prebend had been created from this living (and that of another Wilton abbey parish, West Knoyle near Mere) by 1299. The prebendaries were intended to derive an income from the tithes of the parish, but serve as priests to the abbey; by Leland's time this office had become a sinecure, and it continued as such until 1869, more than three centuries after the abbey was dissolved. Leland was himself a priest, and was the last pre-dissolution holder of the prebend of North Newnton.

Despite its trouble with water the village of North Newnton was probably marginally larger in the middle ages than Hilcott. Hilcott is a linear village, possibly with a back lane to its south and a pond where the lane converges on the village street at its western end. Its name, first recorded in 1196, may mean a shed or hovel, but despite this modest beginning it gradually usurped North Newnton in importance, to the extent that in the nineteenth century there were plans to replace the parish church with a new building at Hilcott. In the event a school-cum-mission room was erected, which is now a private dwelling.

The tithing of Hilcott had its own common fields on the chalk and Greensand (distinguished in normal Pewsey Vale fashion as 'the Clays' and 'the Sands'). North Newnton also had common fields south of the village and extending beyond Woodbridge. These were farmed by the tenantry, but the lord's fields were elsewhere in the south-west corner of the parish, towards Wilsford. When the manor farmhouse, close to the church, burnt down in the 1530s it was not rebuilt *in situ*, but a new structure, Cuttenham Farm, replaced it next to its fields.

Curiously, the present population is concentrated in areas away from the historic settlements. Woodbridge, in the extreme south of the parish, was the name given to one of North Newnton's common fields by the sixteenth century, and so the bridge presumably existed by that date, replacing Stint's Ford mentioned in a Saxon charter as crossing the river in this area. The turnpiking and realignment of the Upavon road in 1840 probably led to the erection of the *Woodbridge Inn* at the cross-roads, and later housing has developed to the south and south-west.

Housing also developed in the nineteenth century along the roads in the extreme north-west of the parish, in the area formerly known as Gores, but which is now usually regarded as part of Bottlesford (Bottlesford was until recently in Manningford parish, and is discussed there). The stimulus in this area was not only the turnpike traffic, but also Honeystreet wharf on the Kennet and Avon Canal in Woodborough, and later the opening of Woodborough Station. Gores, therefore, enjoyed good communications and was well-placed to develop as a centre for the distribution of agricultural produce and supplies. The firm of R F Ford, established in the nineteenth century, still had its depot in the hamlet until the 1970s and the building survives.

The area around Hilcott and Gores, with an influx of population in the nineteenth century but no established church nearby, seems an obvious target for the dissenting evangelists; indeed Hilcott had been chosen in the 1790s as the centre for Independent missionary activity to Pewsey Vale, but the Independent and later Primitive Methodist bodies do not seem to have prospered, and their premises have long vanished. Not so the *Seven Stars* and the *Woodbridge Inn*, which stand at opposite ends of the parish and still carry on a thriving business.

NOTES: (location: SU1358; area: 558ha; population (2001): 415)
General: *VCH* 10, 126-36.
Saxon burials: *WANHM* 47, 265-7; Hedgerows: *WANHM* 84, 71-82; Farming: Straton, C R, *Survey of the lands of . . . Pembroke*, 1909, vol. 1, 284-98; Saxon charters: *WANHM* 19, 302-6.

Patney

H EMMED IN BY LARGER NEIGHBOURS to north and south, this small parish lies in the centre of the Greensand vale, with no access to chalk downland and no opportunity, therefore, to pasture large flocks of sheep. In the middle ages it was owned by St Swithun's Priory, Winchester, and farmed in tandem with Alton Priors, a nearby manor which lay almost entirely on chalk. Patney's boundaries, which existed in 963, are marked by streams forming part of the headwaters of the Salisbury Avon; they enclose a flat territory which nowhere rises more than 15m from its lowest point. The element *eg*, which has combined with a

personal name *Peattag* to form Patney, is thought to denote dry ground surrounded by marsh, and this is an appropriate description, perhaps referring especially to a low eminence in the north of the parish. Many examples of *eg* names date from the eighth century or earlier, and so Patney may have housed one of the earliest of the Saxon communities in

Pewsey Vale. Its population, in view of the parish's limited economic
potential, has probably always been small; figures for 1377 and 1676
suggest a total between 100 and 150, as today.

The present village, near the southern parish boundary, is ranged
along three roads which meet to form a small triangular green adjacent to
the church. Although Victorian, the church replaced a thirteenth-century
building on the same site, and the remains of a mill, perhaps successor to
a mill mentioned in the thirteenth century, lie nearby. The medieval
nucleus, therefore, was probably in this area. The best and oldest houses
in the village lie along the road running east from the church; the road
leading south was devoid of housing in 1773, according to a sketch map,
and that running north was fronted by houses whose crofts retained the
name of the adjoining field, Puckland (goblin's) field, and so may have
been fairly recent in 1773. North-west of the village, beyond the site of the
railway station, lay a group of fields – Great Hall, Little Hall, Hall's
Ground – with names which may point to an important building on the
site, earlier than or contemporary with the medieval village. This
suggestion is reinforced by aerial photography, which shows a complex of
linear features in the same area.

'All the parishioners live by agriculture,' returned an enquiry in
1341, and this must until the twentieth century have held true throughout
the village's history. Narrow water-meadows encircled the parish, and a
large area of meadow lay west of the village; but most land was under
arable cultivation, in two open fields in the thirteenth century, divided into
four by 1773 and enclosed in 1780. The west or clay field occupied the
chalk outcrop in the north and west of the parish, and the east or sand
field the Greensand between the village and Limber Stone Bridge. Two
smaller fields lay close to the village.

Patney received a non-agricultural boost to its economy in 1900,
with the opening of Patney and Chirton Junction Station north of the
village. Chirton was added in preference to the station's proposed name,
Patney Bridge, which it was felt might be confused with the rather better
known London station, Putney Bridge. A railway line from Pewsey to
Devizes had been laid out across the parish in 1862, but no station was
then built. However, with the construction of a new direct line to the west

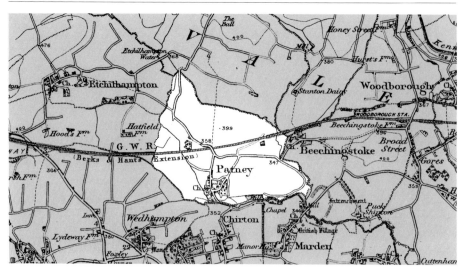

Ordnance Survey 1892 revision, 1 inch = 1 mile

of England via Westbury, branching off the old Devizes line about 1.5km north-west of Patney village, a junction station became necessary.

In its heyday it had four platforms (including one for military traffic) and ten staff. It became an important loading-point for liquid milk and other agricultural produce as well as passengers to and from Devizes. In 1938 no fewer than 32 trains stopped there every weekday. These included main line trains to London and the small local train to Devizes, which was nicknamed 'The Patney Puffer'. The branch line closed in 1966 and the station, apart from its footbridge, was demolished soon afterwards. The main line remains. The railway has affected the village plan, not only by encouraging housing to develop along the lane to the station, but also by extinguishing old routes which ran northwards to All Cannings and Stanton St Bernard; thus was disrupted still further a road pattern already contorted into awkward corners and blind lanes by changing agricultural land use and the need to pick a dry course through a marshy landscape.

NOTES (location: SU0758; area: 358ha; population (2001): 148)
General: *VCH* 11, 203-8.
1773 map: WSRO 490/1057; Station: Priddle, R, and Hyde, D, *GWR to Devizes*, 1996, 203-30.

Pewsey

KING ALFRED is Pewsey's presiding genius, and any account of the town must begin with him. His statue, which is what passers-by remember, was unveiled in June 1913, to commemorate the coronation of George V two years earlier. And his permanent presence at the hub of the community is a reminder of Pewsey's first mention in recorded history a millennium earlier, as one of more than sixty places which Alfred bequeathed in his will. But in fact a more significant royal figure in Pewsey's early history was Alfred's grandson, Edmund. In 940 he granted the royal estate to the new minster at Winchester which his father had founded, and which came later to be known as Hyde Abbey. The grant was quite specific – the income derived from Pewsey was to be used for the monks' clothing. Pewsey remained a possession of Hyde for six centuries, until the monastery was dissolved in 1539.

Included with the royal grant of 940 was a description of the bounds of the estate, and these have been shown to coincide in virtually every particular with the modern parish boundary. The territory thus defined straddles the Greensand vale of the Avon headwaters (to which Pewsey gave its name), and extends on to the chalk escarpments both north and south, from Martinsell to Pewsey Hill and beyond. Only Pewsey and its neighbour Milton Lilbourne bestride the vale in this way. Pewsey's Saxon boundary follows footpaths, hedgelines and present-day roads, including Hare Street and Sunnyhill Lane; included as landmarks are barrows which survive on West Everleigh Down, *Ebban broc*, which is probably the modern Avebrick, and *Hremnes geat*, which must be related to the name (meaning 'raven') underlying Rainscombe.

155

Other information about the Pewsey of Alfred and Edmund can be deduced from names and archaeology. The second element of Pewsey's name, from Old English *eg*, denotes an island, or dry land surrounded by

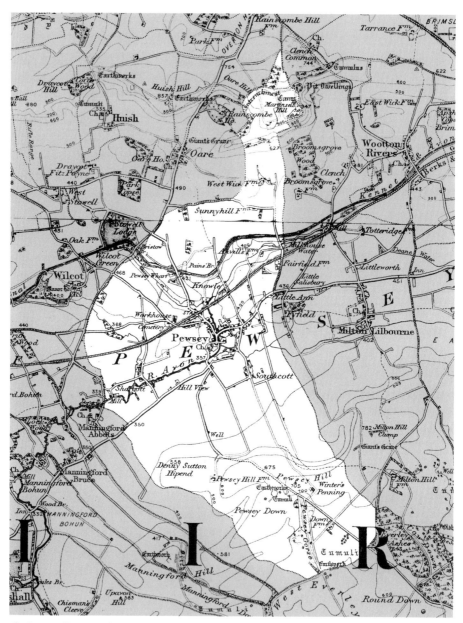

Ordnance Survey 1892 revision, 1 inch = 1 mile

marsh. It often implies an early settlement, and in this instance seems to
be describing the present centre of Pewsey, with its formerly branching
streams of the Avon, and the knoll now occupied by the church. The
rector in 1890 was told that until the eighteenth century the river divided
above the mill (north of the present bridge), and a branch flowed under
the site of the former *Phoenix Hotel*. The first element of Pewsey is a
personal name, probably *Pefe*, and it has been suggested that he may have
been a member of an Anglian, rather than a Saxon, family which settled
in the area, since a pocket of other names of Mercian or Anglian character
is found nearby. A gold pendant found in 1986 near Brunkard's Yard in the
centre of Pewsey is probably of seventh-century date, and it is perhaps not
coincidental that its design has parallels with pendants found in East Anglia.

By the time that the estate was granted to Hyde Abbey in 940 it is
likely that a settlement on the site of modern Pewsey had existed for
several centuries. The abbey's estate was large, thirty hides and seven
mills in 1086, and Pewsey itself was a place of some importance. It seems
to have had a minster church by 940, which did not initially pass to Hyde
Abbey, but had a separate endowment of land. Sarsen foundations
discovered to the west of the present church during Victorian restoration
may have belonged to this Saxon minster. And there must have been a
river-crossing near the present bridge, which carried a Saxon main road,
or *herepath*, known to have existed between Burbage and Manningford. It
probably followed much the same line as the present A345 / B3087.

But *Pefe's* island was not the earliest focus of settlement on the
Pewsey estate. Martinsell, its northern limit, is an impressive Iron-Age
hillfort, which has also yielded evidence of occupation, and perhaps a
pottery kiln site, in use during the Roman period. It stands in the same
relationship to Saxon Pewsey as Chisbury hillfort to Bedwyn, some 12km
to the east. And like Chisbury, Martinsell's inclusion within the bounds of
the Pewsey estate was presumably with an eye to defence, as a refuge if
the valley settlement should ever come under threat. Later it was used as
the venue for a hill fair, which continued until 1860, and for a Palm
Sunday custom of tobogganing down the hillside on the skulls of horses. It
also contained a barn and shepherds' cottages, next to a dewpond and
Scots pines. Stukeley described the dewpond in 1723, which he wrongly

believed to be fed by spring water. The pines suggest that it was used by drovers. The last cottage continued to be occupied by a shepherd and his wife until at least 1910; it was said to be the highest house in Wiltshire, and there was a belief that it was visible from out at sea. That may be far-fetched, but Martinsell's humped form is a landmark from many places in Wiltshire; on a clear day, for example, it can be seen 30km away across Salisbury Plain from the A303 west of Winterbourne Stoke.

Pewsey Hill, with its curiously misnamed spur (apparently the result of a map-reading error), Denny Sutton Hipend, rises from the Greensand to the south of Pewsey, corresponding with Martinsell on the north. Lower and less commanding, its escarpment is nevertheless dramatically steep, and it displays Wiltshire's second youngest white horse, which was cut in 1937 to commemorate George VI's coronation. The trotting horse replaced an earlier beast, probably of eighteenth-century origin, which could then still just be discerned a little below its successor, and to the right. On the downland above these horses has been found evidence of early farming, in the form of Iron-Age or Romano-British circular enclosures. They may represent farmsteads established on marginal land, and colonized from permanent valley settlements. Such a settlement has been excavated in a field significantly named Black Patch (also known as Blacknall Field), at the foot of Denny Sutton Hipend. Not only was it occupied during the Iron Age and later, but in the fifth–sixth centuries the site was reused as a major pagan Saxon cemetery. Over 100 individual graves were excavated, making it one of the two most important such sites in Wiltshire. Scatters of Iron Age and Roman pottery in Southcott Field and elsewhere hint at other farming communities below Pewsey Hill.

Pewsey's medieval history is uneventful. It belonged throughout, as we have seen, to Hyde Abbey, but there seems to have been no attempt to turn the village at the centre of its large rural manor into a small town. The name 'Market Place' which is given to the street beside King Alfred and Phoenix Row probably dates from the urbanisation of Pewsey after the canal put the village on the map in 1810. Phoenix Row bears the date 1823, and a market grant was obtained for Pewsey in 1824. The market for this end of the vale in medieval times was at Upavon. Hyde Abbey did, however, manage to secure control of Pewsey church, which had not

been part of the original grant. During the twelfth century the church was
granted to Cirencester Abbey, which was presumably responsible for
rebuilding it in late Norman style. But by 1306 the monks of Hyde held
the advowson, and the present chancel, which is of this period, may be
attributable to them.

Although medieval Pewsey did not graduate to a town, it boasted a
considerable population. There were over 70 tenants at Domesday, and
probably a total population in the fourteenth century of between 400 and
500. This may have risen above 1,000 by 1676. By 1545 we find the
large parish subdivided for taxation purposes, with entries for *Chercot*
[East and West Sharcott] and Southcott, and for Kepnal. But these were
probably much older hamlets; they all occur by name in thirteenth-
century sources and as tithings had their own open fields and agricultural
regimes. West Wick, below Martinsell, is another example of an outlying
farmstead or hamlet, and traces of a medieval settlement have been
detected from aerial photographs, lying between the present West Wick
House and Sunnyhill Farm. Manningford Abbots, too, was sometimes regarded as a dependent hamlet of Pewsey. In fact, though very small, it was
a separate parish, but it too belonged to Hyde Abbey, and there was a
tendency to administer the two properties together. During the seventeenth
century informal settlements sprang up on outlying areas of waste within
Pewsey parish, including World's End along the Wilcot road, and Raffin
and Swan south of the main settlement (the latter named from a pub).

Pewsey's large arable fields lay for the most part on the chalk loam in the south of the parish, sloping up to Pewsey Hill (there was also some arable beneath Martinsell in the north). William Cobbett's description, as he looked down on the vale from Milton Hill in 1826, admirably summarized the centuries-old regime:

> The shape of the thing is this: on each side downs, very lofty and steep in some places, and sloping miles back in other places. . . From the edge of the downs begin capital arable fields generally of very great dimensions, and, in some places, running a mile or two back into little cross valleys, formed by hills of downs. After the corn-fields come meadows, on each side, down to the brook, or river. The farm-houses, mansions, villages, and hamlets, are generally situated in that part of the arable land which comes nearest to the meadows.

Beyond the river, north of the village, lay Pewsey Common, a large area of pasture ground on Greensand. The River Avon above Pewsey is too insignificant in itself to support floated water meadows, but they were nevertheless achieved from water supplied from ponds fed by springs. After water meadows became redundant in the later-nineteenth century the springs served watercress beds, and later a trout farm. But the meadows have survived, and since 1980 they have been protected as a nature reserve, known as Jones's Mill. They are a rare example in Wiltshire of a fenland habitat, which supports a wide variety of flora and fauna, and may be visited by the public. Jones's Mill was a medieval watermill which had vanished by the sixteenth century, by when the land associated with it had been converted to meadows. Nearby a short-lived windmill was built around 1800, one of two known to have existed during the nineteenth century in the north of the parish; it fed water to the newly built canal, and so was technically a windpump.

In 1770, after a succession of post-medieval owners, the manor of Pewsey was acquired by St Thomas's Hospital in London. This marked the beginning of an innovative period in Pewsey's history. The new landlords set in train the enclosure of the common fields, which involved the first Parliamentary enclosure award (1777) for anywhere in Pewsey Vale. At the same time the parish had an interesting rector, Joseph

Townsend, who started and ran a free medical service for the poor, and developed a practical interest in the problems of poor relief. A remarkable individual, nearer seven than six feet tall, his accomplishments included inventing a preparation ('Townsend's mixture') for the treatment of syphilis, taking to the road as one of the Countess of Huntingdon's itinerant preachers, helping William Smith to establish the chronological sequence of geological strata, and anticipating Malthus's theory of population increase. He wrote an account of his travels in Spain, studied languages, was a friend of Jeremy Bentham, and published a defence of the accuracy of the Old Testament account of the flood, under the title, *The Character of Moses as an Historian*. In 1773 by forcing each of his parishioners to swear their innocence while touching the face of a murder victim, he detected the culprit – who was subsequently executed and hanged in chains on Pewsey Down.

Townsend was rector of Pewsey for more than fifty years, from 1764 to 1816, and lived in the smart Georgian and earlier house known as the Old Rectory, which is approached across a bridge from Church Street. His house later became the offices of the Pewsey Rural District Council. In 1785 he incurred the wrath (and possibly the physical violence) of a parishioner by inviting a Methodist to preach from his pulpit. Among his many good works on behalf of the village was the improvement of roads, and the building of a bridge across the river to connect High Street with River Street and the market place area. If we are to believe the claim that prior to its construction in 1797 (the datestone survives) the river in winter had proved an almost total obstruction to travellers and had often proved fatal to cattle, then he clearly deserved the epithet by which he was known, 'the colossus of roads'. An extraordinary man.

It was perhaps inspired by his researches into the links between population and poor relief that in 1797 the churchwardens drew up a list of all the poor in the parish, 332 individuals, almost 30% of the total population. Among the categories used were: cripple; drunkard; insolent and saucy; lazy; sickly; thief; and bastard. And comments against individuals included: 'children brought up in idleness', 'silly', 'sorry dog', 'a bad one', and 'to some a convenient lady'. Plans were afoot at the time to provide a workhouse for the parish, and in the early nineteenth century the three-storeyed thatched houses in Phoenix Row fulfilled this function. The handsome union workhouse, which in the twentieth century became a colony for mental defectives and later a psychiatric hospital, was built in 1836 as part of the reorganization of indoor relief under the new poor law. Its importance to Pewsey lay not only in the social service it performed; it also established the town (for it was at last taking on urban trappings) as a minor centre of local government. By virtue of its role as the head of a poor law union it became after 1872 the centre of a rural district, and only lost its administrative importance in 1974. Pewsey Hospital continued until closure in 1995; some buildings remain, but most of the site has been redeveloped for housing.

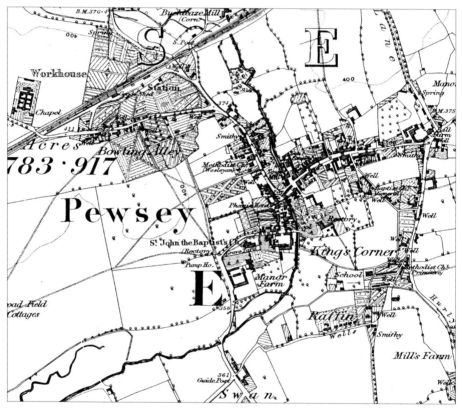

Ordnance Survey 1886 survey, 6 inch = 1 mile

After Townsend's death in 1816 the earls of Radnor presented to the living, and two of their nineteenth-century appointments were members of their own family, the Bouveries. The name is recalled now in Pewsey by the Bouverie Hall of 1989 (replacing its predecessor of the same name in River Street, which was then demolished). Likewise the phoenix, the badge of an earlier landowning family, the Dukes of Somerset, is commemorated in what was generally regarded as the town's principal inn. The Hon. Frederick Bouverie served as rector until his sudden death in 1857 (occasioned by seeing his badly injured son return from the Indian mutiny), and he seems to have followed Townsend's example in pastoral welfare. He is said to have sent a team of oxen with a waggon to Salisbury twice each year to collect provisions for the poor. And many years later, in 1879, one of his daughters, Barbara Haughton, published a short book of vivid reminiscences of Pewsey characters from her childhood – their dignity in the face of abject poverty, their mysterious illnesses, and best of all their broad dialect. In fact Pewsey seems to have been regarded as the last bastion of the pure Wiltshire idiom, since in 1903 a Swedish professor published a technical treatise on the dialect of Pewsey, based on his researches among old men in the workhouse, and the 'worst speakers' at the National school.

The second Bouverie appointment, Bertrand, was rector from 1880 to 1910. He was responsible for restoring the church, and bore most of the cost himself. Above the organ chamber, north of the chancel, he incorporated part of the medieval roof from the refectory of Ivychurch Priory, which had stood on the Radnor estate near Salisbury, and was demolished in 1888. He also carved the font cover himself, and painted angels on the walls of the nave and chancel arch, although these have now been removed. The altar rails which he carved began life adorning the deck of a Spanish ship of the line captured by Lord Nelson in 1797 – Bouverie's wife was a daughter of the third earl Nelson.

Pewsey's population rose steadily after 1800, to a peak of a little over 2,000 in 1861. This is partly explained by the workhouse, and by the attempt to make the town a marketing and shopping centre, helped no doubt by Townsend's bridge and road improvements. But the real stimulus to growth was the construction, between 1807 and 1810, of the Kennet and Avon Canal. This waterway linked Bristol and London, and during the three decades of its success (before the railway era) it not only supplied Pewsey Vale with cheap coal and building materials, but also offered farmers an easy outlet for their produce. A wharf was constructed where the Marlborough road crossed the canal, about 1km north of Pewsey, and gave the little community the access to the outside world which, by-passed by the turnpikes, it had hitherto lacked.

But for many Pewsey residents it was to be another forty years before they ventured very far from home. Barbara Haughton, in her book of reminiscences, wrote that it was the Great Exhibition of 1851 that gave them their first experience of London. The younger and stronger men, she recalled, walked all the way there and back, but others, seized by a perfect mania to see the wonder for themselves, went by train. At that date the nearest railway, opened in 1847, stopped short at Hungerford, but in 1862 the line was extended westward along Pewsey Vale to Devizes. A station was built at Pewsey, north of the town in an area already colonized by cottages and known as World's End, and this has remained open; since 1906 it has been served by trains running on the main line between London and the West Country via Westbury.

Another mode of travel also became significant during the later nineteenth century. Ever since Alfred Reynolds had ridden a penny-farthing bicycle from Pewsey to Hyde Park Corner and back in less than a day during the 1860s, cycling developed as a popular pastime, and a Pewsey Vale Cycle Club was formed. It was during a conversation in Goddard's cycle shop in 1898 that the idea of a carnival was mooted. The first carnival, timed to coincide with the annual Pewsey Feast in mid-September, consisted of about a dozen decorated bicycles riding around the town. The riders raised a sum of money (the amount has been disputed, but is now thought to have been £5 4s. 7½d) in aid of Savernake Cottage Hospital. After this humble beginning the Pewsey and District Carnival became an essential landmark in the vale's calendar. During the 1920s it reached 'stupendous' proportions, with eleven special trains running into Pewsey station. It remains a spectacular event, which attracts up to 100 floats, and thousands of spectators and participants; the centenary carnival, in 1998, was an occasion for particular celebration.

Because Pewsey, historically speaking, is not a town, its centre does not have a particularly urban feel, and most of its prominent buildings have arrived since the canal. A recent locally-produced book describes it first as a village, and then as 'a vibrant town with an active citizenry' in successive sentences. Certainly it now has many urban attributes, including a comprehensive school (opened as secondary modern in 1958), a supermarket (1996), and now an active heritage centre, which occupies the substantial Victorian stone-built premises of a former iron and brass foundry (begun by George Whatley in 1875). Extensive housing estates have been built to the north and west during recent decades, and major redevelopments in the centre (involving the demolition of a motor garage, the old Bouverie Hall, a former cinema and the bus station) have taken place since 1989.

Pewsey's street plan too, with awkward bends around the church, is that of a village away from main roads, and has probably been influenced by areas of former marshy land bordering the river. A map of 1773 depicts houses along Ball Road to Southcott, and along Wilcot Road, in addition to the three built-up streets (High, North and River) later to be linked by Townsend's bridge. Anyone troubling to explore Pewsey beyond the gaze of Alfred's statue, however (he now stares defiantly at the fire station), will be amply rewarded. Many older cottages survive (in Raffin Lane and Ball Road, for example), there are notable timber-framed houses at Ball Corner, and another in Church Street next to the church. This is Court House, probably a former parsonage house, which was later occupied by a lawyer; it is said that he was responsible for naming the cottages opposite his house (which are dated 1734) Quality Court, after the buildings in London's Chancery Lane.

NOTES (location: SU1660; area: 1,909ha; population (2001): 3,237)
General: *VCH* 16, 181-207; Bouverie, B P, *A few facts concerning the parish of Pewsey . . .*, 1890; Haughton, B, *In a Wiltshire valley*, 1879 (reprinted 1980, 1993); Gee, T R, *A brief history of the parish of Pewsey*, 1957 [typescript in T]; Henderson, P, *Pewsey through the ages*, 3 parts, 1993-4; Duckenfield, M, *Pewsey village trail* [1993].
Saxon period: *RMCNHS* 81, 41-8; Pendant: *WANHM* 85, 149-50; Martinsell: *RMCNHS* 73, 48-70; Townsend: *Proc Royal Soc Medicine* 62, 471-8 [copy in T]; *WANHM* 87, 132-3; Poor relief: WSRO 493/49-50; Dialect: Kjederqvist, J, *The dialect of Pewsey (Wiltshire)*, 1903; Church: guide by J C Day, 1988; Carnival: Pewsey Carnival Committee, *Afloat in time: a people's history*, 1999.

Potterne

EVERYONE WHO HAS TRAVELLED out of Devizes on the Salisbury road remembers Potterne. The main road sweeps in two tight curves beneath a stately church perched high above it, and opens into a village street graced by Porch House, one of the most memorable houses in Wiltshire. Narrow intricate lanes, with deep cuttings and sharp turns, and a confusion of building styles and sizes, make Potterne an intriguing village to explore. Its unseen history contains other delights and confusions.

In June 1982 a gravedigger working in Potterne cemetery (north of the village in an area known as Blackberry) uncovered a gold bracelet which proved to be of Late Bronze Age date. Further graves produced artefacts of a similar period, which led to a series of excavations in the area between 1982 and 1985. It became clear that Potterne cemetery lay within an enormous prehistoric midden, approximating to a modern land-fill site, of some 3.5ha, which continued in use for five or six centuries, from about 1200 to 600BC. The principal activity of the people who created the deposit was cattle-rearing, and the site included abundant evidence not only of the waste products associated with husbandry, but also indications that pounds, fences, working areas and huts had been built at various times on parts of the site.

Such a specialist community, perhaps with trading and social links over a wide area, and flourishing on the same site for so long, was at the time of its discovery unique, and has yielded invaluable evidence about the Late Bronze Age and Early Iron Age. Just as the excavation of the Early Iron Age village at All Cannings Cross seventy years earlier provided the 'type-site' or point of reference for a class of archaeological site, so the

Potterne deposit has done the same, and other examples have now been found or re-interpreted, including the midden at East Chisenbury (in Enford) and All Cannings Cross itself (both within the area covered by this volume).

The prehistoric site at Potterne has raised many interesting questions, and it seems likely that it was the venue for ceremonial or trading occasions, drawing people to it from a wide area. Its eventual demise may have occurred when social changes later in the Iron Age produced a more stay-at-home, territorial society, which built enclosures and defensive hillforts. The focus of activity may then have moved away from Potterne, and by the Roman period we find the area being farmed from a settlement at Rangebourne, close to the modern parish's northern boundary with Devizes.

An estate called Potterne was reputedly given to Sherborne Abbey by King Offa in the second half of the eighth century. This presumably was the same as the property eventually inherited by the bishops of Salisbury from their predecessors the bishops of Sherborne. In later centuries the bishop's estate of Potterne (with West Lavington) was reckoned as a half-hundred, also known as Bishop's Rowborough. King's Rowborough, from which it had been separated, comprised the Cheverells and Market Lavington. Rowborough, therefore, 'the land of the rough barrow,' may represent a very early territorial division, which was split by the granting away of Potterne in the eighth century. The bishop's estate at Potterne was always larger than the modern parish. It included Worton and Marston (created separate parishes in 1866) to the west, and on the northern edge it abutted another episcopal estate, Cannings. Along the boundary Devizes ('the dividing line') was built in the late-eleventh or twelfth century, and so Potterne sacrificed part of its territory to the new castle, park and town.

Although both the name and parts of the street pattern are undoubtedly Saxon in origin, the only tangible relic of the period is the font, now in the parish church, which has around its rim in Latin the verse from Psalm 42, which in Nahum Tate's familiar translation begins, 'As pants the hart for cooling streams . . .' The lettering of the inscription dates it to the tenth century or earlier, and the font is thought to have originated

in an earlier timber church which lay south of the present churchyard, at
the back of Porch House garden. This church site was discovered and
excavated in 1962 (the then owner of Porch House happened to be an
archaeologist!), and was found to have a square nave surmounted by a
tower, and with a chancel and baptistery. Nearby in 1975 and 1980 other
wooden structures were investigated, and are believed to have been the
priest's house and stables.

A similar complex of wooden buildings must have existed in many
Saxon communities, to be replaced by the first stonebuilt church after the
Norman conquest. At Potterne the wooden church may have continued in
use until the twelfth century. The excavator considered that the name
Potterne, 'the pot house,' might be a reference to the baptistery building,
containing as it did a large pot-shaped font. One wonders, however,
whether the pots referred to may be the masses of sherds recovered
whenever the prehistoric midden was disturbed.

Medieval Potterne was an important place. In 1091 a block of
property in the village was used to endow a prebend in the new Old
Sarum cathedral, and so was controlled by the dean of Salisbury who
built a house in Potterne. In 1254, by an exchange, the bishop acquired
the prebend from the dean. The bishop may also have had a house in the
village in the twelfth century, and from 1254 until the fifteenth century,
when the manor was leased to private landlords, he was in total control of
the estate. Several bishops, especially between the thirteenth and early
fifteenth centuries, were frequent residents in the village, and a heraldic
roundel bearing the arms of Robert Hallam (bishop from 1407–17) was
found at Potterne in 1983. The most important building in the village was
the bishop's residence, which was perhaps built by Elias de Dereham, the
supposed architect of Salisbury Cathedral, in the thirteenth century, and
enlarged in the fourteenth. It lay on Courthill, north of the lane to Worton,
on the edge of a Greensand ridge overlooking the village. It was
demolished from the 1640s and 1650s onwards and nothing remains on
the site above ground, although many buildings in the present village
have obviously benefited from this supply of second-hand ashlar masonry.
Small-scale excavations were carried out in 1961 and 1973, but missed
the principal buildings. Their location and extent in Great Orchard, north-

east of Courthill House, were confirmed by a geophysical survey conducted in 2001.

The palace had its own chapel, but the parish was also provided with a fine new church in the thirteenth century, contemporary with Salisbury Cathedral and similar in architectural detail. It was not the immediate successor to the Saxon timber building; a previous church occupied either the same site, or, according to local tradition, it may have been further west, near the village hall in Mill Road. The bishop also created for himself a park on land south-east of the village, beyond Potterne Wick, which was in existence by 1353. Potterne Park Farm remains as a reminder in the middle of this area, and nearby, in trees, is a bluebell-covered moat, which presumably surrounded one of the park lodges.

Another episcopal survival may be the *George and Dragon Inn*, om the cemtre of the village, which has been shown to incorporate a fifteenth-century cruck construction encased within an eighteenth-century brick rebuilding. It may have been built by the bishop to accommodate visitors to his manor. Its counterpart across the street, the famous timber-framed Porch House, is probably also a legacy of episcopal control. It seems to have been built during the 1480s, probably as the headquarters for the bishop's staff after the manor and associated buildings had passed to private lessees.

Its later career has been as the home of a farming family until the eighteenth century, then a family of clothiers, a short period in the 1840s and 1850s as the *White Horse Inn*, before it was bought in 1872 by the artist George Richmond, who began a programme of drastic restoration. The most colourful twentieth-century occupant was Mavis de Vere Cole, from 1941-7, who was divorced by her husband, the archaeologist Sir Mortimer Wheeler, after he discovered her there with a lover in 1941. The artist Augustus John was also a frequent visitor. In 1947 she bought Pilgrim Cottage in Chilsbury Lane, from where in 1954 she was removed to Holloway Prison, having shot and wounded another lover after a tipsy evening in the *George and Dragon*.

Under its ecclesiastical landlords Potterne developed into a thriving agricultural community. The Domesday manor, which doubtless encom-

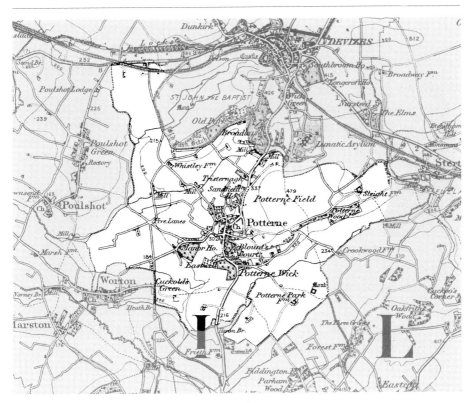

Ordnance Survey 1892 revision, 1 inch = 1 mile

passed a greater area than the modern parish, was large and populous, with extensive woodlands and pasture. The principal area of arable cultivation lay east of the village, on the large dome-shaped hill still known as Potterne Field. Here lower chalk caps the Greensand, in contrast to the heavy and marshy Gault clays stretching westwards from the village. Potterne Wick ('Potterne dairy-farm') and Sleight ('sheep-walk') Farm south and east of Potterne Field suggest the land use here. Woodland probably existed north and west of the village as well as in the area of Potterne Park and on the southern slope of the Greensand ridge, where Potterne Wood still remains. Water from the Greensand drained in streams across the clay and powered mills in the north-west of the parish.

The components of the village plan are not easy to determine. The present main road (A360) is an awkward superimposition, and presumably owes its pre-eminence to the turnpiking of the Devizes–Lavington

road in 1750/1. An earlier north–south route must have passed to the east
of the village, continuing due south at the Butts along Silver Street, in one
of the many deep Greensand cuttings, and then finding its way by one of
several tracks to Potterne Wick and Lavington. Another road south from
Devizes skirted Old Park and Hartmoor, passing west of the village to Five
Lanes and Worton. This was the route taken in 1712 by Mrs Sarah Hickes
on her way from Avebury to Tinhead; near Five Lanes she found 'a great
depe myer acrosse the lane' which resulted in her manservant having 'a
very daingous fall' after his horse had floundered in the mud and broken
its tackle. Similar problems must have endangered any traveller who
ventured off the greensand on to the clay. Main roads apart, the streets of
the village suggest a basically north–south alignment along the line of
High Street and Duck Street, with roads and lanes converging on both its
northern and southern ends. East of this axis, on the better drained slope,
lies the church, Porch House and the site of the timber church; west of the
street most of the properties share a common rear boundary line. Irregular
clusters of buildings surround the northern and southern foci. Away from
the village the parish contains various minor settlements mentioned in
medieval documents, but only Rangebourne, Blount's Court and
Woodbridge appear to have achieved any kind of autonomy.

To the eighteenth- and nineteenth-century traveller Potterne
presented a rather drab and rough appearance. 'Pottern is only remarkable for giving its name to the hundred, which shows that anciently it was
the most noted town in it, how mean so ever it be now', remarked a
guidebook of 1731, and Cobbett, a century later, described it as 'now a
mere ragged village'. The inhabitants earned a reputation for drunken and
quarrelsome behaviour, and were known as 'Potterne lambs', either
ironically or because the policeman stationed to control them was
Superintendent Wolfe. 'They were characterised by a sort of spontaneous
volition which vented itself in one direction or another, and not always in
accord with decorum and good manners,' wrote an old inhabitant. A
government report of 1834, after noting that they were 'a very dis-
contented and turbulent race', described how the paupers of Potterne had
clubbed together to buy a legal handbook so as to be able to bewilder the
magistrates. In 1857 a skimmington, involving a rough music procession

with obscene effigies of a disapproved couple, took place over three evenings. The proceedings degenerated into a riot, and turned on policeman Wolfe; as a result six 'lambs' stood trial and were bound over to keep the peace.

High spirits and an unkempt appearance are not noticeable in Potterne today, which has become an attractive and desirable place to live. Modern housing estates north of the village, in the Butts area, and in the grounds of Blount's Court, have boosted the population, which has practically doubled since 1801. It provides all the services – shops, schools, public houses, chapel and village hall – which might be expected of a large village, and has preserved a good blend of architectural styles in a varied and interesting landscape.

NOTES (location: ST9958; area: 1,245ha; population (2001): 1,570)
General: *VCH* 7, 207-17; *WANHM* 16, 245-86; WSRO 1172/193; Smith, T, *In a Wiltshire village: Potterne 1850-1900*, new ed. 1993.
Prehistoric site: *WANHM* 78, 31-40; *WANHM* 79, 101-8; Lawson, A J, *Potterne 1982-5: animal husbandry in later prehistoric Wiltshire*, 2000; Timber church complex: *WANHM* 59, 116-23; *WANHM* 83, 57-69; Font: Taylor, H M, *Anglo-Saxon architecture*, vol. 3, 1978, 1064-5; Bishop's residence: *WANHM* 69, 85-96; *WANHM* 95, 274-8; Roundel: *WANHM* 89, 136-8; George and Dragon: *WANHM* 77, 87-92; Porch House: Haycock, L, *Porch House, Potterne*, 1992; Mavis Cole: Owen, R, *Beautiful and beloved*, 1974; 1712 journey: *WANHM* 57, 225-6; Skimmington: *WANHM* 83, 147-54.

Poulshot

TIS A WETT, DIRTY PLACE, wrote Aubrey. This is no longer true, of course – Poulshot is one of the more attractive of the clayland villages between Potterne and Steeple Ashton – but there are still suggestions of its seventeenth-century squalor. A stagnant pond lurks in an odd corner of the green, and the altered road line near Manor Farm (a little south of the green), has been built up to avoid a very muddy precursor. Poor drainage and a defective water supply (around 1650 regarded as mineral waters but never developed commercially) led to typhoid in 1883; throughout the winter pools of water stood over the rectory lawns in the nineteenth century.

The village lies on a plateau of Greensand, slightly raised above the level of the clay surrounding it on south and east. Its boundaries run north to the main Devizes–Melksham road at the foot of Caen Hill, where a toll-house survived until demolished in 1968. The parish has a flat appearance, although the north-west is undulating, and Barley Hill Lane makes quite a steep descent towards Summerham Bridge on the parish boundary. The village is ranged around a large rectangular green, its north-eastern corner now enclosed, and with a minor road running diagonally across it, approximately north–south. Irregularities at both the northern and southern ends of the green suggest that former encroach-ments have been swept away. They are absent on a map of 1773, which does however mark a ribbon of houses along the road south of the green, few of which survive.

The buildings around the green include several farmhouses, an attractive village school built in about 1884, closed in 1974 and converted to a village hall, and a wooden chapel-of-ease of 1897 (now disused) practically in the garden of the curious old rectory of 1781. There had been a charity school in the village since 1733, and a forerunner of the rectory had been occupied by Isaac Walton, son of the angler, and rector from 1680 to 1719. A wide lane runs parallel with the green some 200m to the west and driftways feed into the green on either side.

Regular village greens of this magnitude are rare in Wiltshire (although a large green at Marden, in this volume, was built over in the nineteenth century); and Poulshot is the more unusual in that the green seems not to have been the original, or at least not the principal, focus of settlement. The church lies 1km south-west, near the parish boundary and on the clay, and is accompanied by a farmhouse and outbuildings, with a few other houses nearby. The explanation given for this inconvenient position – that it in fact also served the neighbouring settlements of Worton, Marston and Bulkington – is implausible (Bulkington had its own chapel, attached to Keevil, and Worton and Marston were connected by a causeway to their parish church at Potterne). Irregularities in the surrounding fields suggest that an earlier Poulshot lay around its church. A circular feature south of the church may have been a moat enclosing a medieval house ('wrought stones' were dug up there in the nineteenth century) or perhaps a duck decoy; and nearby are the remains of a possible medieval fishpond. The church itself, which contains work of the twelfth century and later, was severely damaged by fire in 1916 when a stove pipe overheated, set fire to the roof and destroyed the nave. The tower and chancel were saved, but the nave was not rebuilt for a decade.

The documentary record does not explain the circumstances behind Poulshot's northward migration from the church to the green, nor the period when it may have occurred. If the church points to the site of the earliest settlement, then it is likely that the creation of the regular green was a later development, and accompanied the laying out of open fields in the late-Saxon or early-Norman period. The three medieval fields appear to be focussed on the green rather than the church. North Field lay between the green and Summerham Bridge; West Field around Byde Mill Lane and Leighball Lane; and East Field along Eastnell Lane.

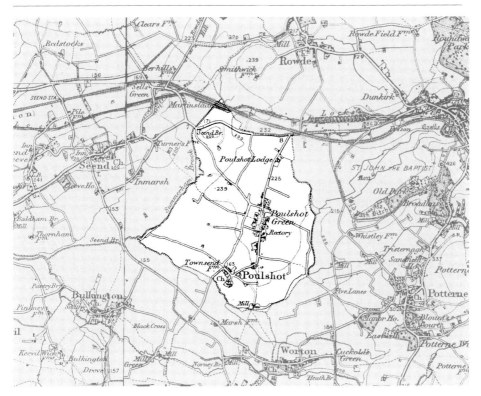

Ordnance Survey 1892 revision, 1 inch = 1 mile

Alternatively the green may have developed rather later. Two separate manors functioned in the village from at least the thirteenth century until the nineteenth, so it is possible that one, known as Poulshot manor, was centred on the church (a church at *Paveshou*, which may be Poulshot, is mentioned in Domesday Book), while the other, Burdon's manor, may have given rise to the second settlement laid out around a green in a period of expansion in the twelfth or thirteenth century.

No dramatic change of fortune may be detected in population figures, with about 200 inhabitants in 1377 and 1676, and a fairly consistent 300 or so at every census since 1801, rising a little during the past twenty years. In fact it has been claimed that 66 new houses were built in the parish between 1950 and 2000.

Like its clayland neighbours, Poulshot's agricultural regime is, and probably always has been, based on its heavy pasture lands. It seems in

the medieval period to have had more land under arable cultivation
(three carucates in one manor in 1273) than at the time of the tithe
award in the nineteenth century (a mere 141 acres). Some enclosure of
common fields by agreement is mentioned in a glebe terrier of 1608 as
having taken place about thirty years before. Until the sale in 1911 of the
Long family estate all farming in the parish took place from a dozen or so
farms within Poulshot.

For fuel and perhaps building materials both Poulshot manors in
the medieval period relied on small portions of Melksham Forest
(probably the area around Rhotteridge Farm between Melksham and
Lacock), which formed detached parts of the parish. The name Poulshot,
however, 'Paul's wood,' suggests that at an earlier period an area of
cultivated woodland ('holt' seems to mean a single-species wood) was a
distinguishing feature of Poulshot itself.

Agriculture apart, the village appears to have had few other means
of support. Poulshot Mill, in common with many in the area, was
adapted for use as a textile mill between about 1791 and 1830, and then
reverted to corn milling again. Photographs taken in the 1930s show a
large three-storey building, but it was demolished soon afterwards. In its
pre-industrial days it had been the birthplace and occasional refuge of
Thomas Boulter, the son of disreputable parents who ran the mill. His
brief career as an infamous highwayman began in 1775, and was spiced
with the usual narrow escapes and derring-do. He acquired Turpin's
high-speed horse, Black Beauty, but even she could not save him from
the gallows after trial at Winchester in August 1778.

NOTES (location: ST9759; area: 621ha; population (2001): 376)
General: *VCH* 7, 121-5; Hooke, N and J, and Stevenson, S, *Poulshot*, 1966 [typescript
in WANHS Library]; Dixon, N, '*Down Poulshot*', 2002.
Mineral water: *WANHM* 55, 7-8; Church: Harper, S, and Dennis, W, *Historical sketch of
Poulshot church*, rev. ed, 1990; Boulter: Waylen, J, *Highwaymen of Wiltshire* [c.1864];
Regan, J, *Gentleman of the road*, 1976.

Roundway

S TANDING NOW at the northern tip of Roundway Hill Covert, part of a
favourite Sunday walk for Devizes people, with west Wiltshire spread
below to the far distance, it is not hard to imagine the chaos of the rout
which ended the civil war battle in July 1643. Roundway Down was fought
between an attacking Parliamentary army, cocksure of victory, and Royalist
reinforcements marching to relieve their battle-scarred colleagues holed up
in Devizes. The action took place over a large tract of downland in Roundway
and neighbouring parishes. The dramatic denouement came when the
Royalists forced their opponents' cavalry to gallop pell-mell over the
precipice on either side of the spur which became known as Oliver's Castle
(Cromwell was not in fact present). Dead and injured, men and their horses,
were strewn in confusion down the hillside, 'where never horse went down
or up before'; and the doomed king's army scored their sweetest victory.

Outside Wiltshire the battle is the only reason for most people
having heard of Roundway. But within the county, until 1995, the name
was more likely to be associated with the large psychiatric hospital, which
began life in 1851 as the county asylum for pauper lunatics. Like the
workhouses of a dozen years earlier it was a purpose-built institution,
resulting from legislation and pressure by central government. Designed
by T H Wyatt, whose sister married its first superintendent, John Thurnam
(also a distinguished archaeologist), it was too small even when it was
built, in consequence of the grudging county authority's cheeseparing
attitude – but its deficiencies were softened by enthusiastic and efficient
management. Responsibility remained with the county as it gradually
expanded; new buildings and extensions were added during each decade

MC

since it was built (except perhaps the 1940s), and in 1948 it became part
of the National Health Service. As a modern psychiatric hospital it earned
a high reputation, and became a major employer in the area. It pioneered
many of the drug-based treatments which led ultimately to the concept of
care within the community rather than in hospitals. In consequence, like
other similar facilities elsewhere, its numbers were gradually run down
during the 1980s and 1990s, and it closed in 1995. Its impressive buildings
have been converted to houses and apartments, and a smaller psychiatric
unit, known as Green Lane Hospital, has been built in its grounds for
those patients who needed to remain.

A second instutution, Le Marchant Barracks, also lies in Roundway
parish. The home of the Wiltshire Regiment from 1878 (when it was built)
until that regiment's demise in 1959, it has for long had a run-down
appearance. The grandeur of its architecture (it has the look of a hybrid
prison-cum-public school) is not seen from the main road, but can be
appreciated from the minor road to Coate. It is said to have been designed
by a Royal Engineer, and to have been copied elsewhere.

Roundway's extraordinary shape, like a pair of jaws gripping
Devizes, resulted from boundary changes consequent upon the town's
suburban expansion, which have claimed Southbroom and Wick and will
presumably one day absorb much of the rest. But the present civil parish
(along with Southbroom and Wick) lay in Bishops Cannings until the
nineteenth century; it consists now of three of that parish's former tithings
– Nursteed (the southern portion), Bedborough (along the main road and
around the barracks) and Roundway itself. They were probably townships
within the bishop of Salisbury's large Domesday manor of Cannings,
although their names do not occur until the twelfth and thirteenth centuries and do not imply settlement. Nursteed is 'the place where nuts
grow' and Bedborough refers to a barrow (now lost) associated with an
individual (?*Beotta*). Roundway is 'the cleared road,' perhaps referring to
the north–south track which branches from the Roman road near Morgans
Hill, runs across Roundway Hill and through the village, over the main road
to Etchilhampton Hill and thence along the Lydeway towards Salisbury.

At the time of enclosure in 1812 much of the present parish,
especially in the south and east (Bedborough and Nursteed), already

consisted of small fields and closes. Roundway village, which from its complicated plan of roads and empty crofts gives the appearance of having once been more populous, was surrounded by three fields – north, east and south – separated by the three roads which meet in the village. In 1597 the same three fields were certainly under open cultivation, and many of the strips were less than half an acre. The picture is complicated, however, not only by Roundway's shrunken appearance, but also by its position adjacent to Devizes New Park, much of which lay in the area of the modern parish. The park existed by 1157, and assarting had begun to nibble away at it by the fourteenth century. In the seventeenth century New Park became associated with Roundway and in the eighteenth the owners of Roundway forsook their house in the village (Nicholas Place at the end of Quakers Walk, of which earthworks survive) and moved into a forerunner of Roundway House, within the area of the park. The house was rebuilt after 1760 and demolished in 1955 (although portions of the stable court remain), thereby permitting housing development in part of its grounds, which had for long been described as Roundway Park.

Ordnance Survey 1892 revision, 1 inch = 1 mile. Note that the present parish is shown. The text considers also land south of Devizes which formerly lay in Roundway parish.

A further complication is presented by the church history of
Roundway. Apart from a twentieth-century reading room, also used for
religious worship, no parish church or chapel-of-ease appears ever to have
existed in the village. The chapel (later church) of Southbroom St James
on Devizes Green acts as the ecclesiastical centre for Roundway, although
now lying in Devizes.

Paradoxically, since the village which gives Roundway its name is so
insignificant, with neither church, nor manor house, and few dwellings,
the parish has a large population. In 1981 rather more than one-third of
the 2,000 inhabitants were residents in Roundway Hospital. The remainder mostly lived in post-war suburban Devizes housing either in the area
of Broadleas Park – Roundway's 'lower jaw' – or in Roundway Park.
Twenty years later the hospital's population has dispersed, but the total is
higher than ever, as new housing fills the narrow neck of land beside
Brickley Lane which joins the two halves of the parish. Excavations
conducted during 1999 in advance of this housing revealed evidence of
an Iron-Age farmstead and extensive Roman activity, including a possible
temple nearby, which was perhaps associated with a villa-estate based on
Wick Green or Pans Lane in Devizes.

As a suburban parish Roundway has been designated not only for
housing but also for light industrial development, and 'Garden' and
'Hopton' industrial estates have taken the place of derelict army huts
opposite Le Marchant Barracks. The Kennet and Avon Canal, which
crosses the parish in the barracks area, appears to have had no effect on
development when it was built and operated commercially. As a leisure
facility, however, it now has a marina close to the barracks.

Roundway, with its stunning hilltop views, has long served Devizes
people as a place of recreation. In 1999 Wiltshire's newest white horse, the
Devizes Millennium Horse, was constructed above Roundway village.
Unlike most of its peers it faces right, and is about 45m tall and long. It is
built of chalk quarried from within itself. Apart from walks and picnics on
Roundway Down a particular attraction lay in the very south of the parish.
Drew's Pond, perhaps originally a fishpond connected with Devizes Castle,
took its name from a family who lived nearby at Rangebourne in the
sixteenth and seventeenth centuries. It became a favourite place for

boating and entertainments – one lavish party in 1819 is recorded by Tom Moore of Bromham, the Irish poet. Some years earlier an impromptu expedition one Sunday led to five drownings – a dreadful warning to sabbath-breakers commemorates the event in St John's churchyard, Devizes.

NOTES (location: SU0163; area: 805ha; population (2001): 2,267)
General: *VCH* 7, 187-97 *passim*.
Battle: Haycock, L, *Devizes in the civil war*, 2000; Hospital: Steele, P, *Down Pans Lane*, 2000; Anon, *Roundway Hospital, Devizes, 1851-1951*, 1951; *WANHM* 84, 96-107; Excavations: *WANHM* 95, 147-239; White horse: *WANHM* 94, 223-5; Drews Pond: Gandy, I, *Round about the little steeple*, 1960, 178-9. I am grateful to Dr Lorna Haycock who has read and commented on a draft of this article.

Rowde

TWO FACTORS ARE IMPORTANT in the history of Rowde: its proximity to Devizes; and the challenge of its steep hill to the traveller. Nowadays, with its considerable housing estates south and west of the main road, the effect on Rowde of Devizes is to give parts of the village a suburban flavour. In the nineteenth century something similar resulted in the capture (in 1835) by the expanding Devizes municipal borough of that part of Rowde parish which lay around Dunkirk and the Bath road, at the top of the hill. Further ribbon development along the Bath road beyond the canal bridge deprived Rowde of more of its ancient territory in favour of Devizes in 1934. In the middle ages the manor of Rowde was usually administered by the constable of Devizes Castle as part of the queen's estate. Devizes usually takes the credit, too, for the famous flight of locks at Caen Hill on the Kennet and Avon Canal, although they nearly all, in fact, lie in Rowde parish.

The Caen Hill flight (the name has nothing to do with Napoleonic prisoners, as is often claimed – it existed at least two centuries earlier) is a series of sixteen adjacent locks, each with its rectangular side pond to conserve water, and part of a larger ascent of 29 locks from Lower Foxhangers, in the south-western corner of Rowde parish, to Devizes top lock. This formed the most difficult engineering feat on the Kennet and Avon (and one of the most impressive monuments of the canal age anywhere), and constituted the last link to be completed, in 1810. It was also the last section of the restored canal to be reopened, by the Queen in August 1990, having lain disused and overgrown since being declared unsafe in 1951. While the flight was being built a makeshift railroad

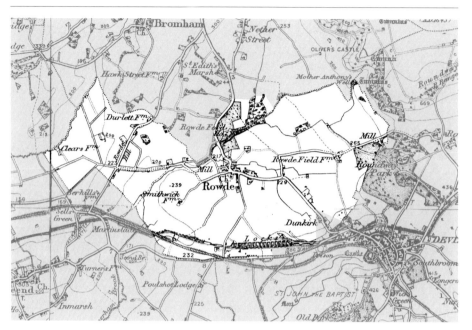

Ordnance Survey 1892 revision, 1 inch = 1 mile

operated between Foxhangers and Devizes, hence the arches which now
take the towpath under the road bridges. This southern extremity of
Rowde parish was later traversed by a conventional railway, opened in
1857 and closed in 1966, from Holt to Devizes; earthworks remain, but
the most memorable structure on this stretch of line, a tubular girder
bridge across the main road, known from its shape as the 'Fish Bridge,'
was demolished in 1968, enabling the road to be straightened and dualled
in 1972. The Fish Bridge of living memory was in fact a replacement, in
1901, of the original railway bridge, which is reputed to have been even
more fish-like.

The complex of road, railway and canal at Caen Hill (to which
might be added the former brickworks and a gruesome car scrapyard)
have little connection with the rest of the parish. It has been the approach
to Devizes from the north – from Calne and Chippenham – that has
affected the topography of the village. Seen on a map the main road
(A342) takes a broad loop to visit Rowde, whereas it could, and perhaps
once did (as a writer in 1922 maintained), continue in a straight line and
avoid the village, like Bromham further north, by about 1km. If a diversion

has taken place it probably occurred before 1228, when a forest peram-
bulation speaks of the high road from Calne to Devizes passing through
Rowde. The position is further complicated by the various lines of the
roads up the hill into Devizes, which until turnpiking in 1706/7 included a
more easterly route near the present Rowde Field Farm.

The turnpike (one of the three earliest in Wiltshire) ran from Devizes,
through the village, to Rowdeford, where a small but elegant three-arched
bridge (repaired and widened in 1815) marks the parish boundary.
Turnpiking was considered necessary on account of the difficult terrain,
and at the Ox House on Dunkirk Hill draught oxen were stabled to assist
heavily-laden waggons. Until 1927 it sported the stone figure of an ox.
The early turnpike suggests also that this was already by 1700 a road of
much more than local importance, and it was referred to shortly afterwards, in 1713, as part of the great road from Winchester and Andover to
Bath and Bristol. To cater for this traffic the *George Inn* existed by 1705,
and between 1842 and 1860 there are records of five named inns in the
parish, including the *Cross Keys* and the *Queens Head*, as well as a
beerseller and other unlocated innkeepers.

Main road apart the drift of communications in the parish has been
east–west, with the broad and doubtless ancient Cock Road and
Consciences Lane crossing from the Melksham Forest area in the west to
Roundway Down in the east. The village has developed where this line –
here fragmented into several strands – crossed the diverted high road. The
village exhibits a triangular green, forcing a swerve in the main road, with
the stately perpendicular church tower perched above it at the southern
base of the triangle. A map of 1721 suggests a degree of regularity in the
house plots along the north side of the main road from the green eastwards to Manor Farm; each house has a croft running down to the stream
and across to meet a now-vanished back lane which ran from Rowde
Lodge to Consciences Bridge.

The village sits on Lower Greensand, although most of the parish is
clay, flat Gault beneath the chalk downs in the east, and gently undulating
Oxford clay in the west. To the north of the village is the parkland of
Rowdeford House, a mansion of 1812, which is now run as a residential
special school for children with special needs. The parish name, first

mentioned in Domesday, describes a 'reedy-place,' and so presumably refers to a settlement near the Rowdeford stream or its tributaries. An extensive Iron-Age and Romano-British settlement lay north-east of the modern village, close to Rowde Farm. The parish had a resident priest at Domesday, and so presumably a church, although the present building, apart from the good fifteenth-century tower, is a rebuild of 1831-3.

In 1225 the parish was reckoned part of Melksham Forest, but by 1300 only the western part remained in the forest; the view westward from Rowde Hill is typical of former woodland country. Arable farming was more important than livestock in the thirteenth century, but here, as elsewhere in the area, enclosure occurred early (apparently in 1619, under some duress) and by the time of the tithe award, 1839-41, less than one-quarter of the parish was in arable cultivation. By the seventeenth century Rowde had in any case developed a domestic cloth industry, so that between 1698 and 1704 (the only period for which the data exist) fewer than half the male workforce were engaged in agriculture – the majority were clothworkers of various trades. In common with neighbouring places, Rowde's mill was converted for use as a fulling mill by 1777. It reverted to a corn mill in the nineteenth century and ceased working in 1947.

The population of the parish, centred in medieval times on the village and on communities recorded at Smithwick, Durlett and perhaps Foxhangers, appears to have been quite large, and by 1676 may have approached 500. As Devizes expanded westwards into the neighbouring part of Rowde, around Dunkirk, the population grew, and exceeded 1,100 in the mid-nineteenth century. But this area was lost by Rowde to Devizes, and until recent expansion the twentieth-century population usually fell in the 800–900 range, rising above 1,000 again by 1981. One modern housing development at the foot of Dunkirk hill has the curious name, Tanis – it appears to be a corruption of Tan House, the name of the farm here in 1773.

A few Rowde inhabitants have made their mark on the wider world. John Maundrell, of a long established Rowde family which leased the principal manor, was a Protestant martyr, burnt at the stake in Salisbury in 1556. The Maundrell Hall in Fisherton Street, Salisbury, formerly commemorated him – it is now a pub. Sir Matthew Digby Wyatt, the architect of Paddington station, and one of a famous architectural dynasty, was born at Rowde in 1820. The vicar of Rowde in 1730, Ferdinando Warner, claimed to have written his church history and another work (in three volumes) with a single pen, 'which was an old one when he began'. And Robert Trotman of Rowde, a moonraker if ever there was one, was buried near Bournemouth in 1765 after picking a fight with a customs officer while smuggling tea.

NOTES (location: ST9663; area: 1,049ha; population (2001): 1,073)
General: *VCH* 7, 217-23; Williams, K R, *A history of Rowde*, 1949 [typescript in WANHS Library]; WANHS MSS box 130: Halcomb papers.
Locks: Jones, P L, *Restoring the Kennet and Avon Canal*, 2002; Fish Bridge: Dixon, N, '*Down Poulshot*', 2002, 87; Roads: *WANHM* 42, 597-8; Innkeepers: WRS 55, 36-47; 1721 map: WSRO 1553/117.

Rushall

T HE APPEARANCE of Rushall today would make more sense to the
inquisitive topographer if the mansion house which Edward Poore
began after he had purchased the manor in 1749 had not been
demolished less than a century later, in 1840. Had the house survived, the
church would not now be standing alone in parkland some 500m east of
the village, and the reason for the disruption of the village plan would be
obvious. Edward Poore and his successors acquired almost everything in
Rushall during the latter half of the eighteenth century, and so had a free
hand to landscape and empark as they saw fit around the mansion which
they created (presumably on the site of an earlier manor house)
immediately north of the churchyard. By the time that they had sold up
and gone (in 1838), and their house had been reduced to the large
grassed mound which still remains, Rushall village had deserted its church
and rearranged itself along the north–south road further west.

The Poore's main area of parkland lay over the river, and their
elegant little bridge of about 1780 survives, serving France Farm –
allegedly so-called because you have to cross the water to reach it.
Another legacy is the line of thatched estate cottages known as Elm Row
south of the cross-roads. Rushall Manor, later remodelled, was also built
by the Poores, and was known as New House in 1803; it resulted from the
partition of the estate between Edward's two sons, which occurred in
1771. The fourteenth-century and later church was rebuilt in brick by the
Poores in 1812, to include the family chapel, pew (described in 1891 as a
kind of royal box), coats of arms and monuments. Since their day the
church has undergone restoration (in 1905) and attractive stained glass,

depicting agricultural scenes in the parish (the *Benedicite* window of about 1980) has been added to a window in the north wall of the nave.

Because of the Poores' activities and the absence of earlier maps it is impossible now to reconstruct the plan of the medieval village. But it seems clear that the road from Devizes continued across the present junction and became the village street leading to the church, and on towards Upavon. This is suggested not only by the road layout and the position of the church and former manor house, but also by earthworks along this 'street', and by a field name, Twintown, which is recorded in the tithe award of 1843. This lay to the north of the church, between (hence the name) this likely village area and the bend at the northern end of the present village. It suggests that Rushall comprised two areas of settlement, one centred on the church, the other on the bend, which is really a T–junction and was formerly a cross-roads.

This northern end of the village is a mixture of old and new houses, a former shop, a village hall and the brick school (still open) of 1872. There appear to be village earthworks to the north of Rushall Bridge (which was widened in 1936). Chapel House, of pebbledash and thatch, is the manse of a former General Baptist chapel which occupied a site (now modern bungalows) north of the road from 1760 until the 1970s. It relied on an endowment of 1743, the theological stipulations of which caused a persistent dispute between the congregation and the trustees

during the nineteenth century. Matters came to a head in about 1850,
when one of the trustees, a Mr Black, came down from London, and
attended a service in the chapel conducted by the minister, a Mr White.
Uproar ensued, and Mr Black, under police escort, had to seek sanctuary
in the inn at Charlton, 'pursued by the roughs of the neighbourhood'. By
strength of feeling, if not of argument, White triumphed over Black, and
he and his descendants continued to occupy Rushall manse until 1932.
The chapel's congregation dwindled after a long-serving minister died in
1956, and it closed in 1973.

Rushall parish, like most of its neighbours, is a long, narrow territory
which includes meadow, arable, and downland pasture. The two headwaters of the River Avon, flowing from north and west, meet in the parish,
near Scales (formerly Cales) Bridge, where there was a fulling mill in the
seventeenth and eighteenth centuries. The name, in the form *Rusteselve*,
is first recorded in Domesday Book, and seems to derive from a personal
name, *Rust* or similar, rather than from the rushy meadows which have
given the name Rusletts (and variants) to fields in neighbouring parishes.
Domesday Rushall was a large estate which had passed to the king from
the Saxon royal family, and clearly embraced an area much greater than
the medieval and modern parish. It seems to have included Upavon and
Charlton. There were at least two churches with land attached on this
estate – at Rushall and Upavon – and Rushall church has preserved its
Norman font. Although the large estate was called Rushall in Domesday
Book, the dominant settlement was probably at Upavon, and what is now
thought of as Rushall was subordinate to it until achieving separate
parochial status in 1395. Apart from the grant of an annual fair in 1285
(perhaps not taken up), medieval Rushall seems not to have been a place
of any great importance; its population in both 1377 and 1801 was
around 150, although somewhat larger in the seventeenth century and
during the Victorian period.

The road system in the parish is complex, reflecting the fact that the
confluence of rivers has made this area a natural cross-roads for travellers
using the Avon valley and Pewsey Vale. Early east–west routes probably
included the present Charlton footpath, which continues as the main road
over Rushall Bridge, and the present Devizes road continuing to Rushall

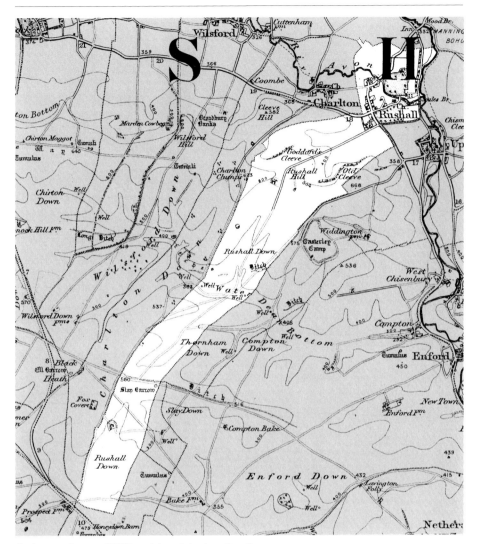

Ordnance Survey 1892 revision, 1 inch = 1 mile

church and Upavon. An early downland track, now designated the Ridgeway Route and open to vehicles, skirts the military land above the village, and Rushall Drove leads up to it from the valley. This drove formerly continued across Salisbury Plain to Tilshead and Shrewton, bisecting the parish along its long axis. Furlong names in the open fields suggest that it was known as the Portway, implying that it once led on to market towns such as Wilton or Salisbury. The present main roads are largely the result of turnpiking in 1762 (now A342 Devizes–Upavon), and 1840 (now A345 Amesbury–Pewsey, although the turnpike headed north at Woodbridge towards Avebury). The latter road replaced an earlier route on the east bank of the river; the new line, which skirts the park, brought the road into Rushall parish, but diverted most of the north–south traffic away from Rushall village.

The conventional pattern of arable and sheep farming in common fields and downs continued until the Poores' arrival and acquisitions in the parish between 1749 and formal enclosure in 1804. Subsequent plough-ing and improving of downland failed to destroy extant archaeology, which includes a Late Bronze or Iron-Age enclosure (Church Ditches – formerly called Church Banks), a prominent bowl barrow (Slay Barrow), and extensive prehistoric field systems, some of which show signs of cultivation during the Saxon period. Since 1898, when it was acquired by the War Department, the downland portion of the parish has fallen within the military firing ranges and is inaccessible. A rifle range was established on Rushall Down soon after the initial purchase, and a century of bom-bardment by shells and missiles has followed.

The remaining farmland within the parish was sold in 1917, and was purchased three years later by a prominent dairy farmer, Joseph Maggs. After farm buildings were destroyed by fire in 1945, Maggs sold the estate to a neighbouring farmer, Percy Wookey of Upavon. His son, Barry, has farmed Rushall (and neighbouring Charlton) along organic lines since the 1970s, and opened a new mill and bakery beside the Devizes road in 1973. The process of converting the farm totally to or-ganic production was achieved between 1970 and 1985, growing wheat and fodder crops, and rearing beef cattle and sheep. Rushall, not only because of its size but also through Mr Wookey's enthusiastic advocacy of the cause in a book published in 1987, has been in the forefront of the now fashionable organic movement.

NOTES (location: SU1255; area: 892ha; population (2001): 134)
General: *VCH* 10, 136-46.
Village layout: WSRO 135/39 (1804 map); Church: *WANHM* 25, 266-7; Baptist chapel: WSRO 1322/29; Farming: Wookey, B, *Rushall: the story of an organic farm*, 1987.

Seend

T HE HIGH-NAVED, squat-towered church stands well away from the main road, unseen by all but a very few of the daily thousands of travellers through the village. Glimpsed from the road along its lane it seems to sit in a walled garden behind its elaborate gates. To appreciate Seend one must park in that lane and stroll to the far side of the church-yard, where a seat is provided for anyone wishing to take in the view. For, beyond everything else (even the accursed traffic) Seend is a place of views.

This is because the village sits along a ridge of ferruginous (or iron-bearing) Lower Greensand, which extends roughly east–west for about 3km, and which stands proud between 20 and 50 metres above the surrounding clay. To the south of this ridge a stream flows – the Summer-ham Brook, which merges with the Semington Brook – and forms the entire southern parish boundary, from the point where westbound travellers enter Seend's territory (Summerham Bridge) to the point where they leave (Baldham Bridge). Gazing north from the ridge another watercourse may be seen, but this is the artificial line of the Kennet and Avon Canal. The parish extends in this direction a further kilometre and more, into the country of isolated farms which occupy land once part of Melksham Forest.

Settlement in the parish lies largely along the sandy ridge that gave Seend its name ('Seend' equals 'sand'), but there are marked contrasts. The irregular scatters of old brick cottages mingled with modern houses and bungalows – some along unmade lanes – at Seend Cleeve in the west, are quite unlike the much grander stone residences and comfortable

rambling farmhouses of Seend itself in the east, which appear to fit within
a regular pattern of planned property boundaries. Off the hill another
hamlet – Martinslade or Sells Green – has developed in the north-east of
the parish, where canal, former railway, and the Melksham road all come
together to skirt around the ridge.

If you are still sitting on the churchyard seat you now have a choice.
You could take the footpath that leads eastward across the parkland of
Seend House; and then turn north along the brief green lane (Love Lane)
to meet the main road. That way you will extend your view from the ridge
and glimpse the quality and affluence of Seend's best houses. But first I
suggest that you should explore the church itself.

The rich clerestoried exterior of later fifteenth-century Perpendicular
almost dwarfs the earlier west tower, and is enlivened by gargoyles and
grotesques (one figure plays the bagpipes, another pulls a grimace). Inside
the monuments to clothiers and landowners have proliferated since John
Stokes, the first of the church's benefactors, who died in 1498, built the
north aisle and emblazoned its west window with carvings of his clothier's
shears and scissors. Above the chancel arch the mere outline of the rood is
preserved – a simple but moving icon. It is apparently a stain caused by oil
which had been used to bring out the colour of fragments of the original

mural painting which was discovered beneath later texts in the 1930s. And in the sunlit south aisle the three-light millennium window, made by Andrew Taylor and dedicated in 2003, tells the story of Seend past and present. It can provide the framework for the rest of this account, most themes of which have already made an appearance.

The lower portion of the window's first light depicts a canal lock and barge, and above it a railway line with guards van. These nineteenth-century means of communication were superimposed on the older network of roads, which must first be considered. That a road ran along the ridge from medieval times or earlier is apparent from the planned layout of Seend village, since it forms the spine; and that it led (as now) between Devizes and Trowbridge may be assumed. 'Sandway', recorded in a deed of 1597, may have been its name. By 1675 it was included in Ogilby's road book as part of the thoroughfare from London to Wells, and in 1750 and 1752 it was turnpiked by two trusts along its whole length from Devizes to Trowbridge and beyond.

The awkward twists at each end of the village street appear to be caused by encroachments on former open spaces or greens where the road forked, with branches leading towards Bromham and Lacock (Spout Lane) at the eastern, and to Melksham (School Lane and Bollands Hill) at the western end. The link with Melksham was particularly important, since although autonomous in most respects Seend remained a dependent chapelry within Melksham parish until 1873, and in the middle ages many functions, including burial of the dead, would have involved a journey to the mother church there. All the more remarkable, therefore, to discover in Seend church so rich a show of tombs, hatchments and heraldry, since until 1873 it was a mere chapel-of-ease.

As coaching increased along the Bath road in the eighteenth century the twisting steep descent by Bollands Hill towards Melksham, which was turnpiked in 1753, proved irksome, and a new turnpike road was constructed in 1780. This, the present A365 road, avoided the ridge altogether and by-passed the village. It turned Sells Green into a roadside hamlet and led to the opening of a 'New Inn' there by 1813, which is now the *Three Magpies*. Meanwhile, by 1769 the lane which drops steeply from the ridge southward to Worton had also been turnpiked – by the over-reaching and incompetent Westbury trust – and during the twentieth century this has become a busy unofficial bypass around Devizes for travellers between south and west Wiltshire.

The Kennet and Avon canal was built, not without financial and engineering problems, across Seend's northern clayland between 1796 and 1800. The works involved five locks below Seend Cleeve, where Seend wharf was built with, in due course, its own beerhouse (the present, very popular *Barge Inn*). A road bridge (one of four in the parish) was necessary at Martinslade to carry the Melksham turnpike, and wharves were built here also and at the foot of Spout Lane (Scott's Wharf). As elsewhere along the canal it was the haulage of coal from, and agricultural products to, these wharves which most affected the local economy. One contractor who had built a section of the canal through Seend, Adam Wragg, later set up as a coal merchant at Martinslade, and his and other haulage businesses continued to derive their livelihood from the canal throughout the nineteenth and into the twentieth century. Since its restoration during the 1970s the canal's increasing leisure use has brought new prosperity to the pubs and businesses along it.

Although the canal may not have had much impact on everyday travel through Seend, the construction of a railway alongside it in 1857 certainly did. The single-track broad gauge line linked Holt (for Melksham, Trowbridge and the network in general) with Devizes, and from 1862, when a connecting line from Devizes to Hungerford was completed, this became a through-route to London. Seend had its own station, where the road down Bollands Hill crossed the line, and from 1909 there was also a halt at Sells Green (misleadingly named Bromham and Rowde). In the line's heyday up to ten Devizes trains stopped at Seend daily and there was a through service to London. The line closed in 1966 and was dis- mantled, but its east–west course across the parish, roughly equidistant between the canal and the A365, is easily traced.

Above the canal and railway view, the millennium window depicts a scene of heavy industry, of furnaces billowing thick smoke, which seems incongruous – shocking even – in the context of a Wiltshire village. But the furnaces were real enough – they stood in a field next to the *Barge Inn*. They were one result of a kind of 'gold rush', which infected Seend for about a decade from 1856, to exploit its newly discovered resources of iron ore. 'Rediscovered' would be the more accurate term, since John Aubrey in the seventeenth century had been well aware of the rich iron-bearing properties of Seend's Greensand. He commented that local people took no notice of this iron ore, 'which every sunshiney day, after a shower, glistered in their eies'. He took samples for smelting, and the results were impressive.

But the resource was not used until in the 1850s – with the canal available and the railway imminent – speculators began buying fields to open as quarries, first on Seend's southern slope and then to the north, between the village, Seend Cleeve, and the wharf by the *Barge*. Twin blast furnaces and extensive works were built around 1860 for processing the

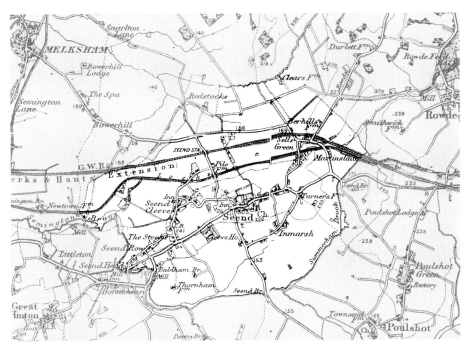

Ordnance Survey 1892 revision, 1 inch = 1 mile

ore, and operated intermittently until the mid-1870s, as successive companies teetered into bankruptcy. A row of workers' cottages, New Buildings, near the canal, and a factory-owner's house on the hillside, Ferrum Lodge, later Ferrum Towers, survive from this period, along with

the scarrings of quarried fields and associated tramways; but the works
themselves, whether through incompetence or market forces, never
prospered and were demolished in 1889. Few traces remain. Quarrying
the ore to transport it away by canal and railway for smelting elsewhere
proved a more viable proposition, however. It continued into the 1880s
and was revived periodically until about 1927.

Returning to our church window, we see that the central light is
devoted to more familiar scenes in the Wiltshire countryside – cattle, sheep
and wheat, with poppies, a tractor and a stream. Thanks to the researches
of Seend's historian, Edward Bradby, we can begin to understand the
community's agriculture and land use from medieval times onwards. In
the middle ages the parish lay along the southern edge of Melksham forest,
the Summerham Brook marking the boundary of both. Forest lodges are
thought to have existed at Moiety Farm near Sells Green (which retains
medieval timber-framing); and by Summerham Bridge, where earthwork
remains can be seen next to the main road. The remote north-western
portion of the parish, now crossed by the canal, was a medieval park,
created in the fourteenth century and enclosed in the seventeenth. Much
of the rest of the parish north of the ridge was low-lying marshland or heavily
wooded, and seems to have been used for rough grazing and wood pasture.
On the higher ground and northern slope of the ridge assarts (or illegal
encroachments) seem to have been widespread, doubtless made from the
forest-edge settlement at Seend Cleeve. In 1624, at the time of final
disafforesting, a large area along the northern limit of the parish, known as
the Clears, was converted to the rectangular closes which still survive.

All this is in marked contrast to the land use in the south of the
parish and around Seend village, where two great open fields, East and
West, divided by the Worton road, extended from the ridge to brook-side
meadows. A third field, north of the village, but never called North Field,
may have been farmed directly by the manorial owner as his demesne. A
vineyard is recorded in a manorial extent of 1283, and this had presumably been planted on the ridge's southern slopes. The East and West
Fields became subdivided, so that names such as Church, Grove and
Sand Fields are encountered while the land was still farmed communally.
But the open field system broke down between about 1650 and 1700 (as

commonly in the clayland parishes of west and north Wiltshire) with the
enclosure of the fields by agreement. Thus from a regular planned settlement, surrounded by open fields, and with its farmhouses ranged along its
street, Seend gradually became a parish of scattered farmsteads surrounded by enclosed fields. Several of the old village farmhouses were either
adapted to new uses (one became the vicarage in the nineteenth century)
or were replaced by the fine gentry houses which now adorn the street.

The stream depicted at the foot of the window reminds us that water
was essential for both settlement and agriculture, but at Seend it was also
important in two other ways. Like Melksham, Holt and other places on the
way to Bath, Seend tried to entice wealthy convalescents to stop and
benefit from the curative properties of its own water. John Aubrey, who
lived at Seend in 1665-6 (when he entered into a disastrous engagement
with his host and friend's sister, Joan Sumner), lavishly praised and
promoted Seend water, and there was a brief possibility around 1684-90
that the village might develop as a spa, focussed on a chalybeate source in
the grounds of what is now Seend Green House. But as with so many of
Aubrey's projects (including his proposed marriage) it came to nothing,
and Seend water maintained only a local reputation.

Seend's other application of water is told in the third (or right hand)
light of the millennium window. A narrow-weaver works at his loom;
finishers are carefully shearing the nap of a roll of cloth, while finished
cloths are folded neatly beside them; a factory-like building is depicted,
with a chapel next door. Medieval fulling mills were powered by the
Semington Brook along the western edge of the parish, at Baldham Mill
(just into Keevil, Seend's neighbour) and probably also at Seend Head.
Peripheral to the main west Wiltshire clothmaking region Seend's clothiers
had nevertheless been able to accumulate sufficient wealth by the fifteenth
century, as we have seen, to rebuild their church in lavish Perpendicular
style.

The Seend clothiers created dynasties – Dugdale, Sumner, Awdry,
Usher – which intermarried with each other and with similar families from
elsewhere. They rose to the status of gentry and built the remarkable series
of fine houses which line the village street. The elaborate monuments to
the dead inside the church complement the elaborate houses – Seend

House, Cleeve House, Seend Green House, the Manor House – in which they had lived. Or they sank back to the artisan level of craft weavers from which they had originated. The clothiers controlled the weavers, spinners and other craftsmen, who worked in more modest cottages and small houses, perhaps with workshops attached. It is the survivors among these that give Seend Cleeve its character.

At Seend as elsewhere the industry was troubled and weakened during the eighteenth century, first by poor labour relations and later by competition from machinery. In its death throes a factory or extended workshop was built in the centre of Seend in 1814, by William Gaisford of nearby Bulkington, in which he installed spinning jennies. The enterprise lasted no more than two decades, but 'Factory Row' remains – since 1971 misleadingly renamed 'Weavers' Cottages', since it seems only ever to have been used for spinning.

The diversity of Seend's economic interests – clothmaking, quarrying and transport in addition to the agriculture and small trades associated with most villages – sets it apart from most of the predominately chalkland communities described in this book. In many ways it has always gazed from its hilltop westward to the Melksham region rather than east-ward to Devizes. As a result it has a strong nonconformist tradition. Meetings held by Presbyterians are recorded between 1702 and 1730, and a cottage at Inmarsh, south of the ridge, was in use by very early Metho-dists (including the celebrated David Saunders) by 1749. In 1774-5 the present exquisite brick chapel was built (soon to be somewhat dwarfed by Factory Row next door), and opened by John Wesley himself, who had previously preached in Seend from the steps of a house in the street, now called Wesley Cottage. The chapel is still in use, working closely with the Anglican congregation, and is beautifully maintained. The village also boasts (another trait of nonconforming villages) no fewer than four thriving pubs. It has achieved a good balance of housing and amenities, including playing fields adjacent to a pleasing 1950s council development at the Lye (defined on its northern edge by the line of a proposed by-pass which never happened). The high status houses have had some high status owners, such as the father of Bloomsbury group member Duncan Bell, and the scandalous politician and diarist Alan Clark (who in the

1970s wrote the church guide, incidentally!). It is also served, in Edward Bradby's book of 1981, by one of the best local histories of any village in Wiltshire.

NOTES (location: ST9461; area: 1,147ha; population (2001): 1,074)

General: *VCH* 7, 91-121 *passim*; Bradby, E, *Seend: a Wiltshire village past and present*, 1981.

Church: Clark, A, *History of the church of the Holy Cross, Seend*, undated; Ironworks: Day, R, in *J Hist Metallurgy Soc* 15, 1981, 18-38; Parkhouse, N, in *Archive* 4, 1994, 58-64; Spa: *WANHM* 55, 8-9; Architecture: Bradby, E, *Seend heritage*, 1985; Chapel: Griffiths, H J, *Seend Methodist Chapel 1775 to 1975*, 1974 (*sic*).

Stanton St Bernard

S<small>T</small> BERNARD, although represented in Victorian stained glass in the church, is an interloper; he is probably a corruption of Burdon, a medieval family of village landholders, whose name as a suffix would have served to distinguish this Stanton from others. Stanton St Bernard to the casual visitor is an unremarkable parish, although it shares with its neighbour All Cannings the distinction of being the highest in Wiltshire – at 294m Milk Hill in Stanton vies with Tan Hill in All Cannings. Its church, too, incompetently rebuilt in 1831-2 and later patched and buttressed, is undistinguished, except for a memorable painting – canvas stuck to the wall – surrounding the chancel arch. Executed in blues and greens it portrays angels and apostles, some with disproportionately small bodies, surrounding the figure of Christ, whose uncanny resemblance to the youthful George V is probably an accurate indication of its date. Curiously, for a feature scarcely beyond living memory, nothing seems to be known about it or its artist, who mysteriously signed him- or herself 'HH'.

For the landscape historian Stanton is an interesting place. It illustrates the dictum that while a settlement's territory seldom alters, the settlement itself is prone to fluctuation. The territory, in common with many Wiltshire parishes, is a long narrow strip, extending from Greensand and alluvial meadowland in the south, up the fertile lower chalk slope of the Marlborough Downs to the upper chalk summit, capped by clay-with-flints. The present boundaries, more or less, were described in a charter of 903, and reiterated in 957 and 960. They may, however, be considerably older, since, in common with neighbouring parishes, they ignore Wansdyke, which probably dates from the fifth or sixth century. It has been suggested that boundaries in this area may be Roman in date. A possible pagan Saxon cemetery near the point where Woodborough, Alton Barnes and Stanton boundaries formerly met at Honeystreet supports this suggestion, since it is believed that Saxon burials often took place at existing boundaries.

Looking down from the gate across the path between Milk Hill and Alton White Horse most of Stanton's eastern boundary is visible as hedge-rows and field divisions. From Milk Hill the village of Stanton, hiding among trees, occupies the middle ground. It sits on the lower chalk in the centre of its parish, and in medieval times presided over two large open fields, which lay north and south of it. By 1784 each had been divided into three – east, middle and west fields above and below the town. Upland pasture was provided by Milk Hill, and Thorn Hill downs beyond Wans-dyke, while an area of lowland pasture, known as the Withicks, lay on the Greensand in the extreme south of the parish around Stanton Mill (now Stanton Dairy). Inclosure of the lowland pastures took place in the early seventeenth century, followed by attempts to increase productivity by floating water meadows, but much of the lower chalk arable remained under open cultivation until 1792.

But if the boundaries have remained static, and the agriculture has been largely determined by the geology, the village itself shows signs of considerable changes. The present settlement has a complicated street plan with an off-centre church, and shares with many of its neighbours a

shrunken appearance. Its 2001 population, 161, was less than 45% of the
1891 total (373) and only 65% of a figure for 1744 (246) recorded in a
parish register. Consequently, earthworks and irregularities, signifying
depopulation, may be seen in several areas around the village, and with
the help of maps and aerial photographs a sequence of abandonment
may be established.

Most recent to go, during the early twentieth century, were houses
and a Methodist chapel south-east of the village. In an area west of the
street a group of buildings existed in 1784 and most survived until 1847
but had been lost by 1886. North of the church only one building
survived until 1784, although the crofts which houses had formerly
occupied still remained. South-west of the village a field name – Cottage
Piece – is mentioned on the 1784 map, although all trace of the cottages
had by then gone. North-east of the village aerial photographs show
rectangular crofts ranged along a holloway, but these are not recorded at
all on the 1784 map.

Immediately west of the church, in the area now occupied by Church
Farrn, the 1784 map describes an enclosure as 'Court,' and further south
'Court Place' is marked. A document of 1602 records the surrender by the
demesne lessee of the 'scite, mansion place and farm,' implying perhaps
that the former 'mansion' was by then derelict. If so, its site may be commemorated in the name 'court,' its grounds stretching south to 'court
gate.' Its occupant some fifty years earlier had been assessed for a tax as
the wealthiest man in Swanborough hundred, so there was perhaps a
building of some opulence in this area in the late medieval period.

Concurrent with the abandonment of parts of the village has doubtless been the rebuilding and re-use of sites within the area of the modern
village, as well as realignment of the road pattern. No major road passes
through the settlement; the only through road to cross the parish, the
minor road from Devizes to Pewsey, passes north of the village. An earlier
pattern of roads and tracks, which must have connected Stanton with All
Cannings, Beechingstoke and Alton, has been largely obliterated by the
Kennet and Avon Canal. This, together with the Devizes branch railway
across the extreme south of the parish, provided better alternative means
of communication through Pewsey Vale in the nineteenth century. One

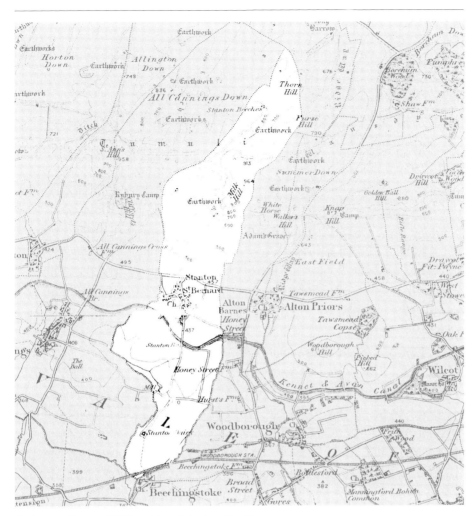

Ordnance Survey 1892 revision, 1 inch = 1 mile

well-known Stanton building is a product of the canal traffic. The *Barge Inn* at Honeystreet, rebuilt after a fire in 1856, is the only public house in the parish; although accessible from the village only by footpath or towpath, it lies just within Stanton's boundary, which runs along the path to its door.

NOTES: (location: SU0962; area: 826ha; population (2001): 161)
General: *VCH* 10, 146-55; Corbyn, N and D, *Stanton and its people*, 1986.
Boundaries: Reynolds, A, *Later Anglo-Saxon England*, 1999, 82-3; Agriculture: Straton, C R, *Survey of the lands of . . . Pembroke*, 1909, vol. 1, 129-40; WRS 9, 63-71.

Stert

IF YOU TAKE A RULER to a map of Wiltshire you will find that the small parish of Stert lies dead centre; and if you stand on the parish boundary where it crosses Monument Hill above the village you will be rewarded with a spectacular view, east along Pewsey Vale to Martinsell and beyond (almost to Hampshire), and south-west to the grey hills of Somerset behind Westbury. Stert is a village of views, as it is built along a ridge or tail (the meaning of the name) of Greensand which overlooks and falls steeply to the clay vale below. It has in consequence attracted a number of twentieth-century houses and bungalows, which appear ordinary enough from the village street, but when seen from the valley reveal their picture windows and conservatories to soak up the south-facing panorama. Below the village springs feed a stream which has cut a secluded wooded valley beneath the tail, before turning to flow westward towards Potterne, and ultimately to join the Bristol Avon. The flat pastures of Hatfield, by contrast, which make up the eastern half of the parish, drain into the Salisbury Avon.

The parish therefore forms a watershed, and this is followed by an early route from Salisbury to Devizes which is known here as the Lydeway. A milestone at the bus stop opposite the former *Clock Inn* persists in giving the miles to Sarum, although the road no longer goes there. The present road alignment across Monument Hill dates only from 1768 (the proud lion monument commemorates its construction). Before that the road struck further north across Etchilhampton Hill, and part of its line is marked by a deep holloway (now part of the Wessex Ridgeway long-distance path) leading up the hill from the present Stert turning.

The modern parish was formed in 1894 by the union of two small territories, Stert and Fullaway. Both were dependent on nearby parishes, Stert on Urchfont, Fullaway on All Cannings, and all four places lay in the ancient hundred of Studfold. Fullaway, 'the muddy way', sat largely on the Gault clay south of Stert, but it also extended up the slope to take in houses on the south side of the village street, including Stert House. The name is first recorded in 1327, although little is known of its medieval history. Uneven ground around the present Fullaway Farm is perhaps the vestige of a once larger settlement, but since the sixteenth century it seems to have consisted of no more than a single farmstead surrounded by its pastures. The Victorians regarded it as having been extra-parochial, and so made it a civil parish in 1858; but with its total population of twenty dwindling to eleven by 1891 it was doomed as a unit of local government, and so was absorbed into Stert in 1894.

Stert was more populous. Its 65 taxpayers in 1377 and 132 adults in 1676 imply total populations at those dates of about 100 and 200 respectively. Since 1800 the population has always fluctuated within these limits, from 193 in 1821 to 112 a century later. Its name is first encountered in Domesday, when it was basically a five-hide estate. An inquisition of 1311 depicts a demesne estate of almost 250 acres of arable and 60 acres of meadow, as well as pasture, woodland, vineyards and a court (the farmhouse or manor house) with a garden. This estate passed in 1393 to New College, Oxford, as part of William of Wykeham's foundation grant. The college let it to tenants, including the influential Topp family of Stockton in the seventeenth century and the Watson Taylors of Erlestoke in the nineteenth; but they continued to own and supervise it for more than five centuries, until sales disposed of it piecemeal to tenants and incomers during the twentieth century.

Stert's arable lands lay on the chalk hillside above the village, and the tenants' two open fields, East and West, displayed remarkable tenacity, since they continued in the traditional way through the nineteenth century, and were not entirely consolidated until 1928. The supposed site of the medieval vineyard, on the sun-soaked hillside sloping south below Barn Cottage, was replanted with vines in 1977, but the enterprise failed twenty years later. The flat area of greensand in the east of the parish was

of poorer quality than the chalk loam – the name given to it, Hatfield
('heath field') is normally a term of reproach – and although the
remaining traces of ridge and furrow imply medieval cultivation, the area
was primarily used for pasture, and much was enclosed in the seventeenth
century. A portion of this remote stretch of country was cultivated again in
the nineteenth century, and the area might have been opened up had the
Great Western Railway's plan to build a station on the Urchfont–Stert
boundary south of Hatfield Farm in about 1900 come to fruition.

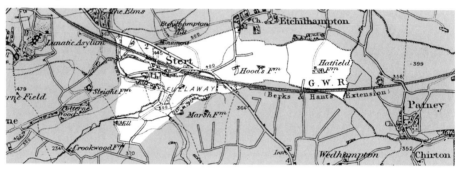

Ordnance Survey 1892 revision, 1 inch = 1 mile

Apart from farming other activities which are known to have taken
place in the parish include milling, brickworks and clockmaking. There
were two working watermills on the stream below the village until the
nineteenth century, probably on the sites of the two mills recorded in
Domesday. A third, Crookwood Mill, lay in Urchfont parish until a recent
boundary change brought it into Stert; the building survives as a private
house, and with many of the mill-workings intact. A windmill between the
village street and the former railway cutting is shown on a map of 1884,
although not present in 1839 or 1899. It has been suggested that it was
the last built and most short-lived working windmill in Wiltshire. Brick pits
and kilns lay near Lower Mill in the Gault clay at the western end of the
parish. Another brick kiln appears near the road west of the former
Hood's Farm on maps of 1817 and about 1843; the kiln has gone, and
Hood's in 1967 was renamed Wabi Farm, after a Canadian foundry,
shares in which enabled its purchase. It may have been the brick pits
serving the Wabi Farm kiln that were the scene of gruesome discoveries
during the 1840s.

On the main A342 road, opposite the former *Clock Inn* and behind the milestone, was formerly an alehouse called *The Shepherd and his Dog*, run in the 1770s by one Thomas Burry, descendant of an old Fullaway family. He seems to have specialized in providing hospitality to pedlars and itinerant travellers, whom he murdered for their belongings and buried in the brick pits. More than a dozen skeletons, some showing evidence of violence, were later discovered there. After his trade declined (quite understandably) members of the Raymond family of clockmakers – Charles, Evi and James – set up beerhouse-keeping as a sideline from their thatched cottage opposite. From surviving examples they are known to have made clocks between 1761 and 1811, and the *Clock Inn* remained in the family until the 1870s. Outside over the door a large clock dated 1773 could be seen until the 1970s, when it disappeared; the pub itself has recently ceased trading.

The nucleus of Stert is the triangle formed at the western end of the village street where it divides, the left fork (Mill Lane) descending the hillside to a footbridge across the stream in Stert Valley. It then continues as a right of way towards Potterne, and is probably part of an early route between Potterne and Pewsey Vale, which may pre-date the creation of Devizes. The right fork keeps to high ground, and leads past the church and Manor Farm to Stert's 'tail'. The church, a reconstruction in 1844-5 of a very small (about 7 x 8m) medieval building on the same site, is built in a vaguely coffin-shaped churchyard perched on the hillside, and abuts the garden of Manor Farm. Since the thirteenth century or earlier it has been a chapel-of-ease to Urchfont, although in the seventeenth century it was regarded as a separate living. Until 1845, when it was rededicated to St James, it bore the uncommon dedication to St Faith.

Manor Farmhouse, according to a document of 1662, had used oaks from Hatfield in its construction, and it retains seventeenth-century work, although it was partly rebuilt after arson destroyed farm buildings in 1846. Until renovation and some demolition during the twentieth century it almost touched the churchyard; and it still dwarfs the little church which, when viewed from the driveway, seems to be trying to hide behind it. The farm complex sports a fine pond, and it is well known in Stert that every midnight the lion leaves his post on the monument and strolls down the drive to drink from it.

Early estate maps (of 1638, 1766 and later) show a regular rear boundary line running parallel with the village street on its northern side, which suggests a planned linear settlement. They also depict more buildings than survive in the area of Manor Farm and Manor Cottages, and slight earthworks are still visible near the pond. North-east of the churchyard the 1638 map depicts 'Bowling Close' and 'Football Close', one of a number of early Wiltshire references to a national obsession. It might be expected that the church house, mentioned in a court roll of 1660, also lay somewhere nearby.

Traces of the Devizes branch railway, built in 1862 and closed in 1966, may also be seen just north of the Manor Farm buildings. Further east, although its sizeable cutting has been completely filled and levelled, the railway bridge which carried the village street over it remains. The line, originally broad gauge, served as a through east–west route until 1900, when a second line was built to become the main London–Exeter route, which it remains. This line leaves the old Devizes branch just south of Hatfield, and now forms the parish boundary between Urchfont and Stert. The line has not been without its problems; collapses at the *Clock Inn* in 1936 and Crookwood in 1961 involved major engineering works and disruption.

Despite several older cottages, the east end of the street, from the main road to Stert House, is architecturally disappointing. But along Mill

Lane are a number of well-kempt timber-framed and thatch cottages which revel in their picturesque surroundings. Most were built or rebuilt in similar style by New College in the mid-seventeenth century, and some were in poor condition when the college relinquished ownership in the twentieth. Vale Cottage, everyone's idea of the perfect country cottage, is particularly well documented. It was built as a farmhouse in about 1574, has a detailed probate inventory listing its furniture in 1621, and was extensively restored and studied during the 1990s. Further up the hill Barn Cottage fell victim to a disastrous fire in 1994 and has been sensitively rebuilt. Between the fork and the substantial brick Stert House stands the former Baptist chapel, closed in 1957, and converted to a private house (Maitland). Nearby the village school, closed in 1927, was sold by the parish council in 1961 in order to pay for a bus shelter. It too was converted to a house during the 1960s, but has since been replaced.

Stert today is an affluent, spick-and-span village, whose community spirit is evidenced by the research for and publication of their millennium history. During its months of preparation more of Stert's inhabitants visited New College, Oxford (the college archivist asserted) than at any time during their more than six centuries of association.

NOTES (location: SU0359; area: 417ha; population (2001): 153)
General: *VCH* 10, 155-9; Stert Millennium Project, *Stert: the hidden village*, 1999.
New College connection: WRS 13; Pub murders: Chandler, J, *The day returns*, 181-3;
Maps: WSRO 1234/29; X3/47H; Miscellaneous records: *WNQ* 4-6 *passim*.

Upavon

IF I WERE IN CHARGE of Upavon (which rest assured I am not) I might
be tempted to demolish the petrol garage and Spar shop which
dominate the square, and then put down to grass the open space thus
created. Aesthetically speaking, this would be an improvement, but from a
historical point of view it would be quite misleading. The centre of
Upavon is not a despoiled village green; it is the market square of a small
town, and the garage and shop are the successors of other buildings which
probably first encroached on to the square when the market flourished
during the middle ages. Shops in the market place are recorded in the
fifteenth century, and the name 'Shamelplace' occurs in 1488 (shambles
were market stalls). The first map of Upavon, of 1729, depicts market
infill, not only where the garage is now, but also further north, in front of
the *Ship*. These buildings had disappeared by 1838, and their site was
open space in 1886. The first market grant dates from 1220 (the year,
incidentally, in which Salisbury Cathedral was begun), and marketing
continued until some date between 1688 and 1792. The decline of
Upavon as a commercial centre for the surrounding villages seems to have
corresponded with the rise of Pewsey, which by the nineteenth century
had taken over this role. It is pleasing, nevertheless, to see that one
Upavon shopkeeper has been immortalised in stone. The face of George
Carter, grocer here a century ago, stares down from above the door of his
corner shop.

Because of these urban aspirations Upavon is rather different from
its neighbours to north and south. Manningford and Enford are both large
parishes made up of the territories of three and six settlements

respectively. But Upavon, although its land extends up on to downland above both sides of the Avon valley (where there may have been outlying medieval farms), has always been a compact, nucleated community. It is first mentioned in about 940, when it was a royal estate, and the name is derived from the river ('Up-' or 'Upper-' to distinguish it from Netheravon further downstream). The naming of an estate directly from a river is sometimes an indication of importance in the Saxon period (Wylye and Kennet – the old name for Avebury – are other Wiltshire examples); in the case of Upavon, this possibility is strengthened by its possession of a church with a substantial landholding at the time of Domesday. It had probably, therefore, begun as a minster church, and there are indications that Rushall, Charlton and Wilsford churches were all once dependent upon it.

If Upavon was successful in establishing itself as a focal point during the later Saxon period, this must partly have been the result of geography. Its position at the head of the Avon valley means that, like Wylye and Avebury, it stands at one of the great natural cross-roads of Wiltshire. Valley routes following the two principal headwaters of the Avon converge here and turn south; and a downland road sometimes referred to as the Inkpen Ridgeway, which runs along the northern escarpment of Salisbury Plain, has to descend here to cross the river. The crossing at Upavon had been bridged by the end of the middle ages, and after 1762 was used by the turnpike road between Devizes and Andover. A second turnpike, linking Amesbury and Avebury, was created in 1840, and the two roads met and crossed (as the A342 and A345 do today) in Upavon market place. Tollhouses were built to control both roads, near the south-eastern and south-western corners of the market place.

The multiplicity of right-angled bends encountered by traffic using the successors of these routes is a sign that the turnpike trusts for the most part took over sections of existing roads rather than engineering new ones. The pattern was also complicated by the closure of part of an old north–south road, probably when Rushall Park was made in the eighteenth century. This road, which entered Upavon from the north-west across the field called the Ham, was responsible for the line of the road now called Chapel Lane. The name derives from the Strict Baptist chapel converted from a house in 1837–8 and memorably christened 'The Cave of Adullam' (the reference is to an episode in the life of the Old Testament hero, King David). Chapel Lane ends in a group of attractive cottages known as Town End, and Jarvis Street turns the corner to take the explorer back to the market square.

William the Conqueror gave Upavon church, with its lands, to the monks of a Norman abbey, St Wandrille de Fontenelle. It was a valuable possession, and in the thirteenth century the endowment was made into a prebend, to support a canon in Salisbury Cathedral. St Wandrille's also established a small monastic cell at Upavon, which was occupied by a prior and probably no more than one or two monks. In 1423, after the English lands of French monasteries had been confiscated, the control of the priory estate and the prebend of Upavon was transferred to Ivychurch Priory, near Salisbury, who retained it until the dissolution. The grange or monastic cell known as Upavon Priory stood between the churchyard and the river, in a meadow described on the tithe award of 1838 as Priory Mead. Its occupants were probably expelled in 1378, and it was damaged by fire around 1400, but the last buildings were not demolished until the early-nineteenth century.

The present parish church is mostly of Norman and Early English date, with an unusually large tower of about 1300, and a finely sculptured Norman font depicting a lion, a leopard, and the annunciation. St Wandrille's, which must have been responsible for much of this medieval work, had understandably lost interest in the church by 1411, for in that year it was reported that the chancel roof was so bad that snow and rain fell on the altars, which were also soiled by the droppings of owls, pigeons and other harmful birds, and that the church was so draughty that candles blew out immediately they were lit. Although the roofs were rebuilt during the fifteenth century, the church was at some date reduced in size by demolishing the south aisle and blocking the south arcade, perhaps a symptom of Upavon's failure to hold its own as a town. Less harmful birds, jackdaws, still circle the church, and in deference to them, it is said, Upavon residents take the sobriquet 'tree-jacks'.

Upavon's heyday, in fact, probably came in the thirteenth and fourteenth centuries. It was at this period too that it made its only appearance on the stage of national events, for in 1233 a dispute over ownership of the manor led to a full-scale revolt by the barons against the government of Henry III. The claim was settled in favour of the Basset family, and in 1262 they increased Upavon's potential by securing the first of several charters to hold an annual fair in the town. The fair took place each autumn in a field (now built over) to the west of Chapel Lane, and was not discontinued until 1874.

One consequence of the weekly and annual invasions generated by the market and fair was that Upavon had a thriving innkeeping trade. In 1352 a dozen brewers, two tapsters and a victualler were fined for overcharging, and three centuries later the vicar claimed that, in addition to the three licensed houses, there were sometimes twenty or thirty unlicensed and illegal alehouses operating in the parish. One assumes that he was exaggerating – unless, that is, almost the entire population engaged in this sideline at fair time; eighty years later the total number of dwelling-houses and cottages in Upavon (apart from the farmhouses) was only forty-three. One of the licensed premises was presumably the *Antelope*, which is first recorded by name in 1609, although the present inn dates from 1765, with possibly some earlier fabric. Its rival across the square, the *Ship*, is an eighteenth-century house which became an inn about 1865, and is so-named (it is claimed) because the remains of a boat were discovered when its foundations were excavated.

Despite the excitement of market day, and the variety of specialist craftsmen and merchants who lived in medieval Upavon as a consequence, the main concern of most inhabitants must always have been agriculture. Inevitably the standard pattern of chalkland sheep-and-corn farming was practised, with large arable fields on the chalk loam stretching up the hillsides on either side of the valley, from meadowland fringing the river to rough grazing on the downland of the plain. The two halves of the parish, east and west of the river, were virtual mirror images; the 1729 map depicts four common arable fields on each side, still mostly farmed in strips, with four areas of downland east and west beyond them. Parliamentary enclosure took place in 1804, and thereafter most land was concentrated in the hands of five or six large farms. The principal farmhouses and buildings, as so often in late-enclosed parishes with a single,

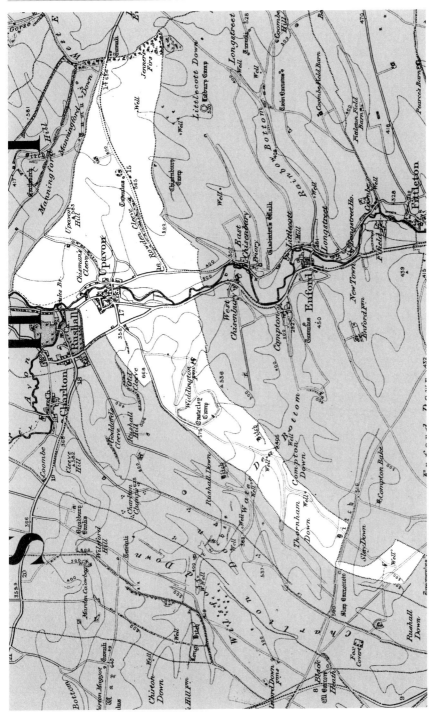

Ordnance Survey 1892 revision, 1 inch = 1 mile

nucleated settlement, stood within or on the edge of the village, and only one, Widdington Farm, lay at a distance.

Despite its habitative-sounding name, Widdington means 'valley of withies', and, although buildings may have existed there in the middle ages, the farmstead dates only from the eighteenth century, and the present buildings are later. But it deserves to be remembered as the birth-place in 1773 of Henry Hunt, the colourful demagogue and reformer, who recorded his memories of the farm in his autobiography, written in a prison cell in Ilchester gaol after the Peterloo massacre in 1819. His father had given him Widdington Farm when he married in 1796, and it was then amply fitted out (after twenty years' disuse) so that he could lead the life of a gentleman farmer. It was, he tells us, a very beautiful farm, with a very good house, and all necessary appendages attached to it.

One effect of enclosure, in Upavon as elsewhere, was that it enabled improving landlords to break up downland for arable. On the corner, as it were, of Salisbury Plain, above Upavon, stands the massive prehistoric enclosure known as Casterley Camp. Colt Hoare visited it and commissioned a survey, not only of the outer bank and ditch (which survive), but also of a number of internal divisions and enclosures. When he returned to the site a few years later, in 1807, he noted: 'Casterley much changed in its appearance having been lately ploughed up. *Nunc seges est ubi Troja fuit* ['where Troy stood there is now a corn-field'].'

Recent fieldwork on the military training area has clarified some aspects, and deepened others, of the lonely, tank-strewn wilderness that stretches away from Casterley deep into Salisbury Plain. Casterley itself is often described as an Iron-Age hillfort – at over 27ha the largest on the plain – but this is an ill-fitting classification for so enigmatic a monument. It is wrongly positioned and too weakly embanked for defence; and finds from the site and its relationship to Bronze-Age linear ditches suggest that it was in use long before the Iron Age. Its purpose in prehistory, and extending into the Roman period, may have been as a collecting and marketing point for sheep, and a place of administrative and ritual assembly for the local population.

That such a population lived not only in the vale is apparent from the survival as earthworks of Romano-British villages south and west of

Casterley, including a settlement of at least thirty houses on Upavon
Down, which was linked to a larger village further west (now in Charlton
and Rushall parishes). These settlements grew corn on the slopes of the
dry downland coombes, notably on Thornham Down, where meticulous
earthwork surveying suggests that the small prehistoric fields were enlarged and re-used in both the Romano-British and medieval periods. In
places, such as the Upavon–Enford boundary following Old Nursery
Ditch, the medieval and modern parishes observed the underlying pattern
of land division; elsewhere, presumably in areas that had reverted to
pasture, the lynchets and ditches were ignored.

As the nineteenth century drew to a close Upavon's downland experienced the two fundamental changes that most Salisbury Plain parishes
underwent at the time. First there was the switch, during the 1880s, from
arable to dairy farming, and then in 1898 acquisition by the War Department for military training. Much of the western downland was taken over
for what became West Down artillery range, and so, from Upavon's point
of view, it was effectively sacrificed. But the military use to which the eastern downland was put was to have a profound effect on the community.

With the formation, in May 1912, of the Royal Flying Corps the
need was identified for a Central Flying School, and this was established
one month later along the Andover road on Upavon Down. Many of the
original buildings, erected between 1912 and 1915, have survived; one
was converted into a museum, and another claimed to be the oldest
officers' mess still in use by the Royal Air Force. Apart from a break of
nine years between the wars *RAF Upavon* continued as a flying school
until 1946, but more recently it has fulfilled various administrative roles. In
addition to sheds and hangars beside the airfield south of the A342, a
complex of buildings, including housing and married quarters, and a
1960s office block, has developed behind security fences to the north of
the road. One unusual modification to the downland landscape was made
in 1912 when archaeologists were called in to watch the levelling of a
Bronze Age barrow close to the airfield, which was regarded as a hazard
to aviators.

RAF Upavon has swollen dramatically the population of the parish.
In both 1801 and 1911 there were 430 inhabitants (the figure having risen

above 500 and fallen again in between); in 1921 and 1931 the total stood at over 700, and reached its peak, 1,668, in 1971. Service families living on the base accounted for a proportion of this increase, but it has also offered civilian employment. For this reason a large estate of local authority housing has gradually taken shape beside the Andover road between the village and the base. It is one of those anomalies that you come to expect on Salisbury Plain – a suburban housing estate, with school and chapel, perched by itself on a chalk hillside. And Upavon itself, although more populous than ever it was when it aspired to being a town, has settled back to being a pleasant village. All it needs now is a village green.

NOTES   (location: SU1355; area: 1,356ha; population (2001): 1,213)
General: *VCH* 10, 159-73; Willis, B A and V H, *A tree-jack's country*, 1992.
Priory: *VCH* 3, 396-7; Church dilapidation: Horn, J M, *Register of Bishop Hallum, 1407-17*, 203-4; Alehouses: Cunnington, B H, *Records of the county of Wilts*, 1932, sv 1648; *Ship*: TS notes by G Charlett [in T]; Hunt: Hunt, H, *Memoirs of Henry Hunt*, 1820; Casterley and downland archaeology: *WANHM* 38, 53-105; *WANHM* 42, 227-30; McOmish, D et al, *Field archaeology of SPTA*, 2002; *RAF Upavon*: Taylor, J W R, *CFS: birthplace of air power*, 2nd ed, 1987.

Urchfont

A WRITER IN 1932 claimed to have found the name 'Urchfont'
spelled in no fewer than 65 ways, and these included forms with
each of the five vowels as the initial letter. Since his day the toponymic
research has continued, so that the tally by 2001 was 111 spellings using
ten different initial letters – such fluidity must surely be a unique distinction. 'Erchfont' was frequently used well into this century (as, for example,
on the village hall inscription of 1929–30), and the pronunciation 'Ushant'
was heard on native lips within living memory. The name probably means
'spring of Eohric', and doubtless refers to the spring now known as 'The
Font' between Rookery Farm and Urchfont Bottom which, it has been
claimed, 'when other springs are at their lowest ebb, flows with greater
rapidity'. When a spring was described by the Saxons as a *funta* (from
Latin *fontana*), rather than the more usual *wielle*, it is thought to imply
that when the name was coined masonry or other evidence of a Roman
construction around the springhead still survived (Teffont and Fovant are
other Wiltshire examples).

Nor is this the sole suggestion of Roman activity in the parish. About
1km west of Urchfont Manor is a considerable area perched on the greensand ridge which is known as Wickham Green. As late as 1820 three
graves were extant belonging to members of the Giddons family, supposedly victims of a plague epidemic in 1644; and modern maps describe this
area as The Three Graves. 'Wickham' place-names (the Urchfont example
is first recorded in 1237) are supposed to derive from *vicus*, the Latin
word for a village, and Wickhams in other parts of England have yielded
evidence of Roman settlements. In the case of Wickham Green a few

Roman and medieval finds have been made in the area, but the existence there of a Roman village is largely speculative at present; however it may be significant that three green lanes, including one which runs north to cut a deep and ancient holloway through the Greensand, meet at the edge of Wickham Green, and there is also a tradition of an underground cavern nearby which was used, perhaps in the eighteenth century, by a robber who was subsequently executed. A third name of some interest in the parish is Crookwood, which is thought to derive from *cruc*, a native British word for a hill, and so (like a similar hill-word underlying neighbouring Conock, in Chirton parish) may be another indication of native Roman and sub-Roman activity in the area continuing into the Saxon period.

Urchfont is one of the largest of the parishes lying along the northern escarpment of Salisbury Plain. In common with many of its neighbours its main settlements – Urchfont itself and Wedhampton – are sited on the rich Greensand, and their strip territories run both south up on to the high chalk downland, and north into the clay vale. There is earth-work evidence of another small settlement within the modern parish at Crookwood, now a single farm complex. The ancient parish was larger, and included Stert, which achieved separate parochial status in 1894, and Eastcott, which was transferred to Easterton in 1934. Wedhampton and Urchfont were both tithings of the larger parish, and Urchfont was for a time subdivided into three smaller units. 'The parish is purely agricultural', wrote a mid-Victorian vicar. The agriculture which he saw from his study window was typical of the area, and dictated by geology – pasture on the claylands, which had been cleared of woodland and enclosed, perhaps by the seventeenth century; market gardening and coppicing on the Green-sand; large, formerly open, arable fields stretching up the chalk escarp-ment; and rough downland grazing for sheep on Salisbury Plain. The downland was purchased for military training before World War One, and public access is restricted by a vedette post on Redhorn Hill. Small streams which emanate from the springline at the base of the chalk flow in deep coombes north and west, and formerly turned mills beside Crookwood Farm, Crookwood Mill Farm and in Peppercombe. The last to work was at Crookwood Mill Farm, which is now in Stert parish. Its leat was about 800m long and powered an overshot wheel made in about 1910.

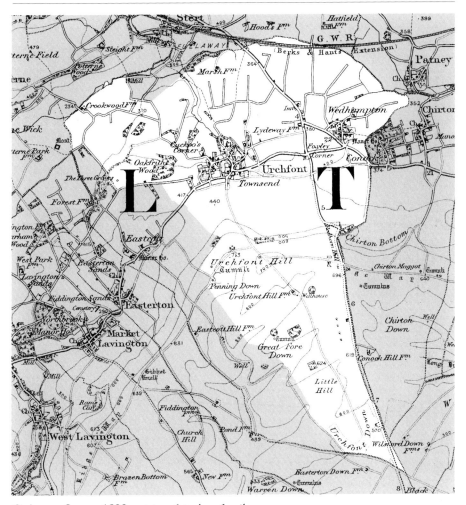

Ordnance Survey 1892 revision, 1 inch = 1 mile

Until closed by the War Department the principal road through the parish connected Salisbury and Devizes. Its northern end is still in use as part of the A342, and has given its ancient name of Lydeway to the small roadside settlement beside the junction where it turned south (the present Urchfont turning). Much of it was turnpiked in 1760–2, and a milestone at Lydeway still proclaims the distance to Salisbury. Some 600m along the turning there is a cross roads known as Foxley Corner (near the former meeting place of Studfold hundred), at which traffic for Urchfont now turns right. The old Salisbury road continued straight on, between the fields and up the escarpment to Redhorn Hill, where there was a turnpike gate. An adjacent field name suggests that near Foxley Corner the road was known as 'Portway'. Multiple trackways may be seen finding alternative routes up the steepest section of the hill. The road's antiquity is suggested by the fact that the parish boundary follows it from Redhorn (which means 'red boundary stone') into the heart of the plain. At Redhorn it crosses another ancient route, supposedly part of the Great Ridgeway, running along the edge of the escarpment, which has now been reopened to (robust) wheeled traffic. At Foxley corner the Salisbury road crossed a second turnpike, the present B3098 through Urchfont village to the Lavingtons. This was the result of a controversial turnpike act in 1769, until which another parallel road running east–west from Conock, via Townsend and Wickham Green, to Easterton Sands, seems to have been at least as important. The section of this road which ran close to Urchfont Manor was diverted on to the turnpike road during the first half of the nineteenth century. It seems strange that no direct road from Urchfont village to its former chapelry at Stert, and on to Devizes, has survived. Peppercombe Lane has been suggested as the Urchfont end of such a route, and modern footpaths perhaps preserve its line in places. Fullaway ('the muddy way') near Stert may be a reference to it, and also to the cause of its abandonment in favour of the Lydeway, a watershed road which was therefore better drained. In 1862 a railway line was built across the northern claylands of the parish – it remains open as part of the London–Exeter main line – and in about 1900 there were plans, which came to nothing, to build a railway station near Stert to serve the Urchfont area.

Urchfont first occurs by name in Domesday Book, although, as we have seen, it is likely that the name, and probably the territory and settlements of Urchfont, date from a considerably earlier period. A Saxon origin has been claimed for foundations of an earlier building discovered beneath the parish church. Urchfont in 1086 was a twenty-hide estate belonging to St Mary's Nunnery, Winchester, in whose hands it remained until the dissolution. The nuns were also patrons of the church, and later appropriated the rectory; it was they or one of their appointees who, at the beginning of the fourteenth century, rebuilt the chancel with its elaborate vault and heavy buttresses. Later the nave was rebuilt, and a perpen-

dicular tower and vaulted porch were added. The nuns' Urchfont estate
was probably administered from a demesne farmhouse on the site of the
present Manor Farm, which lies due south of the church and close to the
picturesque village pond. The present farmhouse retains work which is
contemporary with, or not much later than, an extensive rebuilding known
to have taken place around 1500. The pond has been recently relined,
after the parish council's claim to its ownership was agreed in 1995.

The medieval village, which had an adult population of 209 in 1377
(this figure may include settlements at Crookwood and Wickham Green)
was presumably ranged around the church and pond, and probably
extended along High Street to Townsend, where a late medieval cruck
from a demolished cottage is incorporated into the gable of Townsend
Cottage. In 1676 the adult population of the whole parish (excluding
Stert) was recorded as 1,010; an exaggeration perhaps, this figure
nevertheless suggests a considerable increase in population (despite the
plague epidemic in 1644), which seems to be reflected in the surviving
domestic architecture. Cottages and more substantial houses of this period
are to be found around the Green (or 'Top Green') and Back Lane to the
west of the High Street. They also occur in the secretive part of Urchfont –
rarely discovered by the casual visitor and passer-by – to the east of the
High Street. Here, in Urchfont Bottom and Uphill, many of the cottages
have been built directly against the cliff edge of the deep Greensand
coombes. Informal building around and beside greens and commons, and
along strips of wasteland, occurred at this period all over this part of
Wiltshire, and there is probably no need to explain the triangular green at
the west end of Back Lane as a second medieval nucleus which then
coalesced with Urchfont proper. An estate map of 1784 describes this as
Lower Green, and refers to Upper Green as lying due south of Urchfont
Manor. As so often, it was the settlement around the green which attracted
the chapel (1817–1971) and the beerhouse (*The Lamb*), while the church,
former National school and former inn (recently closed) are to be found in
the older, High Street area.

The Lamb is an attractive timber-framed and thatched building of
the seventeenth century, with evidence of a former brewery in its skittle
alley. The school was replaced by a new building at Cuckoo Corner

behind the manor in 1974. It is approached from the main road along
Blackboard Lane which, however appropriate it may seem, in fact refers
to its former surface of tarred elm boards. During the twentieth century
council and private housing filled the space between the High Street,

green, and road to Lavington, and there has been substantial development also near the church and at Uphill. In consequence the gradual
population slide which continued until after the last war has been reversed,
and Urchfont is once again a large and thriving village community.

Urchfont Manor dates from about 1680, and is regarded by Pevsner as one of the best houses of its type in Wiltshire. It is thought to have been built on the site of an earlier house (from which it retains a fireplace and some other internal fittings) and so it cannot be regarded as simply a very grand example of the process, described above, of informal building on common land. The new house was the creation of a successful London lawyer, Sir William Pynsent, who came to Urchfont in 1678. Nearly ninety years later his son astounded fashionable society by leaving the Urchfont estate, and others, to William Pitt the Younger; whether this was prompted by strong political views or out of spite for his family is not entirely clear. A succession of owners followed, including members of the Watson Taylor family of Erlestoke. The last private owner, like the first, was a lawyer. Hamilton Rivers Pollock bought Urchfont Manor in 1928, and adopted the lifestyle (as his son described it) of 'a romantic but unrealistic eighteenth century squirearchy', which was shattered by the war and concluded by his untimely suicide in 1940. Ten years earlier he had been instrumental in an enterprising communal project, the Urchfont (or rather 'Erchfont') village hall, which, as its plaque declares, was built entirely by voluntary labour – and this included the squire's own clumsy attempts at bricklaying. Since the war Urchfont Manor has taken on a new career, as Wiltshire's adult education college, and so the exquisite house, its vistas and village, have become known and enjoyed by thousands of residential students.

'Wedhampton only' until recently read the sign to Urchfont's other settlement, and in consequence it is little known and rarely visited. The name first occurs in 1249 ('Wed-' refers to weeds), so at Domesday its land was presumably reckoned as part of Urchfont's twenty hides. As one of Urchfont's tithings it shared the same agricultural regime, with its strip of pasture, arable and downland, and its village plan, which now appears to be a simple loop of houses, bears some affinity to Urchfont's. The southern part of the village – or perhaps hamlet – is graced by substantial houses of very high quality, including a manor house and timber-framed farmhouses, whereas at the northern end, where the street divides into Green Gate Road and the Cartway, are humbler cottages, including some shown as cottages on the waste in the tithe award of 1840–2. Rough, overgrown ground along the lane leading north-east (the Cartway) probably denotes the sites of other cottages, as well as two ponds shown on the tithe map. Earlier settlement to the east of Manor Farm is suggested by a field name, Dark Croft, and part of the slope beneath Redhorn Hill, where the hamlet's common field lay, was known as Black Furlong, and may refer to earlier occupation in this area also. As at Urchfont, nonconformity found its home among the cottages on the waste, and the Wesleyan chapel of 1867 (closed in 1964 and since 1969 a private house) lies at the northern end. There has never been an Anglican church, nor was there a medieval chapel-of-ease, in Wedhampton. Fleece Cottage, an industrial building of 1860 (the date and initials WR are picked out in coloured bricks), may have been built by William Romain, bricklayer and parish clerk, for a woolstapler, with areas for sorting, washing and baling wool. It later served as the village shop.

NOTES (location: SU0457; area: 1,980ha; population (2001): 954)
General: *VCH* 10, 173-90; *Urchfont by any other name: a history of the parish*, 2001; *WNQ* 4-6, *passim*; Hamilton, K, and Stark, A, *Urchfont remembered*, 1982.
Name: *WANHM* 46, 47-8; Victorian vicar: WANHS Library, MS 41, no. 43; Wickham names: *Landscape History* 24, 27-45; Crookwood Mill: *Wiltshire Industrial Archaeology* 3, 21-9; Manor: *WANHM* 46, 35-49; Barklem, T, *Urchfont: the evolution of a house in its setting*, 1977.

West Lavington

I T LIES FAR AWAY from the coming and going of the great busy world,'
wrote an inhabitant in 1875. Today, and for many decades, the great
busy world speeds along the A360 from Salisbury to Devizes and threads
its way precipitously through the chicane formed by the churchyard and
the almshouses. In fact the main road spends about 8km in West Lavington parish, from the high downland south of Gore, the 'buried village of
Salisbury Plain', past Gore Cross, where it is intersected by an important
ridgeway, down a long descent beside landscaped woodland (known as
The Warren) and into the pleasant valley where the village sits, then along
some 2km of ribbon development associated with the linear village of
Littleton Pannell, before leaving the parish north of the railway bridge.
This journey is familiar to most Wiltshire travellers, and even without
realising that chalk is giving way to Greensand and clay, many must feel
as they pass along that here south Wiltshire ends and west Wiltshire begins.

Since 1884 the parish has consisted of three units – Gore, formerly
in Market Lavington, West (or Bishops) Lavington and Littleton Pannell.
Previously Fiddington, now in Market Lavington, was in West Lavington,
and all seem to have been constituent parts in Saxon times of a territory
known as Rowborough, which had been split up between the king and the
bishop of Salisbury by the thirteenth century. West Lavington, like
Potterne its northern neighbour, belonged to the bishop, hence its
alternative name. Littleton ('the small farmstead') acquired its suffix from
the Paynell family who owned it in the thirteenth century; and Gore,
which means a triangular piece of land, is an accurate description of the
former tithing's territory.

Gore as a village has disappeared; it is represented now solely by a rather fetid pond at Gore Cross, and by St Joan à Gore farmhouse further south. They stand at the head of the Till valley, on the watershed between the Salisbury and Bristol Avon river systems. The name is apparently corrupted from a chapel of St John which stood to the west of the house. It existed in 1322 but was disused by 1550; its foundations, along with evidence of houses, were uncovered in 1877, but had disappeared by 1926. The chapel has been located again by geophysical survey, which showed it to have been a simple apsidal structure, about 17 x 5m in plan. A twelfth-century wheel cross grave-marker found nearby was re-used as a memorial to John Thurnam at Roundway Hospital.

High on the plain, Gore was probably always a small community, but it existed in the eleventh century, and so cannot be explained as a product of land hunger in the twelfth and thirteenth. Some evidence of former Roman occupation in the area has also been recorded. Traditionally the village is supposed to have met its end by fire in the seventeenth century, its inhabitants taking refuge at Market Lavington because West Lavington would not help; but this is probably merely a folk explanation of why Gore came under the jurisdiction of Market, rather than West, Lavington, coupled with vague memory of a real fire which occurred at West Lavington in 1689. In fact the population of Gore in 1691, seventeen, was probably about the same as in 1377, and it was left to the War Office after 1900 to provide the final straw.

Littleton Pannell possesses few buildings earlier than the nineteenth century, but there is nothing to indicate that its layout has been altered since medieval times. Indeed the regularity of the village plan on a map of about 1767 suggests that it was laid out as a linear settlement along an important road. The tithing had the normal allowance of clay in the north (early enclosed as pasture and meadow), Greensand in the centre, on which lay the village and, unusually, the arable fields – east, middle and west, and still partially open in 1767 – and a thin tongue of chalk downland, described as 'over the hill,' extending now to the remote (and aptly named) New Zealand Farm. The slow-coach road from Salisbury to Bath across Salisbury Plain crosses the extremity of the parish here.

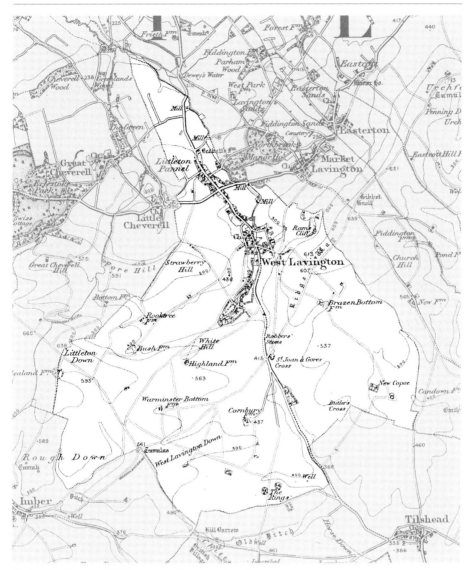

Ordnance Survey 1892 revision, 1 inch = 1 mile

The most substantial group of buildings in Littleton Pannell is
Dauntsey's School, moved to its present site in 1895; and the largest
house, almost invisible from the road, is Becketts, of 1904, rebuilt from an
earlier manor house (William Beckett owned part of the manor in 1542).
The house is notorious for the murder there in 1644 of Captain Henry
Penruddocke. Another anecdote of lawlessness in Littleton Pannell dates

from 1825, when the tollgates leases in the area were taken by local villagers (see Market Lavington), and the gates near the cross-roads were removed, paraded along the streets and ceremoniously burnt; the gatekeeper, apparently, narrowly escaped a similar fate. In a gentler vein, David Saunders, immortalised as the model of piety by Hannah More in her famous and influential religious tract, *The Shepherd of Salisbury Plain*, was born in the village. He became a notable evangelist in the Methodist cause throughout this part of Wiltshire in the late-eighteenth century, and was buried at West Lavington in 1796.

West Lavington has a complicated village plan, and it is not possible to interpret it with any certainty. The church, portions of which date from about 1200, has its main approach from the west, and here too is the Old Manor House. Perhaps, therefore, an early village centre lay in this area. Like Great Wishford in the Wylye valley, the churchyard is entirely sur-rounded by roads. A second focus may be represented by the triangular green-like area some 200m south of the church along the main road, beside the stream and at the foot of a long holloway. A third area of development, east of the village, is represented by the name New Town, and also by extensive disturbances and earthwork features in the Duck Street and Lime Kiln Hill areas. Other elements are the almshouses and former school complex (apparently erected on a vacant site in the mid-sixteenth century) to the north-east of the church, and further north along the main road a manor house (probably of sixteenth-century origin), and later ribbon development.

West Lavington in the middle ages appears to have been a place of some importance. In 1334 it was the seventh most highly rated community in Wiltshire; it was still in 1523/4 assessed as worth more than Potterne. It may be reasonable, therefore, to assume that a large area, including the land from the church eastwards to New Town, was built over in the middle ages. In 1689 a catastrophic fire engulfed the village, and destroyed 226 'bayes of buildings.' About 26 owners seem to have lost buildings and 34 lost goods (three deaths noted in the burial register may also be connected), and it is tempting to imagine the fire to have occurred in the area of the settlement earthworks. But one of the buildings destroyed was the parsonage. The house now known as the Parsonage lies immediately

south of the church, and seems to date from shortly after the fire. Another
house, Dial House, by the supposed triangular green, dates from 1691,
and so was presumably built to replace a casualty. It is more likely,
therefore, that the area laid waste in 1689 included these two buildings
and so lay south of the church. There is no record of the fire having
affected the almshouses further north. This fire, and piecemeal rebuilding
thereafter, are doubtless to blame for the confused topography. The
resulting rather untidy plan has been further modified since 1800 by the
tendency of West Lavington and Littleton Pannell to grow towards each
other along the main road. One building beside this road is equipped with
long hooks for removing thatch from burning buildings.

If it is the ambition of a landed family to leave its mark on a place,
the Dauntseys may be well pleased with their success. They were lessees
of land in West Lavington from 1474 or earlier until 1630, when their
holding passed by marriage to the Danvers, and later the Bertie, families.
They beautified the church, embellishing the rebuilt south transept with
their 'D' monogram, and turning it into a Dauntsey Chapel. In 1542
William Dauntsey left money to found three public buildings in the village,
a church house (this was probably never built), a school and a group of
eight almshouses. The charity survived, and the almshouses, which were
rebuilt in 1810 but derelict in 1974, have been restored. They lie on their
original site, east of the church, and almost facing an earlier and humbler
group of three, the South Bank Almshouses (endowed in 1499 and rebuilt

in 1831). In the nineteenth century Dauntsey's Almshouses were known
as Mercers' Almshouses, and behind them ran Mercers' Lane. The school
was also on this site. By then it was moribund and poorly regarded; its
renaissance dates from 1891, when the charity was reorganised to endow
an elementary school, opened in 1898, and an agricultural college, which
has become the modern public school. Both were established on new sites
at Littleton Pannell.

   The transformation of Dauntsey's School began in the 1920s under
the inspirational leadership of its head, George Olive, which continued
until 1956. Lavington Manor (the manor house of Market Lavington, but
approached from and regarded as part of Littleton Pannell) was acquired
for boarders in 1929. Extensive new buildings, to some extent built by the
staff and pupils, were added during the 1950s and later, as the school
grew. Important developments during the 1970s were the links it forged
with Lavington comprehensive school by teaching the latter's sixth form
pupils; and the move to become co-educational, which was achieved in
1976. Thus the Dauntsey name lives on.

   Their successors, the Danvers, also made their mark. Sir John
Danvers, who acquired the property by marriage after 1630, 'had a very
fine fancy', according to Aubrey, 'which lay chiefly for gardens and
architecture'. He rebuilt West Lavington manor house (although the
present house is largely a 1908 Arts and Crafts remodelling) and laid out
extensive gardens in the Italian style along either side of the stream below
the house. From Aubrey's description they appear to have been
comparable to those at Wilton House, and to have extended from the
present main road by the great arch (which survives), north-eastwards
towards Market Lavington and up the hillside opposite the house to give
views across the fields.

   This garden, and the later landscaping (as wooded parkland with a
series of ponds) of the valley above West Lavington village known as The
Warren have not, so far as I am aware, received the attention from garden
historians that they deserve. The Warren perhaps lay on the estate built up
by the Hunt family after 1700 from a house at the southern end of the
village known until 1979 as The Lodge, but now renamed Hunt's House.
William Hunt, who died there in 1753, was a magistrate whose justicing

notebook covering the years 1744-9 has survived and been published; it provides a fascinating window on to the frailties and parochial concerns of the local society which he strove to govern.

Of the agriculture and communications of the parish little more need be said, since they follow the pattern set by its neighbours. The railway station to serve this area was opened in 1900 and closed in 1966; it lay near the railway bridge across the main road north of Littleton Pannell, where a station hotel was built, and later known as the *Chocolate Poodle*. The busy A360, although doubtless an ancient route, has only taken on its present importance during the twentieth century, with the closure of the Salisbury–Devizes roads across the military areas of Salisbury Plain. It was turnpiked as far south as West Lavington village in 1750/1, but the ascent to Gore and beyond was never a turnpike, although there was sufficient traffic along it in October 1839 for it to be a haunt of highwaymen, as an inscribed stone testifies, commemorating the robbery of an Imber farmer on his way home from market, and the subsequent fate of his assailants; it stands beside the road a little north of Gore pond.

NOTES (location: SU0053; area: 2,395ha: population (2001): 1,281)
General: *VCH* 7, 198-206; 10, 82-106 *passim* (Gore); Awdry, R W, notes on West Lavington [typescript in WANHS Library]; WANHS Library, Wilts Cuttings, 16, 268-72. Gore chapel: *WNQ* 2, 87; McOmish, D, *et al*, *The field archaeology of Salisbury Plain*, 2002, 126, 130-1; David Saunders: Evans, G E, *Pastoral pedigree*, 1977; 1689 Fire: Cunnington, B H, *Records of the county of Wilts*, 1932, 275; Dauntsey's School: Olive, G W, *A school's adventure*, 1951; Hodges, J, *How does your garden grow?*, 1992; Italianate garden: Aubrey, J, *Natural history of Wiltshire*, 1847 ed, 93; Hunt: WRS 37; Robber stone: Sawyer, R, *Little Imber on the Down*, 2001, 11.

Wilcot

T WO PROMINENT LANDMARKS fix the eastern and western edges of this
confusing parish. Giant's Grave, a spur of Martinsell Hill fortified as
an iron age promontory fort, towers above Oare and Rainscombe, the
parish's eastern settlements. In the west Picked Hill (perhaps once known
as Cocklebury), as near conical as one can expect of a hill, was a
traditional place of assembly on Good Friday, and was perhaps a landmark associated with Swanborough Tump, 1km south (in Manningford
parish), the meeting place of the hundred. The parish rises more than
150m from its lowest point near Wilcot church to the edge of the scarp
near Withy Copse. Apart from Rainscombe, which sits in a huge chalk
bowl, all the modern settlements lie on the Upper Greensand of Pewsey
Vale, drained by minor tributaries of the Salisbury Avon flowing south.
North of the scarp the views are towards Marlborough and beyond, and
here the chalk is capped by clay-with-flints.

The backbone of roads in the parish is a saltire cross, formed by a
north–south route from Marlborough to the Avon valley known as Hare
Street, and a continuation of the Workway Drove from Pewsey towards
Wansdyke, which in the thirteenth century formed the south-western
boundary of Savernake Forest. As its name implies Hare Street was a
Saxon *herepath*, or military road; north of Oare, where it climbed the hill
in a now overgrown holloway slightly west of the present course, it was
also called Portway, the market road to Marlborough.

Several Romano-British settlements have been discovered in the
parish, including lowland sites north-east of Draycot Farm, north of
Sunnyhill Lane beneath Giant's Grave, and in the area known

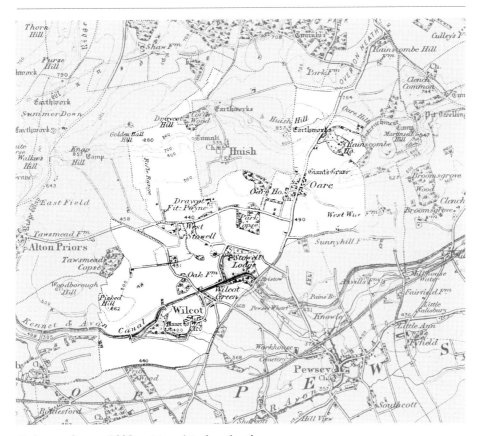

Ordnance Survey 1892 revision, 1 inch = 1 mile

significantly as Castle Ground on the parish boundary between East and
West Stowell (no doubt associated with the villa site at nearby Stanchester
in Alton parish). But the most important Romano-British site seems to
have been an industrial colony of potters who in the mid-first century
began to produce pottery for the Roman army, and later for civilian
markets, from a base at Withy Copse high on the downs in the north of
the parish. Where these potters came from is unclear. It has been
suggested that they followed the Roman army as it moved west, and
finding that suitable clay (the clay-with-flints deposit overlying the chalk)
was readily available here they began an industry which later spread to
various sites nearby. The characteristic grey, lumpy pottery that their kilns
produced is known as Savernake Ware by archaeologists, and from its
marketing centre at *Cunetio* (Mildenhall) it became widely dispersed

through southern England in the Roman period. In later centuries the same raw material was used for brickmaking in the vicinity.

Although other Romano-British settlements may remain to be discovered, none of the sites (except possibly Draycot) so far known corresponds with the five principal foci of Saxon and medieval settlement, at Wilcot, Draycot, East Stowell, Oare and Rainscombe. Wilcot, 'the cottages by the spring,' is first mentioned in a charter of 940, and this implies that it then lay at or near the point where Hare Street crosses a stream some 500m south-east of the parish church. A spring is marked nearby on modern maps, and earthworks are visible from the air extending south-east from the later village centre beside the church. The present positions of church and adjacent manor house were probably settled in the eleventh century. The first recorded owner of Wilcot, Edward of Salisbury, built a new church shortly before 1086. His house was then described as very fine (and so may also have been new) and he had a good vineyard. His grandson gave the manor in the mid-twelfth century to Bradenstoke Priory, who retained it until the dissolution, probably as a monastic grange, of which fishponds south of the village are the only obvious survival.

Between 1572 and 1900 Wilcot, together with East Stowell, belonged to members of a single family, with the surnames Wroughton and Montagu. Their influence has been profound, not only in their building work around the church and manor house, with fine thatched barns and ornamental grounds, but also at East Stowell and Wilcot Green. Their work in restoring the church in 1835, however, was spoilt by a disastrous fire in 1876, possibly caused by sparks from a chimney in the manor house, and the present church fabric, except the tower, dates largely from after that date. Another building which has undergone successive renewals is the vicarage. The present house of 1969 replaced a Victorian building which succeeded a humbler vicarage, said to have been haunted in the seventeenth century by a continually tolling bell, a 'debauched person's' revenge on an uncooperative vicar. One more recent (around 1950) resident of Wilcot was the actor David Niven, who briefly lived in the manor house after many years in Hollywood, and whose autobiography recalls his surprise one autumn morning at finding the local hunt enjoying its opening meet, according to tradition, in his garden.

Two events which occurred almost simultaneously at the beginning of the nineteenth century conspired to change the parish dramatically. The Wroughton family permitted the Kennet and Avon canal to cross their land on two conditions: that it be widened to form an ornamental lake, known as Wide Water, west of their manor house; and that the view of the lake be closed by an ornate bridge over the canal. The resulting Ladies' Bridge, which was designed by John Rennie and carries the date 1808, is a well-known canal landmark. The ladies (not Ladies) in question were both named Susannah Wroughton, mother and daughter. The construction of the canal also led to the diversion of the lane from Wilcot to East Stowell, which formerly ran north from near the green, past a group of (long-vanished) cottages and along a causeway known as Stoneham Bridge. A private suspension footbridge was built in 1845 to cross the canal near this point by a Bath engineer, James Dredge, to his own innovative patent, and it survives; but the lane was carried alongside the canal to join the main road north of Wilcot Bridge.

While these alterations were being made the Wroughton family was also engaged in creating Stowell Lodge, a grand house completed in 1813, and surrounded by a park. Emparking involved the destruction of East Stowell village, which lay along either side of the north–south lane, and the removal of its inhabitants to Wilcot Green. Such wholesale displacement of communities was by no means uncommon at this period, but there are not too many examples in Wiltshire; this is one of the most substantial if not the most ornate – for which see Erlestoke elsewhere in this volume. The large triangular village green, the most memorable feature of the present village, was fronted by some houses, including an inn, in the eighteenth century. The village pound and stocks lay at its south-western corner, and until the late-nineteenth century it was graced by large elm trees. By 1779 there were said to be eleven cottages around the green, and further building work took place before 1803. Soon afterwards the symmetrical row of seven pairs of cottages along the western side and three in similar style at the south-east corner had been constructed, apparently using materials salvaged from demolished buildings at

East Stowell. A school was built overlooking the green in 1841, but it is now a private house. The present inn, the *Golden Swan*, was built around 1859 at the south-east corner of the green. It succeeded the *White Swan*, which lay with other buildings further south-west, and this in turn succeeded the *Black Swan* or *Swan* at the Hare Street crossroads.

This reordering of villages and the lives of their inhabitants occurred when power was concentrated in the hands of a single owner. Oare, the other sizeable village in the parish, presents a contrast, since until consolidation in the nineteenth century it was divided between many owners. The name, first recorded as *Motenesora* in 934, means 'flat-topped hill,' and the prefix is apparently an owner's name, used to distinguish it from *Matteles ore* (Martinsell) further east. Recent work on this interesting word has shown that it probably came into Saxon parlance from Latin *ora* ('shore'), which was shouted by sailors when they spotted 'land ahoy'. It came to be used of a hill which was a prominent landmark, whether guiding mariners to a known point on the coast, or – as here – pointing overland travellers to their route up the escarpment, the former *herepath*.

Oare is a busy linear village, with a seldom-observed speed limit, built along Hare Street, which is here now part of the A345 Salisbury–Marlborough road. Until 1857 it had no church, and was therefore receptive to nonconformity. In 1851 the Wesleyan chapel, tucked down a lane east of the main road, enjoyed a larger attendance than Wilcot parish church. Largely from a single benefaction a church was built in Oare in 1858 and was granted parochial status in 1892. A simple, clean Victorian brick building, said to have been modelled on a public school chapel, and set on rising ground against a backcloth of trees, it hardly deserves Pevsner's judgement (later half-heartedly retracted) of the ugliest church in Wiltshire.

It stands close to Oare House, a fine eighteenth-century mansion made of local brick, with a spectacular vista (usually missed by the hurrying motorist) to the main road along an avenue of lime trees. The house and gardens were remodelled in 1921-5 by Clough Williams Ellis, the distinguished architect and creator of Portmeirion in north Wales, who was also responsible for building several of the more humble dwellings in the village at this period, and a more substantial house, Cold Blow. For Oare House he re-used local bricks from a derelict house and a chapel on Huish Hill. His client, Sir Geoffrey Fry, was private secretary to two prime ministers, and during World War Two cabinet meetings were held in the house.

Oare was the scene of rickburning during the agricultural riots of 1830, and a second case of arson in 1834 devastated the farm and fortune of the leading family in the village. A labourer, Charles Kimmer, was subsequently hanged for the offence, after some astute detective work by a Bow Street Runner (there being no Wiltshire constabulary until 1838), and a sermon was preached in Wilcot church entitled 'Satan's workshop,' to dissuade other prospective malcontents. The Old Oxyard, a seventeenth-century yeoman's house, hidden behind a long thatched shed which backs on to the main road, was spared a similar fate. It became the home of the eminent historian, G M Young, during the 1930s and 1940s.

Draycot, 'the cottages by the slope,' is a Domesday manor which has taken the name of a fourteenth-century owner, Fitzpayne, doubtless to distinguish it from the other Wiltshire Draycots. Fitzpayne's predecessor had made arrangements with Bradenstoke Priory in the late-thirteenth century to endow a chantry chapel on his estate; a grave-slab from the chapel was allegedly dug up north-east of Draycot Farm in 1879. Traces of the moat and fishponds which surrounded the medieval manor house still exist south of the farm. The owner in 1545, Walter Skylling, was the second wealthiest man in Swanborough hundred; his descendants adhered to the catholic faith, and their house sheltered sick and elderly Jesuits in the seventeenth century.

Most secret of the Wilcot settlements is Rainscombe, 'the valley of ravens.' The early nineteenth-century house lies centre-stage beneath a towering natural theatre formed by Oare Hill and Giant's Grave, but it is hardly seen from the main road. Until 1885 it lay not in Wilcot parish, but was a detached portion of North Newnton, perpetuating an anomaly which can be traced back to a Saxon grant of 934 to Wilton Abbey. Much of its territory was wooded in the early medieval period, and it fell within Savernake Forest jurisdiction until 1330. When transferred to Wilcot in 1885 its population was about 35, and by then a new farm had been built beside the main road. Its farmer during the 1930s was a noted (and knighted) agriculturalist, Anthony Hurd, whose son Douglas spent his childhood here, before rising to political prominence as a minister in the Thatcher administration.

NOTES (location: SU1461; area: 1,223ha; population (2001): 512)
General: *VCH* 10, 190-204; Ibberson, D, *Two Wiltshire villages*, 1963; WSRO 1739/26, 28, 31.
Roman buildings: *WANHM* 66, 71-5; Savernake pottery site: *WANHM* 36, 125-39; *Britannia* 6, 36-61; Timby, J, in Ellis, P (ed.) *Roman Wiltshire and after*, 2001, 73-84; Niven: Niven, D, *The moon's a balloon*, 1972; Dredge: *Civil Engineering* 102 (Feb. 1994), 34-42; The name *ora*: *J English Place-Name Soc* 21, 15-22; 22, 26-41; Arson: Goddard, H, *Memoirs of a Bow Street Runner*, 1956; Rainscombe: *VCH* 10, 128, 130, 132; Hurd, D, *Memoirs*, 2003.

Wilsford

THERE IS LITTLE REMARKABLE about Wilsford. It typifies the strip parishes of chalkland Wiltshire. Its territory extends from the normally tranquil branch of the River Avon which flows through Pewsey Vale, to Ell Barrow, a solitary tattered mound high on one of the most desolate and shell-shocked landscapes of Salisbury Plain. The parish shares its name with a village in the Woodford valley north of Salisbury, both of which may be derived from a form of the word 'weevil' (beetle), or from a personal name. Two Saxon charters of neighbouring North Newnton, dated 892

and 934, refer to this ford, and imply that it lay not at the present causeway and bridge by Cuttenham Farm (this was called 'Teolta's ford'), but further upstream, near Puckshipton. In prehistoric and Saxon times it was

probably one of the river-crossings used by travellers along the Great
Ridgeway as they picked their way across the vale from one chalk massif
to the other.

The village, however, is not aligned on this north–south route, but
sits on the valley gravel along an east–west street, which presumably once
formed part of a road connecting the ribbon of settlements, from Urchfont
to Rushall, which lie on the southern side of the vale. Fortunately for them,
the turnpike road of 1761/2, now part of the A342 Devizes–Andover road,
took a more southerly course across their parishes on firmer ground at the
foot of the lower chalk slope. The layout of the settlement suggests a
planned medieval village, with buildings lining both sides of its street. On
the south side a common rear croft boundary runs almost parallel with
the street, and a second boundary lies a further 200m south, now
marked by a track. The tithe map of 1844 shows a similar croft
boundary north of the street, although by then (as now) there were few
buildings on this side. Several houses disappeared on the southern side
between 1844 and 1886, their sites now represented by faint earthworks;
these losses were doubtless in consequence of a rapidly declining
population. In fact from a peak of 306 in 1851 the number of inhabitants
had dipped to 128 by 1901.

But long before this the village had probably tended to polarise
about the two manor houses which lie at either end of the street, Wilsford
Manor and Wilsford House. The division of the parish into two estates had
occurred by the thirteenth century, and although the present brick and
slate manor houses are only a couple of centuries old or less, they are
doubtless on or near the sites of their predecessors. The more important,
Wilsford Manor, lies at the eastern end, where are also the church, and
former vicarage and mill. The church retains a re-set Norman doorway, an
unspoilt thirteenth-century chancel and a Perpendicular tower and nave,
but its medieval north chapel (later used as a school and a bakehouse)
was demolished as recently as 1957. From the middle ages until 1939 the
nearby village of Manningford Bohun formed part of the ecclesiastical
parish of Wilsford, and its Victorian chapel of ease was dependent on
Wilsford church. Between Wilsford churchyard and the mill are substantial
earthworks. A National school, built in 1848 and closed in 1965, also lay

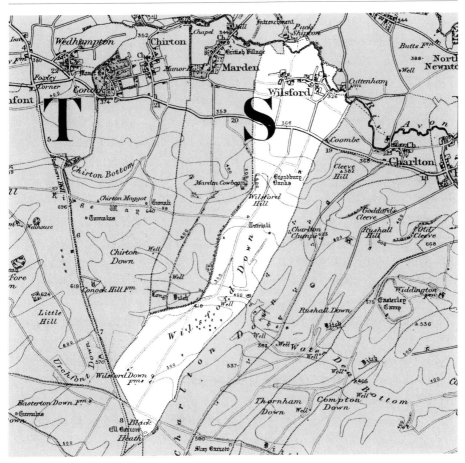

Ordnance Survey 1892 revision, 1 inch = 1 mile

in the built-up eastern part of the village. It site, north of the street, is now occupied by two modern houses.

The western end of the street accommodates Wilsford House, successor to the demesne house of the Wilsford Dauntsey estate, as well as a former malthouse and dwelling, and the former *Poores Arms*, marked as a beerhouse on the tithe map of 1844, and later an off-licence, but now a smart private house. Cheek by jowl across the lane in 1844 was an Independent Methodist chapel, built in 1823; it had gone by 1886, when the site (as now) was deserted.

Wilsford's geology and agricultural history are typical of chalkland strip parishes. Meadows lay north of the village beside the Avon and a tributary stream, the Cadburne; south of the village to the foot of the scarp, where the lower chalk produced a suitable loam, lay the common arable fields, enclosed in 1808; rough sheep pasture was on the high downland of Salisbury Plain, about half the total acreage of the parish, and this became after 1897 part of the military ranges. Unmolested by medieval and later agriculture, these sad, inaccessible downs have retained extensive field systems, enclosures and linear earthworks of their prehistoric farmers. Finds of Iron-Age and Romano-British material along the escarpment imply settlement sites in this area, related perhaps to the extensive settlement nearby on Charlton Down. Air photographs taken in 1981 have been interpreted as showing traces of a henge monument between Wilsford House and the river, less than 1km from the well-known Marden Henge. Earthworks on the hillside, known as Broadbury Banks, have long been thought to be the remains of an unfinished Iron-Age hillfort. Colt Hoare dug into them and found nothing; and a recent archaeological survey concluded that they are merely part of a medieval or later curving holloway leading up on to the downs.

Though unremarkable Wilsford is far from unattractive. The older village houses which remain are mostly thatched, and two (Cruck End and no. 18) retain medieval crucks. Around its church the village poses for a handsome group portrait. Quiet, small and without most facilities Wilsford nevertheless does not seem remote. Nine or ten other villages lie within a five-minute drive, and the main road to Devizes is reassuringly visible across the fields.

NOTES (location: SU1057; area: 709ha; population (2001): 73)
General: VCH 10, 204-14.
Prehistoric enclosures: WANHM 87, 159; Broadbury Banks: McOmish, D et al, Field archaeology of SPTA, 2002, 79, 81.

Woodborough

THE HILL WHICH GIVES Woodborough its name lies in the extreme north of this small parish. It is not wooded now, but the few trees which cling under the lee of its summit give it a distinctive appearance. The Kennet and Avon Canal crosses from east to west between the hill and the village, and marks the division between chalk to the north and Greensand to the south. In common with most Pewsey Vale villages the main settlement at Woodborough developed away from the main roads; the village street is a cul-de-sac, leading past a Victorian church to a few houses and a former Methodist chapel of about 1820. By the church the street widens, and is depicted on a map of 1773 as a considerable triangular green; the churchyard, grazed by sheep, offers a peaceful view across the vale to the Alton white horse and Marlborough Downs.

Apart from the nearby Church Farm, the church is the most northerly building in the village, and there are no signs of earthworks in the field beyond. The medieval settlement, therefore, presumably lay around a thin wedge-shaped green, its apex to the south, with lanes leading off north-east to Woodborough Hill and north-west to Alton. There are hints of a boundary bank running south-east from the former chapel; perhaps (and this is no more than conjecture) this could have marked the western edge of the village, and its eastern boundary may now be followed by the lane past Church Farm.

The main lines of communications through Woodborough seem always to have been independent of the village plan, and consequently secondary settlements have sprung up beside them away from the village. (As early as 1249 there is a reference to a three-acre housing development on common pasture land.) The Great Ridgeway, which had to abandon high ground in order to cross Pewsey Vale, probably picked one or more routes from north to south through Woodborough parish, and it has been suggested that the name Honeystreet (first recorded in 1773, but perhaps much older, and referring to a farm near the site of a Roman villa) may be a comment on the sticky nature of the ridgeway at this point.

A north–south route lay some 300m west of the present line, and Little Woodborough grew up along the lane to meet it. An important inn, the *Rose and Crown,* stood at the junction, but now the lane consists mostly of modern housing and a social club. The lane itself, which continues eastwards to meet Woodborough village street, is of some antiquity. It is mentioned in a charter of 941, when it was sufficiently important to have a stone ford across the brook near the present mill house, and it still forms Woodborough's southern parish boundary. In 941 an 'old farmstead' lay somewhere along it near the modern cross roads. The present north–south road is in part the product of a turnpike trust constituted in 1840 (and therefore one of the last in England) to build and improve the route from the Bath road at West Kennet to Amesbury, thus linking north and south Wiltshire. Its rerouting in Woodborough in about 1842 stimulated development at the new road junction, including the former *Station Hotel* of the early-twentieth century. The site of the station itself, together with Woodborough School, lie in Beechingstoke parish.

The fortunes of two farming families, whose influence has been felt far beyond Woodborough, can be traced back to the parish. James Stratton, a saddler and harness-maker, who died in 1809 and has his tombstone in Woodborough churchyard, is claimed as the patriarch of a dynasty which ramified across Wiltshire and beyond during the nineteenth century – to the extent that in farming circles the county was sometimes dubbed 'Stratton-shire'. His stroke of fortune came, according to family tradition, when, having supported the squire against a bogus claim to the estate, he was entrusted with Woodborough Farm.

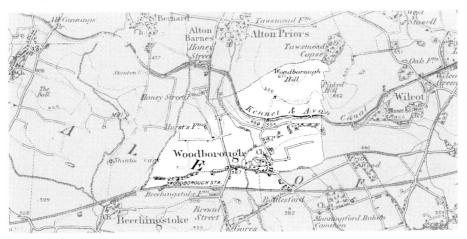

Ordnance Survey 1892 revision, 1 inch = 1 mile

The Robbins family had lived and farmed in Woodborough since the seventeenth century, and occupied the manor farm from 1802. Samuel Robbins, a leading figure in the promotion of the Kennett and Amesbury Turnpike Trust, was a member of this family. Not having the acreage nor the potential for agricultural improvement of many neighbouring parishes, Woodborough's farming community welcomed the opportunities to diversify offered by the completion of the Kennet and Avon Canal in 1810. In the following year Samuel Robbins began to build a wharf alongside the canal at Honeystreet (then in the extreme north of Woodborough parish, although recently transferred to Alton). It became not only an important distribution centre for the surrounding villages (hence his interest in the turnpike), but also fostered a successful boatbuilding enterprise. To an area of chronic depressed agricultural wages this nineteenth-century industrial estate was an important source of revenue – a labourer in 1830 who could earn eight shillings for a week in the fields might earn twenty at the wharf. The wharf's clock tower of 1854, and some other Victorian buildings (many rebuilt after a fire, also in 1854), have been demolished in recent years. But a tall chimney (incongruously attached to a greenhouse) and some industrial and domestic buildings remain, together with a sawmill and the *Barge Inn* – this, however, lies just beyond the old and new parish boundaries, in Stanton St Bernard.

Honeystreet is still an attractive industrial hamlet, of a type not usually associated with Wiltshire, and its future, as canal leisure grows in popularity, seems assured.

NOTES: (location: SU1160; area: 416ha; population (2001): 267)
General: *VCH* 10, 214-24.
1249 reference to commons: WRS 26, 52; Strattons: Stratton, R F, *A history of the Wiltshire Strattons*, 1987; Robbins: Robbins, M, *Gleanings of the Robins or Robbins family . . .*, 1908, 90-103.

Wootton Rivers

W HICHEVER WAY you approach it – except by canal – a visit to Wootton Rivers involves several miles of twisting narrow lanes. And yet everyone seems to have heard of it, and been there, and come away with a favourable impression. As well they might, for it is among the most attractive of Wiltshire's thatched villages, and, although few of its present-day residents are natives, it still seems imbued with a sturdy, slightly old-fashioned independence, born of its isolation.

The village appraisal, a self-examination undertaken in 1985, is full of commonsense and intelligent comment. In 2000 the parish council invited each household to write for publication something about themselves (76 of 116, almost two-thirds, responded), and then distributed copies of the resulting booklet to everyone in the village. But something of its character is caught too in anecdotes from its earlier history. Peter Waterman, vicar during the civil war, was a clubman who described the Earl of Essex as cuckold and rebel, and Parliament as a company of tinkers and pedlars. He farmed his glebe in person, encouraged card-playing, and skittles on Sunday, and his wife sold mead.

Better known is the story of John Kingstone Spratt, dubbed the village genius, who, when plans for a new church clock to commemorate George V's coronation were found to be too expensive, volunteered to make one from odds and ends. A broom handle for its pendulum, a cattle-trough for its face, and a blacksmith's hammer for its striker, the job took him four months, and achieved national fame for the village when it was unveiled in 1911. It still works, having undergone restoration in 1977.

Wootton, the farm by the wood, existed in the early ninth century, when land there was acquired by the bishop of Winchester. The wood in question is presumably a reference to Savernake, within whose forest jurisdiction Wootton lay during the early middle ages until 1300. The affix distinguishes the village from Wootton Bassett, and refers to the Rivers or de Ripariis family, manorial owners from the thirteenth to the fifteenth century. Domesday Wootton, with nearly thirty hides and two churches, seems too large for the present small parish, and the entry probably embraces part or all of Easton and perhaps Milton Lilbourne as well.

East Wick is a nice example of an outlying dairy farm (the common meaning of Wick) and is well seen from the chalk escarpment beneath which it shelters. Brimslade House within its park lay outside any parish until 1857 when it was grouped with Savernake. It was transferred to Wootton Rivers in 1987, but has already been discussed in this series under Savernake (vol. 1, p. 217). Apart from Brimslade and a few houses called Cuckoo's Knob, south of the village, East Wick is now the only satellite settlement in the parish, although until the nineteenth century cottages existed along Cock Lane near the southern parish boundary, and were known (after one of the many copyhold estates) as Streches or Searches. East Wick is first recorded in the thirteenth century, and village earthworks associated with the farm complex have been identified abutting the western (or Milton Lilbourne) side of the lane.

The parish church, drastically rebuilt by G E Street in 1860/1 and memorable now chiefly for its clock, is set well back from the village street and is approached by a footpath. This position must have been dictated by that of the manor house, 'an impressively large version of a local thatched cottage' (as the village appraisal describes it), which sits next to it and is overlooked from the churchyard. The house retains fifteenth-century work, and is presumably successor to the capital messuage of the Rivers family mentioned in an inquisition of 1314. That the present manor house and church represent the site of the Saxon farmstead and proprietary church of Wootton is confirmed by the pattern of lanes approaching the village. From south and south-east, and from north-west, the present lanes seem to have been deflected away from an earlier course to the church and channelled into the village street. The lane from East

Wick approaches the village in a deep greensand cutting and is continued
as a footpath right up to the churchyard.

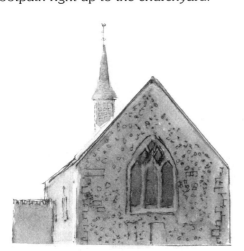

Properties along the east side of the village street retain to some
extent the regular rear boundary line which is a marked feature of
nineteenth-century maps of the village; this suggests that the street is a
planned medieval addition, along what may have become a significant
north-south route. A copy of a rough late-medieval map of Savernake
seems to mark a Marlborough way in the vicinity of Wootton, and an
estate map of 1732 describes as the Marlborough road the present bridleway leading up the hill north of the village before veering eastwards; its
southern continuation may be clearly seen as the lane by Cuckoo's Knob,
and the presumably ancient track past the *Bruce Arms* which is followed
by a parish boundary. Such a route would have been adversely affected by
the emparking of areas of Savernake forest further north in around 1600.
Later disruption occurred at the southern end of the village when the
Kennet and Avon Canal was built across the parish in 1809. It follows
closely a headwater of the River Avon, and a pond is shown on a map of
1773 at the point where the village street crossed the stream. Now there is
a lock-keeper's cottage here, a small wharf, and the last lock (restored in
1986) on the canal travelling westwards before the long pound of some
24km through Pewsey Vale to Devizes. Parallel with the canal a railway was
built in 1862, which became in 1906 part of the main line from London to

Exeter. It remains open, although a halt built to serve the village in 1928 was closed in 1966. Its lay opposite St Andrew's Close. The halt was un-staffed, but tickets could be purchased at the *Royal Oak Inn* in the village.

Control of the manor and the advowson of the church remained with the Rivers family until 1441, when they were sold to Sir John Seymour, warden of Savernake Forest, whose family had previously acquired property in the parish. They descended with the Seymour estates until 1692, when Sarah, Duchess of Somerset, bequeathed manorial lands to endow scholarships at St John's College, Cambridge, and gave the advowson to St John's and to Brasenose College, Oxford, to present alternately former Somerset scholars to the living. St John's remains the principal landowner in the parish, and has been responsible for building or maintaining most of the thatched houses and cottages which are such an attractive part of the village scene. The arrangement over the advowson ensured a supply of gifted and interesting characters to the rectory, of whom the most distinguished was perhaps the Latin scholar, William Brodribb, rector 1860-1905, who was an authority on the Roman historian Tacitus. Another rector, Edward Outram, was a notorious pluralist who was deprived of the living in 1813 after legal action.

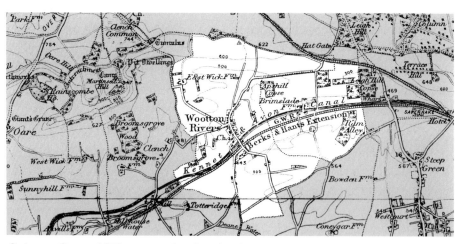

Ordnance Survey 1892 revision, 1 inch = 1 mile

Unlike most of its neighbours in Pewsey Vale Wootton Rivers has virtually no chalk downland, and sits almost entirely on Upper Greensand. A fourteenth-century inquisition suggests that arable farming then predominated, and this was certainly the case in 1842, when more than 90% of the parish was cultivated. A portion of this arable was still farmed under the open field system until enclosure in that year. A windmill, not otherwise recorded, is marked on a map of 1773 lying south-west of the village in an area later described as Berryfields. Could this, one wonders, be an instance of a windmill constructed on a prehistoric barrow?

From plodding on as an agricultural parish for a millennium, the employment profile of Wootton Rivers, as elsewhere, changed very radically during the twentieth century. Most working inhabitants now commute out of the village, especially to Swindon. The largest employer in the parish is probably now its popular pub, the *Royal Oak*; and one self-employed villager in 2000 was building light aircraft.

The medieval population of Wootton may have been small – there were only 51 adult taxpayers in 1377. In the seventeenth century the population was roughly the same as today, although during the canal heyday it rose substantially, achieving a total of 470 in 1841. Poverty, and the consequent lack of decent clothing, were given in 1783 as the reason for non-attendance at church by some inhabitants. There was no formal education available in the village at this date, although by 1846 Sunday and day schools were operating, and later –– partly supported by a bequest in 1848 – school was held in what is now Clock House. A National school was provided in 1863, and after closure in 1979 it was used by Westminster College, Oxford, as a centre for teacher education. It is now a private house. A Methodist group certified a private house for worship in 1821, but no chapel was built until sixty years later; it seems always to have enjoyed amicable relations with the parish church. The chapel closed in 1967 but survives as a private house, and, like the church, has a clock made by the ingenious Mr Spratt. The dial of the church clock spells 'Glory be to God'; that of the chapel clock 'To God be glory'. A mere nuance of dissent.

NOTES (location: SU 1963; area: 486ha; population (2001): 243)
General: *VCH* 16, 229-36; *Wootton Rivers village appraisal*, 1985; *Wootton Rivers: the millennium book*, 2000.
Waterman: Underdown, D, *Revel, riot and rebellion*, 1985, 90; Spratt: *WANHM*, 44, 293; Church: Tomlin, A, *Wootton Rivers, St Andrews Church: a brief history*, 1989; Enclosure: *WANHM* 72/3, 157, 163-4.

Worton

WITH ITS CLOSE NEIGHBOUR Marston, Worton formed the south-western portion of the estate and ancient parish of Potterne. It became a parish in its own right in 1866, although it had been regarded as a separate entity for administrative and fiscal purposes since 1316 at least. But its owners were always the owners of Potterne – the bishops of Salisbury – and it was to Potterne church that its inhabitants resorted on Sundays, using the raised causeway alongside the present lane. In Potterne church Worton and Marston residents each had a portion reserved for them, where they worshipped and for which they were responsible. Only in 1843, five years before the Wesleyan chapel, was a parish church built in Worton for the two communities, and then it was sited several hundred metres west of the village so that it could be convenient for Marston people also. The chapel closed, but has reopened as an independent church dedicated to St Brihtwold.

Worton is a linear village, strung along a busy (although officially a minor) road, which acts as a by-pass around Devizes for motorists from the south and west. Unlike many such villages, however, its raison d'être seems not to have been the road, which as a route linking Market Lavington with Melksham probably dates only from turnpiking in 1769; the road is not marked on a map of 1675, and before the turnpike it was described as 'miry and foundrous.' It was the brainchild of the trouble-some Westbury trust, and its turnpiking was resisted by Worton people (fearing the tolls no doubt) who claimed that a good horse causeway already existed. Speeding heavy traffic along it in recent decades has become the bugbear of life in Worton.

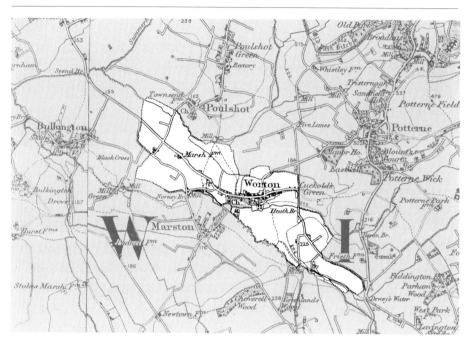

Ordnance Survey 1892 revision, 1 inch = 1 mile

The choice of site was probably dictated by the terrain. The parish consists largely of poorly-drained, heavy Kimmeridge clay, and the village is perched on a slight eminence, surrounded by an almost fenland landscape. The houses south of the road (from Park Farm westwards) have a back lane running along behind them, and so regular are many of the property boundaries on a map of 1656 that this area of the village must have been planned and laid out as a single operation, presumably in the medieval period. Its form is reminiscent of the planted villages laid out on their estates by great monastic landowners such as Glastonbury, and suggests that here, as on their large property of Bishops Cannings, the bishops of Salisbury were founding villages on new sites.

The village is first mentioned by name in a document of 1173. The name means 'farmstead with a herb-garden or kitchen garden,' and so perhaps the original nucleus was a community with this specialised function within the episcopal manor of Potterne. By 1334 Worton was assessed for tax at about two-thirds the total for the rest of Potterne (excluding Marston) and in 1377 another tax roll suggests a total population of 120-150. The map of 1656 marks about forty houses in the village, and so accommodating perhaps 150-200 people. Between 1801 and 1971 the population rarely fell outside the 300-400 range, although a 1970s housing development was built south of the road over a field belonging to John Gaisford on a map of 1735, and was accordingly named Gaisford Chase. This and subsequent new housing, Mill Head and Cedar Close, have boosted the total, which exceeded 600 in 1991.

Exploiting the waterlogged clays must always have presented problems. Traces of medieval ridge and furrow cultivation, and of hedgerows formed when they were consolidated, may be seen on either side of the road west of the village. Some show the slightly curved 'aratral' profile characteristic of former open-field furlongs, and they run back on the north side to a long regular boundary which would have separated the field from the meadows beyond. By 1656 most of this area had been taken out of the open fields and enclosed; although Furlong Field (north of the village) and South Brook Field (south of the village) remained open, along with Worton Common on higher ground to the south-east. By the nineteenth century enclosure was complete, and in 1841 over 85% of the agricultural land was described as meadow (i.e. pasture). Dairy farming continued to be the principal land use until recently, but now the milking herds which used to stroll along the main road have become a memory.

Park Farm, a large timber-framed house, is the most impressive of the farmhouses, and Marsh Farm, near the Poulshot turning, presents a modest but ornate front to the road. Worton Mill, new in 1855 as a corn mill, but on the site of an earlier fulling mill, is an imposing landmark west of the village; it continued working until about 1970. No trace remains of the tollhouse which stood in 1812 by the Poulshot turning, but Turnpike Cottage survives at the east end of the village by the Potterne turn (known as Cuckolds Green). A village hall was built in 1911, and was originally known as the Library Hall, because it was partly funded by Andrew Carnegie, the American philanthropist who was responsible for promoting many of England's public libraries (including Calne in Wiltshire).

Although not the most picturesque village on the claylands Worton has a very strong and friendly community spirit, with an annual newcomers party, a vibrant local pub (*Rose and Crown*), and a modern primary school. Its inhabitants boast a wide range of attainments and interesting occupations, working for the most part away from the village. The principal business still operating, from its garage in the High Street, is Bodmans Coaches, begun in 1922 by the grandfather of the present proprietor; Bodman's vehicles are a familiar sight throughout Wiltshire. Worton shares with Marston its church and school, but the two are also fostering other links through a kind of twinning organization which restored the footpath between them as a millennium project.

Perhaps the most remarkable Worton resident was the affable Frederick Kempster (1889-1918). Dubbed the English giant, he stood 2.56m (8ft 4½in) tall and weighed 171.5 kilos (27 stone). He lived intermittently at Grange Lodge with his sister and brother-in-law between 1911-16, entering the house on hands and knees, lighting cigarettes from streetlamps, shaking hands with people at upstairs windows, and playing darts in the pub while kneeling.

NOTES (location: ST9857; area: 396ha; population (2001): 586)
General: VCH 7, 207-17 *passim*; *Worton and Marston Domesday Book 2000*, 2001.
Church: Maggs, F H C, *History of Christ Church, Worton and Marston (1841-1991)*, 1991;
1656 map: WSRO Ch Comm Maps 42; Kempster: Alexander-Jones, C, *An introduction to Frederick the English giant*, [c.1999].

Note on Sources

THIS BOOK is not intended primarily as a work of reference, and I do not anticipate that most readers will wish or need to be told chapter and verse for every assertion made. Nevertheless its value to students and historians is clearly enhanced if the source of statements made in the text can be readily identified, and if pointers are given for further research. To each parish history, therefore, has been appended a note, describing the principal published (and in some cases manuscript) sources peculiar to that place or relevant to particular topics discussed in the text.

To save space in these notes (and below), certain frequently cited sources are abbreviated, as follows: *HR = Hatcher Review; RMCNHS = Reports of the Marlborough College Natural History Society; VCH = Victoria History of Wiltshire; WANHM = Wiltshire Archaeological and Natural History Magazine; WF = Wiltshire Folklife; WNQ = Wiltshire Notes and Queries;* WRS = Wiltshire Record Society (formerly Wiltshire Archaeological and Natural History Society, Records Branch). In each case such abbreviations are followed by volume (or issue) number, and page numbers.

In addition to these specific sources, I have adopted a checklist of standard sources which I have used throughout as the basis for my research, covering topics such as archaeology, place-names, geology, buildings, etc. These are rarely cited in the notes appended to histories, but I set them out in detail below, and generally give sufficient clues in the text for the serious student to identify which of them is my source. Not all the following sources are relevant to every parish. (Note that T = Trowbridge Reference Library (Local Studies Library); WANHS = Wiltshire Archaeological and Natural History Society Library, Devizes; WSRO = Wiltshire and Swindon Record Office, Trowbridge.)

Bibliographies and Guides to Sources

Goddard, E.H., *Wiltshire bibliography...*, 1929 [also Goddard's fuller typescript
      bibliography on which the published work is based, copies at T and WANHS]

Green, R.A.M., *A bibliography of printed works relating to Wiltshire 1920-1960*, 1975

For work published since 1960 the library catalogue at T has been used, as well as the
      volume indexes to *WANHM* and other periodicals. In certain cases the exhaustive
      card index to *WANHM* at WANHS has been consulted, as well as the cumulative
      indexes in *WANHM* 8, 16, 24, and 32.

For unpublished sources footnotes in *VCH* articles are invaluable, and the subject and
      place catalogues in WSRO have also been checked. Gover *et al*, 1939 (see below:
      Names) is useful in citing documents which refer to specific places.

Names

Gover, J.E.B., *et al*, *The place-names of Wiltshire*, 1939. This, the standard work, is now
      very dated, and the following have also been used for specific names:

Mills, A.D., *A dictionary of English place-names*, 1991

Gelling, M., and Cole, A., *The landscape of place-names*, 2000

Smith, A.H., *English place-name elements*, 2 vols., 1956

Field, J., *English field names: a dictionary*, 1972

Boundaries

Sawyer, P.H., *Anglo-Saxon charters: an annotated list and bibliography*, 1968. This
      identifies places with early boundary charters, many of which are described (not
      always convincingly) by -

Grundy, G.B., 'The Saxon land charters of Wiltshire', *Archaeological Journal*, 2nd series,
      vol.26, 1919, pp.143-301; vol.27, 1920, pp.8-126

Youngs, F.A., *Guide to the local administrative units of England, vol.1: Southern England*,
      1979. This dates changes to ancient, civil, and ecclesiastical parish boundaries, but
      without maps or detailed descriptions. For 19th- and 20th- century changes the
      footnotes to the parish population tables in *VCH* 4, 339-61 can be useful.

Communications

Timperley, H.W., and Brill, E., *Ancient trackways of Wessex*, 1965, should be taken with a
      pinch of salt. Documentary references to early roads have been collected by -

Grundy, G.B., 'The ancient highways and tracks of Wiltshire, Berkshire, and Hampshire,
      and the Saxon battlefields of Wiltshire', *Archaeological Journal*, 2nd series, vol.25,
      1918, pp.69-194.

Margary, I.D., *Roman roads in Britain*, 3rd ed., 1973.

Jervoise, E., *The ancient bridges of the south of England*, 1930.

For turnpike roads, and the dates of opening of canals and railways, the articles in *VCH* 4,
254-93 are invaluable.

Buildings

Pevsner, N., and Cherry, B., *Wiltshire*; 2nd ed., 1975 (The Buildings of England)

Department of the Environment, *Lists of buildings of special architectural and historic
interest*. Most of Wiltshire was relisted during the 1980s, and a bound set of the
resulting lists (known as 'greenbacks') with key map is in T.

For medieval chapels J.E. Jackson's article in *WANHM* 10, 253-322 is still worth consulting.

Stell, C., *An inventory of nonconformist chapels and meeting-houses in south-west
England*, 1991 (RCHM). Dates of pre-1852 nonconformist chapels and their
precursors are generally found in my edition of meeting-house certificates, WRS 40.

Rogers, K.H., *Wiltshire and Somerset woollen mills*, 1976.

Geology

Barron, R.S., *The geology of Wiltshire: a field guide*, 1976. This has been used in
conjunction with the relevant sheets of the British Geological Survey on Ordnance
Survey 1-inch base.

Geddes, I., *Hidden depths: Wiltshire's geology and landscapes*, 2000.

Archaeology

Wiltshire Sites and Monuments Records, maintained by County Archaeologist, Wiltshire
County Council. This has been used in conjunction with *VCH* 1, parts 1 and 2
(Part 1 is the gazetteer compiled by L.V. Grinsell), and the annual summaries of
archaeology and fieldwork in *WANHM*.

McOmish, D., *et al*, *The field archaeology of the Salisbury Plain Training Area*, 2002

Historic Maps

Ogilby, J., *Britannia, volume the first*, 1675.

Andrews J., and Dury, A., *A map of Wiltshire (taken from an actual survey)*, 1773
(facsimile edition in WRS 8).

Other early printed maps of Wiltshire, notably Greenwood, 1820, are reproduced in my
edition, WRS 52.

Ordnance Survey, 1-inch first series. Most of Wiltshire falls on sheets 14 (1817), 15 (1811),
and 34 (1828). Convenient facsimile editions were published by Harry Margary in
1981 and 1986.

Ordnance Survey, 6-inch first series. Wiltshire sheets were surveyed c.1880-c.1890.
Original sheets in T and WRO. Later Ordnance Survey maps have been used to
answer specific questions.

Most manuscript maps in WSRO, including tithe, enclosure, and estate maps, of various
        dates, 16th-19th century, have been examined where relevant, including copies of
        maps held elsewhere.

Population and Ownership

Thorn, C., and F., *Domesday Book 6: Wiltshire*, 1979. Also, for Domesday and the Geld
        Rolls, *VCH 2*.

Rotuli Hundredorum, vol.2, pp.230-81, 1818 (Record Commissioners).

The 1316 *Nomina Villarum* is printed in *WANHM*12, 1-43.

Editions of tax lists and assessments have been consulted for the following dates: 1332
        (by D.A. Crowley in WRS 45); 1334 and 1377 (*VCH* 4, 294-313); 1524-5 (by
        Sheail, J., *The regional distribution of wealth in England as indicated in the 1524/5
        lay subsidy returns*, List and Index Soc, special series 28, 1998, copy in T); 1545
        and 1576 (by G.D. Ramsay in WRS 10).

Abstracts of Wiltshire inquisitiones post mortem, 3 vols, 1893, 1908, 1914 (British Record
        Society, Index Library, vols.23, 37, 48). Covers the period 1242-1377, 1625-49.

Whiteman, A., *The Compton census of 1676: a critical edition*, 1986.

Summaries of Wiltshire enclosure awards and tithe apportionments by R.E. Sandell in
        WRS 25 and 30.

Population tables, 1801-1951, in *VCH* 4,339-61. Subsequent decennial totals are to be
        found in 1961 and 1971 Wiltshire census reports, 1981 OPCS Wiltshire ward and
        civil parish monitor, and Wiltshire County Council 1991 census headcounts, all in T.

Miscellaneous

Smith, L.T., *The itineraries of John Leland...*, 1908-12.

Aubrey, J., and Jackson, J.E., *Wiltshire: the topographical collections*, 1862.

Hoare, Sir Richard Colt, *The history of modern Wiltshire*, 6 vols., 1822-44. This covers
        only the southern half of Wiltshire, and is not relevant to the present part of my
        history.

Gomme, G.L., *Topographical history of Warwickshire, Westmoreland, and Wiltshire*, 1901
        (Gentleman's Magazine Library).

Kelly's directory of Wiltshire, various issues, 1848-1939.

VCH 4, 391-460. Wiltshire forests, by R. Grant and E.H.L. Poole.

WANHM 89, 88-98, Wiltshire deer parks, by K. Watts.

Richardson, J., *The local historian's encyclopaedia*, 1974, pp.232-69, lists of market
        grants, markets and fairs, derived from a not wholly accurate government report of
        1889.

WRS 55, *Devizes area income tax assessments, 1842-1860*, ed. by R. Colley

WRS 56, *Wiltshire glebe terriers 1588-1827*, ed.by S. Hobbs

Index

THIS IS PRIMARILY an index of persons and places. The principal parish entries are given in **bold** type. All locations, including streets, houses and farms, within the parishes covered by this volume are separately indexed by name, followed by their parish name. Places outside Wiltshire are followed by the name of their historic county. The more important entries relating to selected subjects have also been indexed, but topics such as geology, railways, churches, schools, etc, which are regularly covered parish by parish, have not.